Why Do You Need This New Edition?

If you're wondering why you should buy this new edition of *The Longman Reader*, here are a few great reasons!

1. Eleven new readings have been added in Chapters 3–11 on current topics such as e-mail style, "Gen Nexters," friendship, and teenage driving that are **models for the different patterns of writing** that you'll be learning and practicing.

2. New Development Diagrams illustrate at-a-glance how the distinctive features of different patterns of development are used in essay writing, **summarizing key concepts in an easily referenced format** (Chs. 3–11).

3. New Essay Structure Diagrams outline visually the structure of one professional reading for each pattern of development **to help you see how the reading is organized and supported**, a skill that will help you plan your own writing (Chs. 3–11).

4. Concrete guidelines for integrating quotations, summaries, and paraphrases into your papers tell you **what you need to know to avoid unintentional plagiarism** and its consequences (App. A).

5. New material in the revised Appendix A, "A Guide to Using Sources," will **help you with the research tasks of evaluating, analyzing, and synthesizing research sources.**

6. A sample student essay updated to show MLA style for in-text citations and Works Cited lists offers a **model of how to write a research paper for your course** (Ch. 11).

7. Examples for MLA documentation style are completely updated to illustrate the **2008 guidelines published by the Modern Language Association** (App. A).

8. New material on reading illustrations gives insight into how you can **evaluate graphics and photos** you find in your research (Ch. 1).

9. You can use *The Longman Reader* alongside Pearson's unique MyCompLab and find a world of resources developed specifically for you!

PEARSON

ABOUT THE AUTHORS

Judith Nadell was until several years ago Associate Professor of Communications at Rowan University (New Jersey). During her eighteen years at Rowan, she coordinated the introductory course in the Freshman Writing Sequence and served as Director of the Writing Lab. More recently, she has developed a special interest in grassroots literacy. Besides designing an adult-literacy project, a children's reading-enrichment program, and a family-literacy initiative, she has volunteered as a tutor and tutor trainer in the programs. A Phi Beta Kappa graduate of Tufts University, she received a doctorate from Columbia University. She is author of *Becoming a Read-Aloud Coach* (Townsend Press) and coauthor of *Doing Well in College* (McGraw-Hill), *Vocabulary Basics* (Townsend Press), and *The Longman Writer*. The recipient of a New Jersey award for excellence in the teaching of writing, Judith Nadell lives with her coauthor husband, John Langan, near Philadelphia.

John Langan taught reading and writing courses at Atlantic Cape Community College in New Jersey for more than twenty years. He earned an advanced degree in reading at Glassboro State College and another in writing at Rutgers University. Active in a mentoring program, he designed a reading-enrichment program for inner-city high school students and wrote a motivational and learning skills guidebook, *Ten Skills You Really Need to Succeed in School*, for urban youngsters. Coauthor of *The Longman Writer* and author of a series of college textbooks on both reading and writing, he has published widely with McGraw-Hill Book Company, Townsend Press, and Longman.

Eliza A. Comodromos taught composition and developmental writing in the English Departments of both Rutgers University and John Jay College of Criminal Justice. After graduating with a B.A. in English and in French from La Salle University, she did graduate work at the City University of New York Graduate School and went on to earn an advanced degree at Rutgers University. A freelance editor and textbook consultant, Eliza Comodromos has delivered numerous papers at language and literature conferences around the country. She lives with her husband, Paul, and daughters, Anna Maria and Sophia Mae, near Philadelphia.

THE LONGMAN READER

NINTH EDITION

Judith Nadell

John Langan

Eliza A. Comodromos

Longman

New York   San Francisco   Boston
London   Toronto   Sydney   Tokyo   Singapore   Madrid
Mexico City   Munich   Paris   Cape Town   Hong Kong   Montreal

Acquisitions Editor: Lauren A. Finn
Development Director: Mary Ellen Curley
Development Editor: Linda Stern
Senior Supplements Editor:
 Donna Campion
Senior Marketing Manager:
 Sandra McGuire
Production Manager: Eric Jorgensen
**Project Coordination, Text Design, and
 Electronic Page Makeup:** Elm Street
 Publishing Services

Cover Design Manager: Nancy Danany
Cover Design : Nancy Sacks
Cover Image: San Juan National Forest,
 Colorado, © James Randkley/The
 Image Bank/Getty Images, Inc.
Visual Researcher: Rona Tuccillo
Senior Manufacturing Buyer:
 Dennis J. Para
Printer and Binder: R R Donnelley &
 Sons Company/Crawfordsville
Cover Printer: Coral Graphic Services, Inc.

For permission to use copyrighted material, grateful acknowledgment is made to the copyright
holders on pp. 665–667, which are hereby made part of this copyright page.

Library of Congress Cataloging-in-Publication Data

Nadell, Judith.
 The Longman reader/Judith Nadell, John Langan, Eliza A. Comodromos.—9th ed.
 p.cm.
 Includes bibliographical references and index.
 ISBN 978-0-205-63256-5
 1. College readers. 2. English language—Rhetoric—Problems, exercises, etc. 3. Report
writing—problems, exercises, etc. I. Langan, John, 1942- II. Comodromos, Eliza A.
III. Title.

PE1417.N33 2009
808'.0427—dc22   2008046764

Please visit us at www.ablongman.com

1 2 3 4 5 6 7 8 9 10—DOC—11 10 09 08

Longman
is an imprint of

www.pearsonhighered.com

ISBN 13: 978-0-205-63256-5
ISBN 10:   0-205-63256-4

CONTENTS

3 DESCRIPTION   72

Maya Angelou   SISTER FLOWERS   87
Hidden deep within herself after the trauma of a rape, young Angelou is escorted back into life by the grand lady of a small town.
Figure 3.2   Essay Structure Diagram: "Sister Flowers" by Maya Angelou   92

Gordon Parks   FLAVIO'S HOME   95
Having battled poverty and prejudice himself, writer-photographer Gordon Parks visits a Brazilian slum and finds, among the wretched thousands forgotten by the outside world, a dying yet smiling boy.

David Helvarg   THE STORM THIS TIME   103
Three weeks after Hurricane Katrina, an environmentalist tours New Orleans and the Gulf Coast to assess damage and the prospects for recovery.

Gary Kamiya   LIFE, DEATH AND SPRING   111
This author muses about cycles of growth and decay as he remembers visits to a family ranch.

7 PROCESS ANALYSIS   282

9 CAUSE-EFFECT   383

Examining an Issue: Gender-Based Education

Examining an Issue: Torture

Examining an Issue: Illegal Immigration

APPENDIX B: AVOIDING TEN COMMON WRITING ERRORS   638

THEMATIC CONTENTS

FAMILY AND CHILDREN

GOVERNMENT AND LAW

HEALTH AND PSYCHOLOGY

HUMAN GROUPS AND SOCIETY

HUMOR AND SATIRE

MEANING IN LIFE

MEDIA AND TECHNOLOGY

MEMORIES AND AUTOBIOGRAPHY

MEN AND WOMEN

NATURE AND SCIENCE

PREFACE

As computers have become firmly established in the lives of students and instructors, the ways in which we acquire information and communicate with one another have been profoundly transformed. Moreover, the ways teachers teach, as well as the ways students learn, have been deeply affected. Perhaps now, more than ever, the need for students to develop sound writing skills has become as essential as it is fundamental. It's to this mission that we continue to be committed.

As in the first eight editions, in this ninth edition we have aimed for a different kind of text—one that would offer fresh examples of professional prose, one that would take a more active role in helping students become stronger readers, thinkers, and writers. *The Longman Reader* continues to include widely read and classic essays, as well as fresh new pieces, such as Gary Kamiya's "Life, Death and Spring" and Amy Sutherland's "What Shamu Taught Me About a Happy Marriage." We've been careful to choose selections that range widely in subject matter and approach, from the humorous to the informative, from personal meditation to polemic. We've also made sure that each selection captures students' interest and clearly illustrates a specific pattern of development or a combination of such patterns.

As before, we have also tried to help students bridge the gap between the product and process approaches to reading and writing. Throughout, we describe possible sequences and structures but emphasize that such steps and formats are not meant to be viewed as rigid prescriptions; rather, they are strategies for helping students discover what works best in a particular situation.

WHAT'S NEW IN THE NINTH EDITION OF *THE LONGMAN READER*

In preparing this edition, we looked closely at the reviews completed by instructors using the book. Their comments helped us identify new directions the book might take. Here are some of the new features of this edition of *The Longman Reader*.

- **Eleven of the fifty-eight selections are new.** Whether written by a journalist such as Anna Quindlen ("Driving to the Funeral"), an academic writer such as Eric G. Wilson ("The Miracle of Melancholia"), or a literary figure such as Joan Murray ("Someone's Mother"), the new selections are bound to stimulate strong writing on a variety of topics—education, technology, interpersonal relationships, gender, and morality, to name a few. When selecting new readings, we took special care to include pieces written from a personal point of view (for example, Marion Winik's "What Are Friends For?") as well as those citing academic research (for example, Kurt Kleiner's "When Mañana Is Too Soon"). Finally, honoring the requests of many instructors, we also made an effort to find compelling pieces on technology and contemporary life, such as Eric Weiner's "Euromail and Amerimail" and Ann Hulbert's "Beyond the Pleasure Principle."

- **Nine new Essay Structure Diagrams**—one for the first professional essay in each pattern-of-development chapter—are unique among rhetorical readers: each diagram outlines the essay's organization, development, and support, paragraph by paragraph, using the visual pedagogy valued by today's students to model an often-taught "outlining" assignment (Chs. 3–11).

- **Nine new Development Diagrams** have been added to the pattern-of-development chapters. Also unique among rhetorical readers, these flowcharts illustrate visually for students how a particular development pattern is expressed at each stage of the writing process, summarizing key chapter content succinctly in innovative and useful at-a-glance pedagogy (Chs. 3–11).

- **Appendix A, "A Guide to Using Sources," has been rewritten** and includes guidelines for students on how to evaluate, analyze, and synthesize printed and Internet source materials. An extensive section that discusses effective uses of summaries, paraphrases, and the incorporation of quotations includes numerous examples. Finally, the appendix gives completely updated information on the most recently published MLA citation guidelines, with examples of major entries in a Works Cited list.

- **A student-authored MLA model paper in the argumentation-persuasion chapter has been redesigned** for ease of use and fast reference as well as revised in accordance with the new MLA documentation standards published in 2008. The paper not only provides students with an easy-to-find, clear, and up-to-date model for documentation, it also serves as a model for formatting an MLA paper.

- **A new pair of pro-con essays** in the argumentation-persuasion chapter further expands coverage of refutation strategies: Gerry Garibaldi's "How the Schools Shortchange Boys" and Michael Kimmel's "A War Against Boys?"—two readings that explore the debate on whether gender discrimination exists in elementary education (Ch. 11).

• **Instruction on reading images critically has been added** in Chapter 1 and again in Appendix A so that students have some guidance on how to understand and interpret images they encounter in their research.

ORGANIZATION OF *THE LONGMAN READER*

Buoyed by compliments about the previous editions' teachability, we haven't tinkered with the book's underlying format. Such a structure, we've been told, does indeed help students read more critically, think more logically, and write more skillfully. Here is the book's basic format.

Chapter 1, "The Reading Process"

Designed to reflect current theories about the interaction of reading, thinking, and writing, this chapter provides guided practice in a three-part process for reading with close attention and a high level of interpretive skill. This step-by-step process sharpens students' understanding of the book's selections and promotes the rigorous thinking needed to write effective essays.

An activity at the end of the chapter gives students a chance to use the three-step process. First, they read an essay by the journalist Ellen Goodman. The essay has been annotated both to show students the reading process in action and to illustrate how close critical reading can pave the way to promising writing topics. Then students respond to sample questions and writing assignments, all similar to those accompanying each of the book's selections. The chapter thus does more than just tell students how to sharpen their reading abilities; it guides them through a clearly sequenced plan for developing critical reading skills.

Chapter 2, "The Writing Process"

As an introduction to essay writing and to make the composing process easier for students to grasp, we provide a separate section for each of the following stages: prewriting, identifying a thesis, supporting the thesis with evidence, organizing the evidence, writing the first draft, revising, and editing and proofreading. The stages are also illustrated in a *new diagram*, "Stages of the Writing Process."

From the start, we point out that the stages are fluid. Indeed, the case history of an evolving student paper illustrates just how recursive and individualized the writing process can be. Guided activities at the end of each section give students practice taking their essays through successive stages in the composing process.

To illustrate the link between reading and writing, the writing chapter presents the progressive stages of a student paper written in response to Ellen Goodman's "Family Counterculture," the selection presented in

Chapter 1. An easy-to-spot symbol in the margin [symbol] makes it possible to locate—at a glance—this evolving student essay. Commentary following the student paper highlights the essay's strengths and points out spots that could use additional work. In short, by the end of the second chapter, the entire reading-writing process has been illustrated, from reading a selection to writing about it.

Chapters 3–11: Patterns of Development

The chapters contain selections grouped according to nine patterns of development: description, narration, exemplification, division-classification, process analysis, comparison-contrast, cause-effect, definition, and argumentation-persuasion. The sequence progresses from the more personal and expressive patterns to the more public and analytic. However, because each chapter is self-contained, the patterns may be covered in any order. Instructors preferring a thematic approach will find the Thematic Contents helpful.

The Longman Reader treats the patterns separately because such an approach helps students grasp the distinctive characteristics of each pattern. At the same time, the book continually shows the way writers usually combine patterns in their work. We also encourage students to view the patterns as strategies for generating and organizing ideas. Writers, we explain, rarely set out to compose an essay in a specific pattern. Rather, they choose a pattern or combination of patterns because it suits their purpose, audience, and subject.

Each of the nine pattern-of-development chapters follows the format below.

1. **A striking visual** opens every pattern-of-development chapter. The photo reappears in thumbnail form following the "How [name of pattern] Fits Your Purpose and Audience" section. There, the image prompts a pattern-related writing activity that encourages students to consider issues of purpose and audience in a piece of real-world writing.
2. **A detailed explanation of the pattern** begins the chapter. The explanation includes (a) a definition of the pattern, (b) a description of the way the pattern helps a writer accommodate his or her purpose and audience, and (c) step-by-step guidelines for using the pattern.
3. **A Development Diagram,** *new to this edition,* in each chapter illustrates how the pattern is expressed in each stage of the writing process.
4. **An annotated student essay** using the pattern appears next. Written in response to one of the professional selections in the chapter, each essay illustrates the characteristic features of the pattern discussed in the chapter.

5. **Commentary** after each student essay points out the blend of patterns in the piece, identifies the paper's strengths, and locates areas needing improvement. "First draft" and "revised" versions of one section of the essay reveal how the student writer went about revising, thus illustrating the relationship between the final draft and the steps taken to produce it.

6. **Professional selections** in the pattern-of-development chapters are accompanied by these items:

   - **An Essay Structure Diagram,** *new to this edition,* for the first essay in each section shows how the essay makes use of patterns of development.

   - **A biographical note** and **Pre-Reading Journal Entry assignment** give students a perspective on the author and create interest in the piece. The journal assignment encourages students to explore—in a loose, unpressured way—their thoughts about an issue that will be raised in the selection. The journal entry thus motivates students to read the piece with extra care, attention, and personal investment.

   - **Questions for Close Reading,** five in all, help students dig into and interpret the selection's content. The first question asks them to identify the selection's thesis; the last provides work on vocabulary development.

   - **Questions About the Writer's Craft,** four in all, deal with such matters as purpose, audience, tone, organization, sentence structure, diction, and figures of speech. The first question in the series (labeled "The Pattern") focuses on the distinctive features of the pattern used in the selection. And usually there's another question (labeled "Other Patterns") that asks students to analyze the writer's use of additional patterns in the piece.

   - **Writing Assignments,** five in all, follow each selection. Packed with suggestions on how to proceed, the assignments use the selection as a springboard. The first two assignments ask students to write an essay using the same pattern as the one used in the selection; the next two assignments encourage students to experiment with a combination of patterns in their own essay; the last assignment helps students turn the raw material in their pre-reading journal entries into fully considered essays.

     Frequently, the assignments are preceded by the symbol ![chain symbol], indicating a cross-reference to at least one other selection in the book. By encouraging students to make connections among readings, such assignments broaden students' perspective and give them additional material to draw on when they write. These "paired assignments" will be especially welcome to instructors stressing recurring ideas and themes. In other cases, assignments are preceded by the symbol ![keyboard symbol], indicating that students might benefit from conducting library and/or Internet research.

7. **Prewriting and revising activities** in shaded boxes at the end of each chapter help students understand the unique demands posed by the pattern being studied.

8. **Two sets of Additional Writing Assignments** close each pattern-of-development chapter: "General Assignments" and "Assignments with a Specific Purpose, Audience, and Point of View." The first set provides open-ended topics that prompt students to discover the best way to use a specific pattern; the second set develops their sensitivity to rhetorical context by asking them to apply the pattern in a real-world situation.

Chapter 12, "Combining the Patterns"

The final chapter offers a sample student essay as well as two essays each by three very different prose stylists. Annotations on the student essay and on one of the professional selections show how writers often blend patterns of development in their work. The chapter also provides guidelines to help students analyze this fusing of patterns.

Appendixes and Glossary

Appendix A, "A Guide to Using Sources," has been extensively rewritten and provides guidelines for evaluating, analyzing, and synthesizing sources; using quotations, summaries, and paraphrases to integrate sources into a paper; and documenting sources following the latest MLA style guidelines. **Appendix B, "Avoiding Ten Common Writing Errors,"** targets common problem areas in student writing and offers quick, accessible solutions for each. The **Glossary** lists and defines all the key terms presented in the text.

SUPPLEMENTS FOR STUDENTS AND INSTRUCTORS

Instructor's Manual

A comprehensive Instructor's Manual contains the following: in-depth answers to the "Questions for Close Reading" and "Questions About the Writer's Craft"; suggested activities; pointers about using the book; a detailed syllabus; and an analysis of the blend of patterns in the selections in the "Combining the Patterns" chapter.

The NEW MyCompLab Website

PEARSON
mycomplab

The new MyCompLab integrates the market-leading instruction, multimedia tutorials, and exercises for writing grammar and research that users have come to identify with the program with a new online composing space and new assessment tools. The result is a revolutionary application that offers a seamless and flexible teaching and learning environment built specifically for writers.

Created after years of extensive research and in partnership with composition faculty and students across the country, the new MyCompLab provides help for writers in the context of their writing, with instructor and peer commenting functionality, proven tutorials and exercises for writing, grammar and research, an e-portfolio, an assignment-builder, a bibliography tool, tutoring services, and a gradebook and course management organization created specifically for writing classes. Visit www.mycomplab.com for more information.

ACKNOWLEDGMENTS

At Longman, our thanks go to Lauren Finn for her perceptive editorial guidance and enthusiasm for *The Longman Reader*. We're also indebted to Linda Stern, our Development Editor, and to Heather Johnson of Elm Street Publishing Services and Eric Jorgensen of Longman for their skillful handling of the never-ending complexities of the production process.

Over the years, many writing instructors have reviewed *The Longman Reader* and responded to detailed questionnaires about its selections and pedagogy. Their comments have guided our work every step of the way. We are particularly indebted to the following reviewers for the valuable assistance they have provided during the preparation of the ninth edition of *The Longman Reader:* Martha Bachman, Camden County College; Kamala Balasubramanian, Grossmont College; Andrew Ball, Bluegrass Community and Technical College; Samone Polk Brooks, Lane College; Mary Cantrell, Tulsa Community College; Holly Carey, Lamar University; Joseph Couch, Montgomery College; Darren DeFrain, Wichita State University; Jonathan Fegley, Middle Georgia College; Billy Fontenot, Louisiana State University at Eunice; Hank Galmish, Green River Community College; Barbara Goldstein, Hillsborough Community College; Richard Lee, State University of New York College at Oneonta; Dolores MacNaughton, Umpqua Community College; Raphael Okonkwor, Moraine Park Technical College; Dana Resente, Montgomery County Community College; Mary Simpson, Central Texas College; April Van Camp, Indian River Community College; Deborah LeSure Wilbourn, Northwest Mississippi Community College; and Darcy A. Zabel, Friends University.

Some individuals from our at-home office deserve special thanks. During the preparation of the ninth edition, Marion Castellucci provided valuable assistance with the apparatus. Finally, as always, we're thankful to our students. Their reaction to various drafts of material sharpened our thinking and helped focus our work. And we are especially indebted to the eleven students whose essays are included in the book. Their thoughtful, carefully revised papers dramatize the potential of student writing and the power of the composing process.

JUDITH NADELL
JOHN LANGAN
ELIZA A. COMODROMOS

THE READING PROCESS

More than two hundred years ago, essayist Joseph Addison commented, "Of all the diversions of life, there is none so proper to fill up its empty spaces as the reading of useful and entertaining authors." Addison might have added that reading also challenges our beliefs, deepens our awareness, and stimulates our imagination. And the more challenging the material, the more actively involved the reader must be.

The essays in this book, which range from the classic to the contemporary, call for active reading. They contain language that will move you, images that will enlarge your understanding of other people, and ideas that will transform your views on complex issues. They will also help you develop a repertoire of reading skills that will benefit you throughout life.

The novelist Saul Bellow has observed, "A writer is a reader moved to emulation." As you become a better reader, your own writing will become more insightful and polished. Increasingly, you'll be able to employ the techniques that professional writers use to express ideas.

The three-stage approach outlined here will help you get the most out of this book's selections and ultimately improve your own writing too.

STAGE 1: GET AN OVERVIEW
OF THE SELECTION

Ideally, you should get settled in a quiet place that encourages concentration. Once you're settled, it's time to read the selection. To ensure a good first reading, try the following hints.

☑ FIRST READING: A CHECKLIST

❏ Start by reading the biographical note that precedes the selection. By providing background information about the author, the biographical note helps you evaluate the writer's credibility as well as his or her slant on the subject. For example, if you know that Leslie Savan has written extensively about advertising for major broadcast and print media, you can better assess whether she is a credible source for the material she presents in her essay "Black Talk and Pop Culture" (page 206).

❏ Do the *Pre-Reading Journal Entry* assignment, which precedes the selection. This assignment "primes" you for the piece by helping you to explore—in an easy, unpressured way—your thoughts about a key point raised in the selection. By preparing the journal entry, you're inspired to read the selection with special care, attention, and personal investment. (For more on pre-reading journal entries, see pages 16–17 and 658.)

❏ Consider the selection's title. A good title often expresses the essay's main idea, giving you insight into the selection even before you read it. For example, the title of Yuh Ji-Yeon's "Let's Tell the Story of All America's Cultures" (page 520) suggests that the piece will advocate multiculturalism. A title may also hint at a selection's tone. Paul Roberts's "How to Say Nothing in 500 Words" (page 316) points to an essay that's light in spirit, whereas George Orwell's "Shooting an Elephant" (page 148) suggests a piece with a serious mood.

❏ Read the selection straight through purely for pleasure. Allow yourself to be drawn into the world the author has created. Just as you first see a painting from the doorway of a room and form an overall impression without perceiving the details, you can have a preliminary, subjective feeling about a reading selection. Moreover, because you bring your own experiences and viewpoints to the piece, your reading will be unique. As Ralph Waldo Emerson said, "Take the book, my friend, and read your eyes out; you will never find there what I find."

❏ After this initial reading of the selection, focus your first impressions by asking yourself whether you like the selection. In your own words, briefly describe the piece and your reaction to it.

STAGE 2: DEEPEN YOUR SENSE
OF THE SELECTION

At this point, you're ready to move more deeply into the selection. A second reading will help you identify the specific features that triggered your initial reaction.

There are a number of techniques you can use during this second, more focused reading. You may, for example, find it helpful to adapt some of the strategies that Mortimer Adler, a well-known writer and editor, wrote about in his 1940 essay "How to Mark a Book." There, Adler argues passionately for marking up the material we read. The physical act of annotating, he believes, etches the writer's ideas more sharply in the mind, helping readers grasp and remember those ideas more easily. And "best of all," Adler writes, the "marks and notes...stay there forever. You can pick up the...[material] the following week or year, and there are all your points of agreement, doubt, and inquiry. It's like resuming an uninterrupted conversation."

Adler goes on to describe various annotation techniques he uses when reading. Several of these techniques, adapted somewhat, are presented in the checklist below.

☑ SECOND READING: A CHECKLIST

Using a pen (or pencil) and highlighter, you might . . .

❏ Underline or highlight the selection's main idea, or thesis, often found near the beginning or end. If the thesis isn't stated explicitly, write down your own version of the selection's main idea.

❏ Place numbers in the margin to designate the main points that support the thesis.

❏ Circle or put an asterisk next to key ideas that are stated more than once.

❏ Take a minute to write "Yes," "No," or a brief comment beside points with which you strongly agree or disagree. Your reaction to these points often explains your feelings about the aptness of the selection's ideas.

❏ Return to any unclear passages you encountered during the first reading. The feeling you now have for the piece as a whole will probably help you make sense of initially confusing spots. However, this second reading may also reveal that, in places, the writer's thinking isn't as clear as it could be. If that's the case, you might put a question mark in the margin beside the unclear material.

❑ Put brackets around words whose meaning you need to check in a dictionary.

❑ Ask yourself if your initial impression of the selection has changed in any way as a result of this second reading. If your feelings *have* changed, try to determine why you reacted differently on this reading.

STAGE 3: EVALUATE THE SELECTION

Now that you have a good grasp of the selection, you may want to read it a third time, especially if the piece is long or complex. This time, your goal is to make judgments about the essay's effectiveness. Keep in mind, though, that you shouldn't evaluate the selection until after you have a strong hold on it. A negative or even a positive reaction is valid only if it's based on an accurate reading.

At first, you may feel uncomfortable about evaluating the work of a professional writer. But remember: Written material set in type only *seems* perfect; all writing can be finetuned. By identifying what does and doesn't work in others' writing, you're taking an important first step toward developing your own power as a writer. You might find it helpful at this point to get together with other students to discuss the selection. Comparing viewpoints often opens up a piece, enabling you to gain a clearer perspective on the selection and the author's approach.

Evaluate the Writing

To evaluate the essay, ask yourself the following questions.

☑ EVALUATING A SELECTION: A CHECKLIST

❑ *Where does support for the selection's thesis seem logical and sufficient? Where does support seem weak?* Which of the author's supporting facts, arguments, and examples seem pertinent and convincing? Which don't?

❑ *Is the selection unified? If not, why not?* Where does something in the selection not seem relevant? Where are there any unnecessary digressions or detours?

❑ *How does the writer make the selection move smoothly from beginning to end?* How does the writer create an easy flow between ideas? Are any parts of the essay abrupt and jarring? Which ones?

❑ *Which stylistic devices are used to good effect in the selection?* Which *pattern of development* or combination of patterns does the writer use to develop the piece? Why do you think those patterns were selected? How do paragraph development, sentence structure, and word choice contribute to the piece's overall effect? What *tone* does the writer adopt? Where does the writer use *figures of speech* effectively? (The next chapter and the glossary explain the terms shown here in italics.)

❑ *How does the selection encourage further thought?* What new perspective on an issue does the writer provide? What ideas has the selection prompted you to explore in an essay of your own?

Evaluate the Images

Some readings use graphics (such as charts, tables, graphs, and diagrams) or illustrations (such as photographs, paintings, and drawings) to support their message. You can read and evaluate these just as you would text.

Preview images.   As you get an overview of a text, ask yourself questions about its images. Who created the image? Is the source reliable? What does the caption say? Is information clearly labeled and presented? What mood, feelings, or other impression does the image convey?

Analyze and interpret images.   Deepen your understanding of images as you read the text. What is the author's purpose? Does the image make assumptions about viewers' beliefs or knowledge? How is the image explained in the text? Are data accurate, up-to-date, and presented without distortion? Do illustrations tell a story? What elements stand out? What mood do the colors and composition (arrangement of elements) convey?

Integrate image evaluations.   Integrate your findings into your evaluation of the reading as a whole. Are the images adequately discussed in the text? Do graphics give relevant, persuasive details? Are illustrations thought-provoking without being sensationalistic? In general, do the images improve the reading and support the writer's main points? For a reading that uses photos, see David Helvarg's "The Storm This Time" (page 103).

It takes some work to follow the three-step approach just described, but the selections in *The Longman Reader* are worth the effort. Bear in mind that none of the selections sprang full-blown from the pen of its author. Rather, each essay is the result of hours of work—hours of thinking, writing, rethinking, and revising. As a reader, you should show the same willingness to work with the selections, to read them carefully and thoughtfully. Henry David Thoreau, an avid reader and prolific writer, emphasized the importance of this kind of attentive reading when he advised that "books must be read as deliberately and unreservedly as they were written."

To illustrate the multi-stage reading process just described, we've annotated the professional essay that follows: "Family Counterculture" by Ellen Goodman. Note that annotations are provided in the margin of the essay as well as at the end of the essay. As you read Goodman's essay, try applying the three-stage sequence. You can measure your ability to dig into the selection by making your own annotations on Goodman's essay and then comparing them to ours. You can also see how well you evaluated the piece by answering the questions in "Evaluating a Selection: A Checklist" and then comparing your responses to ours on pages 7–11.

Ellen Goodman

The recipient of a Pulitzer Prize, Ellen Goodman (1941–) worked for *Newsweek* and the *Detroit Free Press* before joining the staff of *The Boston Globe* in 1967. A resident of the Boston area, Goodman writes a popular syndicated column that provides insightful commentary on life in the United States. Her pieces have appeared in a number of national publications, including *The Village Voice* and *McCalls*. Collections of her columns have been published in *Close to Home* (1979), *Turning Points* (1979), *At Large* (1981), *Keeping in Touch* (1985), *Making Sense* (1989), and *Value Judgments* (1993). Most recently, she coauthored *I Know Just What You Mean* (1999), a book that examines the complex nature of women's friendships, and *Paper Trail* (2004). The following selection is from *Value Judgments*.

Pre-Reading Journal Entry

Television is often blamed for having a harmful effect on children. Do you think this criticism is merited? In what ways does TV exert a negative influence on children? In what ways does TV exert a positive influence on youngsters? Take a few minutes to respond to these questions in your journal.

Marginal Annotations

Interesting take on the term "counterculture"

Time frame established

Light humor; easy, casual tone

Time frame picked up

Thesis, developed overall by cause-effect pattern

First research-based example to support thesis

Family Counterculture

1   Sooner or later, most Americans become card-carrying members of the counterculture. This is not an underground holdout of hippies. No beads are required. All you need to join is a child.

2   At some point between Lamaze and the PTA, it becomes clear that one of your main jobs as a parent is to counter the culture. What the media delivers to children by the masses, you are expected to rebut one at a time.

3   The latest evidence of this frustrating piece of the parenting job description came from pediatricians. This summer, the American Academy of Pediatrics called for a ban on television food ads. Their plea was hard on the heels of a study showing that one Saturday morning of TV cartoons contained 202 junk-food ads.

4   The kids see, want, and nag. That is, after all, the theory behind advertising to children, since few six-year-olds have their own trust funds. The end result, said the pediatricians, is obesity and high cholesterol.

5   Their call for a ban was predictably attacked by the grocers' association. But it was also attacked by people

assembled under the umbrella marked "parental responsibility." We don't need bans, said these "PR" people; we need parents who know how to say "no."

Relevant paragraph? Identifies Goodman as a parent, but interrupts flow

Well, I bow to no one in my capacity for naysaying. I agree that it's a well-honed skill of child raising. By the time my daughter was seven, she qualified as a media critic.   6

Transition doesn't work but would if ¶6 were cut

But it occurs to me now that the call for "parental responsibility" is increasing in direct proportion to the irresponsibility of the marketplace. Parents are expected to protect their children from an increasingly hostile environment.   7

Series of questions and brief answers consistent with overall casual tone

Are the kids being sold junk food? Just say no. Is TV bad? Turn it off. Are there messages about sex, drugs, violence all around? Counter the culture.   8

Brief real-life examples support thesis

Fragments

Mothers and fathers are expected to screen virtually every aspect of their children's lives. To check the ratings on the movies, to read the labels on the CDs, to find out if there's MTV in the house next door. All the while keeping in touch with school and, in their free time, earning a living.   9

More examples

In real life, most parents do a great deal of this monitoring and just-say-no-ing. Any trip to the supermarket produces at least one scene of a child grabbing for something only to have it returned to the shelf by a frazzled parent. An extraordinary number of the family arguments are over the goodies—sneakers, clothes, games—that the young know only because of ads.   10

Another weak transition—no contrast

But at times it seems that the media have become the mainstream culture in children's lives. Parents have become the alternative.   11

Restatement of thesis

Second research-based example to support thesis

Barbara Dafoe Whitehead, a research associate at the Institute for American Values, found this out in interviews with middle-class parents. "A common complaint I heard from parents was their sense of being overwhelmed by the culture. They felt their voice was a lot weaker. And they felt relatively more helpless than their parents.   12

Citing an expert reinforces thesis

Restatement of thesis

"Parents," she notes, "see themselves in a struggle for the hearts and minds of their own children." It isn't that they can't say no. It's that there's so much more to say no to.   13

Without wallowing in false nostalgia, there has been a fundamental shift. Americans once expected parents   14

Comparison-
contrast pattern—
signaled by
"once," "Today,"
"Once," and
"Now"

to raise their children in accordance with the dominant
cultural messages. Today they are expected to raise their
children in opposition.

Once the chorus of cultural values was full of ministers, 15
teachers, neighbors, leaders. They demanded more con-
formity, but offered more support. Now the messengers are
Ninja Turtles, Madonna, rap groups, and celebrities pushing
sneakers. Parents are considered "responsible" only if they
are successful in their resistance.

Restatement
of thesis

It's what makes child raising harder. It's why parents 16
feel more isolated. It's not just that American families
have less time with their kids. It's that we have to spend
more of this time doing battle with our own culture.

Conveys the
challenges that
parents face

It's rather like trying to get your kids to eat their green 17
beans after they've been told all day about the wonders of
Milky Way. Come to think of it, it's exactly like that.

Annotations at End of Selection

Thesis: First stated in paragraph 2 (". . . it becomes clear that one of your main jobs as
a parent is to counter the culture. What the media delivers to children by the masses,
you are expected to rebut one at a time.") and then restated in paragraphs 11 ("the
media have become the mainstream culture in children's lives. Parents have become the
alternative."); 13 (Parents are frustrated, not because ". . . they can't say no. It's that
there's so much more to say no to."); and 16 ("It's not just that American families have
less time with their kids. It's that we have to spend more of this time doing battle with
our own culture.").

First reading: A quick take on a serious subject. Informal tone and to-the-point style
gets to the heart of the media vs. parenting problem. Easy to relate to.

Second and third readings:
1. Uses the findings of the American Academy of Pediatrics, a statement made by
   Barbara Dafoe Whitehead, and a number of brief examples to illustrate the relentless
   work parents must do to counter the culture.
2. Uses cause-effect overall to support thesis and comparison-contrast to show how
   parenting nowadays is more difficult than it used to be.
3. Not everything works (reference to her daughter as a media critic, repetitive and
   often inappropriate use of "but" as a transition), but overall the essay succeeds.
4. At first, the ending seems weak. But it feels just right after an additional reading.
   Shows how parents' attempts to counter the culture are as commonplace as their
   attempts to get kids to eat vegetables. It's an ongoing and constant battle that makes
   parenting more difficult than it has to be and less enjoyable than it should be.
5. Possible essay topics: A humorous paper about the strategies kids use to get around
   their parents' saying "no" or a serious paper on the negative effects on kids of
   another aspect of television culture (cable television, tabloid-style talk shows, and
   so on).

The following answers to the questions in "Evaluating a Selection: A Checklist" on pages 4–5 will help crystallize your reaction to Goodman's essay.

1. *Where does support for the selection's thesis seem logical and sufficient? Where does support seem weak?*

Goodman begins to provide evidence for her thesis when she cites the American Academy of Pediatrics' call for a "ban on television food ads" (paragraphs 3–5). The ban followed a study showing that kids are exposed to 202 junk-food ads during a single Saturday morning of television cartoons. Goodman further buoys her thesis with a list of brief "countering the culture" examples (8–10) and a slightly more detailed example (10) describing the parent-child conflicts that occur on a typical trip to the supermarket. By citing Barbara Dafoe Whitehead's findings later on (12–13), Goodman further reinforces her point that the need for constant rebuttal makes parenting especially frustrating: Because parents have to say "no" to virtually everything, more and more family time ends up being spent "doing battle" with the culture (16).

2. *Is the selection unified? If not, why not?*

In the first two paragraphs, Goodman identifies the problem and then provides solid evidence of its existence (3–4, 8–10). But Goodman's comments in paragraph 6 about her daughter's skill as a media critic seem distracting. Even so, paragraph 6 serves a purpose because it establishes Goodman's credibility by showing that she, too, is a parent and has been compelled to be a constant naysayer with her child. From paragraph 7 on, the piece stays on course by focusing on the way parents have to compete with the media for control of their children. The concluding paragraphs (16–17) reinforce Goodman's thesis by suggesting that parents' struggle to counteract the media is as common—and as exasperating—as trying to get children to eat their vegetables when all the kids want is to gorge on candy.

3. *How does the writer make the selection move smoothly from beginning to end?*

The first two paragraphs of Goodman's essay are clearly connected: The phrase "sooner or later" at the beginning of the first paragraph establishes a time frame that is then picked up at the beginning of the second paragraph with the phrase "at some point between Lamaze and the PTA." And Goodman's use in paragraph 3 of the word *this* ("The latest evidence of *this* frustrating piece of the parenting job description...") provides a link to the preceding paragraph. Other connecting strategies can be found in the piece. For example, the words *once, Today, Once,* and *Now* in paragraphs 14–15 provide an easy-to-follow contrast between parenting in earlier times and parenting in this era. However, because paragraph 6 contains a distracting aside, the contrast implied by the word *But* at the beginning of paragraph 7 doesn't work. Nor does Goodman's use of the word *But* at the beginning of paragraph 11 work; the point there emphasizes rather than contrasts with the one made in paragraph 10. From this point on, though, the essay is tightly written and moves smoothly along to its conclusion.

4. *Which stylistic devices are used to good effect in the selection?*

Goodman uses several patterns of development in her essay. The selection as a whole shows the *effect* of the mass media on kids and their parents. In paragraphs 3 and 12, Goodman provides *examples in the form of research data* to support her thesis, while paragraphs 8–10 provide a series of *brief real-life examples*. Paragraphs 12–15 use *contrast*, and paragraph 17 makes a *comparison* to punctuate Goodman's concluding point. Throughout, Goodman's *informal, conversational tone* draws readers in, and her *no-holds-barred style* drives her point home forcefully. In paragraph 8, she uses a *question-and-answer format* ("Are the kids being sold junk food? Just say no.") and *short sentences* ("Turn it off" and "Counter the culture") to illustrate how pervasive the situation is. And in paragraph 9, she uses *fragments* ("To check the ratings..." and "All the while keeping in touch with school...") to focus attention on the problem. These varied stylistic devices help make the essay a quick, enjoyable read. Finally, although Goodman is concerned about the corrosive effects of the media, she leavens her essay with dashes of *humor*. For example, the image of parents as counterculturists (1) and the comments about green beans and Milky Ways (17) probably elicit smiles or gentle laughter from most readers.

5. *How does the selection encourage further thought?*

Goodman's essay touches on a problem most parents face at some time or another—having to counter the culture in order to protect their children. Her main concern is how difficult it is for parents to say "no" to virtually every aspect of the culture. Although Goodman offers no immediate solutions, her presentation of the issue urges us to decide for ourselves which aspects of the culture should be countered and which should not.

If, for each essay you read in this book, you consider the preceding questions, you'll be able to respond thoughtfully to the *Questions for Close Reading* and *Questions About the Writer's Craft* presented after each selection. Your responses will, in turn, prepare you for the writing assignments that follow the questions. Interesting and varied, the assignments invite you to examine issues raised by the selections and encourage you to experiment with various writing styles and organizational patterns.

Following are some sample questions and writing assignments based on the Goodman essay; all are similar to the sort that appear later in this book. Note that the final writing assignment paves the way for a student essay, the stages of which are illustrated in Chapter 2.

Questions for Close Reading

1. According to Goodman, what does it mean to "counter the culture"? Why is this harder now than ever before?
2. Which two groups, according to Goodman, protested the American Academy of Pediatrics's ban on television food ads? Which of these two groups does she take more seriously? Why?

Questions About the Writer's Craft

1. What audience do you think Goodman had in mind when she wrote this piece? How do you know? Where does she address this audience directly?
2. What word appears four times in paragraph 16? Why do you think Goodman repeats this word so often? What is the effect of this repetition?

Writing Assignments

1. Goodman believes that parents are forced to say "no" to almost everything the media offer. Write an essay illustrating the idea that not everything the media present is bad for children.
2. Goodman implies that, in some ways, today's world is hostile to children. Do you agree? Drawing upon but not limiting yourself to the material in your pre-reading journal, write an essay in which you support or reject this viewpoint.

The benefits of active reading are many. Books in general and the selections in *The Longman Reader* in particular will bring you face to face with issues that concern all of us. If you study the selections and the questions that follow them, you'll be on the way to discovering ideas for your own papers. Chapter 2, "The Writing Process," offers practical suggestions for turning those ideas into well-organized, thoughtful essays.

THE WRITING PROCESS

Not many people retire at age thirty-eight. But Michel Montaigne, a sixteenth-century French attorney, did exactly that. Montaigne retired at a young age because he wanted to read, think, and write about all the subjects that interested him. After spending years getting his ideas down on paper, Montaigne finally published his short prose pieces. He called them *essais*—French for "trials" or "attempts."

In fact, all writing is an attempt to transform ideas into words, thus giving order and meaning to life. By using the term *essais*—or *essays* in English—Montaigne acknowledged that a written piece is never really finished. Of course, writers have to stop at some point, especially if they have deadlines to meet. But, as all experienced writers know, even after they dot the final *i*, cross the final *t*, and say "That's it," there's always something that could have been explored further or expressed a little better.

Because writing is a process, shaky starts and changes in direction aren't uncommon. Although there's no way to eliminate the work needed to write effectively, certain approaches can make the process more manageable and rewarding. This chapter describes a sequence of steps for writing essays. Familiarity with a specific sequence develops your awareness of strategies and choices, making you feel more confident when it comes time to write. You're less likely to look at a blank piece of paper and think, "Help! Now what do I do?" During the sequence, you do the following:

1. Prewrite.
2. Identify the thesis.
3. Support the thesis with evidence.

4. Organize the evidence.
5. Write the first draft.
6. Revise the essay.
7. Edit and proofread.

We present the sequence as a series of stages, but we urge you not to view it as a formula to be followed rigidly. Most people develop personalized approaches to the writing process. Some writers mull over a topic in their heads and then move quickly into a promising first draft; others outline their essays in detail before beginning to write. Between these two extremes are any number of effective approaches. The sequence here—illustrated in Figure 2.1 —can be streamlined or otherwise altered to fit individual writing styles as well as the needs of specific assignments.

FIGURE 2.1
Stages of the Writing Process

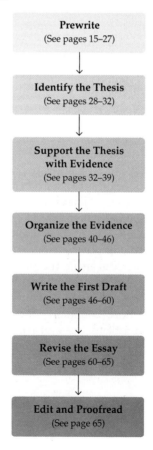

Prewrite
(See pages 15–27)

Identify the Thesis
(See pages 28–32)

Support the Thesis with Evidence
(See pages 32–39)

Organize the Evidence
(See pages 40–46)

Write the First Draft
(See pages 46–60)

Revise the Essay
(See pages 60–65)

Edit and Proofread
(See page 65)

STAGE 1: PREWRITE

Prewriting refers to strategies you can use to generate ideas *before* starting the first draft of a paper. Prewriting techniques are like the warm-ups you do before going out to jog—they loosen you up, get you moving, and help you to develop a sense of well-being and confidence. Since prewriting techniques encourage imaginative exploration, they also help you discover what interests you most about your subject.

During prewriting, you deliberately ignore your internal critic. Your purpose is simply to get ideas down on paper *without evaluating* their effectiveness. Writing without immediately judging what you produce can be liberating. Once you feel less pressure, you'll probably find that you can generate a good deal of material. And that can make your confidence soar.

Keep a Journal

Of all the prewriting techniques, keeping a journal (daily or almost daily) is most likely to make writing a part of your life. Some entries focus on a single theme; others wander from topic to topic. Your starting point may be a dream, a snippet of overheard conversation, a song, a political cartoon, an issue raised in class or in your reading—anything that surprises, interests, angers, depresses, confuses, or amuses you. You may also use a journal to experiment with your writing style—say, to vary your sentence structure if you tend to use predictable patterns.

Here is a fairly focused excerpt from a student's journal:

Today I had to show Paul around school. He and Mom got here by 9. I didn't let on that this was the earliest I've gotten up all semester! He got out of the car looking kind of nervous. Maybe he thought his big brother would be different after a couple of months of college. I walked him around part of the campus and then he went with me to Am. Civ. and then to lunch. He met Greg and some other guys. Everyone seemed to like him. He's got a nice, quiet sense of humor. When I went to Bio., I told him that he could walk around on his own since he wasn't crazy about sitting in on a science class. But he said "I'd rather stick with you." Was he flattering me or was he just scared? Anyway it made me feel good. Later when he was leaving, he told me he's definitely going to apply. I guess that'd be kind of nice, having him here. Mom thinks it's great and she's pushing it. I don't know. I feel kind of like it would invade my privacy. I found this school and have made a life for myself here. Let him find his own school! But it could be great having my kid brother here. I guess this is a classic case of what my psych teacher calls ambivalence. Part of me wants him to come, and part of me doesn't! (November 10)

Although some instructors collect students' journals, you needn't be overly concerned with spelling, grammar, sentence structure, or organization. While journal writing is typically more structured than freewriting (see page 22), you don't have to strive for entries that read like mini-essays. In fact, sometimes you may find it helpful to use a simple list. The important thing is to let your journal writing prompt reflection and new insights, providing you with material to draw upon in your writing. It is, then, a good idea to reread each week's entries to identify recurring themes and concerns. Keep a list of these issues at the back of your journal, under a heading like "Possible Essay Subjects." Here, for instance, are a few topics suggested by the preceding journal entry: deciding which college to attend, leaving home, sibling rivalry. Each of these topics could be developed in a full-length essay.

The pre-reading journal.   To reinforce the value of journal writing, we've included a journal assignment before every reading selection in the book. This assignment, called *Pre-Reading Journal Entry*, encourages you to explore—in a tentative fashion—your thoughts about an issue that will be raised in the selection. Here, once again, is the *Pre-Reading Journal Entry* assignment that precedes Ellen Goodman's "Family Counterculture" (page 7):

> Television is often blamed for having a harmful effect on children. Do you think this criticism is merited? In what ways does TV exert a negative influence on children? In what ways does TV exert a positive influence on youngsters? Take a few minutes to respond to these questions in your journal.

The following journal entry shows how one student, Harriet Davids, responded to the journal assignment. A thirty-eight-year-old college student and mother of two young teenagers, Harriet was understandably intrigued by the assignment. As you'll see, Harriet used a listing strategy to prepare her journal entry. She found that lists were perfect for dealing with the essentially "for or against" nature of the journal assignment.

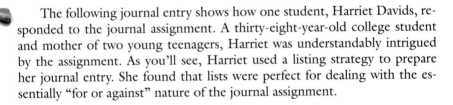

TV's Negative Influence on Kids	TV's Positive Influence on Kids
Teaches negative behaviors (violence, sex, swearing, drugs, alcohol, etc.)	Teaches important educational concepts (*Sesame Street*, shows on The Learning Channel, etc.)
Cuts down on imagination and creativity	Exposes kids to new images and worlds (*Dora the Explorer, Mister Rogers' Neighborhood*)
Cuts down on time spent with parents (talking, reading, playing games together)	Can inspire important discussions (about morals, sexuality, drugs, etc.) between kids and parents

(Continued)

Encourages parents' lack of involvement with kids	Gives parents a needed break from kids
Frightens kids excessively by showing images of real-life violence (terrorist attacks, war, murders, etc.)	Educates kids about the painful realities in the world
Encourages isolation (watching screen rather than interacting with other kids)	Creates common ground among kids, basis of conversations and games
De-emphasizes reading and creates need for constant stimulation	Encourages kids to slow down and read books based on a TV series or show (the *Arthur* and the *Clifford, the Big Red Dog* series, etc.)
Promotes materialism (commercials)	Can be used by parents to teach kids that they can't have everything they see

The journal assignment and subsequent journal entry do more than prepare you to read a selection with extra care and attention; they also pave the way to a full-length essay. Here's how. The final assignment following each selection is called *Writing Assignment Using a Journal Entry as a Starting Point*. This assignment helps you to translate the raw material in your journal entry into a thoughtful, well-considered essay. By the time you get to the assignment, the rough ideas in your journal entry will have been enriched by your reading of the selection. (For an example of a writing assignment that draws upon material in a pre-reading journal entry, turn to page 102.)

As you've just seen, journal writing can stimulate thinking in a loose, unstructured way; it can also prompt the focused thinking required by a specific writing assignment. When you have a specific piece to write, you should approach prewriting in a purposeful, focused manner. You need to:

- Understand the boundaries of the assignment.
- Determine your purpose, audience, and tone.
- Discover your essay's limited subject.
- Generate raw material about your limited subject.
- Organize the raw material.

Understand the Boundaries of the Assignment

Before you start writing a paper, learn what's expected. First, clarify the *kind of paper* the instructor has in mind. Suppose the instructor asks you to discuss the key ideas in an assigned reading. What does the instructor want you to do? Should you include a brief summary of the selection? Should you compare the author's ideas with your own view of the subject? Should you determine if the author's view is supported by valid evidence? If you're not sure about an assignment, ask your instructor to make the requirements clear.

Second, find out *how long* the paper is expected to be. Many instructors will indicate the approximate length of the papers they assign. If no length requirements are provided, discuss with the instructor what you plan to cover and indicate how long you think your paper will be. The instructor will either give you the go-ahead or help you refine the direction and scope of your work.

Determine Your Purpose, Audience, and Tone

Once you understand the requirements for a writing assignment, you're ready to begin thinking about the essay. What is its *purpose*? For what *audience* will it be written? What *tone* will you use? Later on, you may modify your decisions about these issues. That's fine. But you need to understand the way these considerations influence your work in the early phases of the writing process.

Purpose. The papers you write in college are usually meant to *inform* or *explain*, to *convince* or *persuade*, and sometimes to *entertain*. In practice, writing often combines purposes. You might, for example, write an essay trying to *convince* people to support a new trash recycling program in your community. But before you win readers over, you most likely would have to *explain* something about current waste disposal technology.

When purposes blend this way, the predominant one determines the essay's content, organization, emphasis, and choice of words. Assume you're writing about a political campaign. If your primary goal is to *entertain*, to take a gentle poke at two candidates, you might start with several accounts of one candidate's "foot-in-mouth" disease and then describe the attempts of the other candidate, a multimillionaire, to portray himself as an Average Joe. Your language, full of exaggeration, would reflect your objective. But if your primary purpose is to *persuade* readers that the candidates are incompetent and shouldn't be elected, you might adopt a serious, straightforward style. You would use one candidate's gaffes to illustrate her insensitivity to important issues. Similarly, the other candidate's posturing would be presented not as foolish pretension, but as evidence of his lack of judgment.

Audience. To write effectively, you need to identify who your readers are and to take their expectations and needs into account. An essay about the artificial preservatives in the food served by the campus cafeteria would take one form if submitted to your chemistry professor and a very different one if written for the college newspaper. The chemistry paper would probably be formal and technical, complete with chemical formulations and scientific data: "Distillation revealed sodium benzoate particles suspended in a gelatinous medium." But such technical material would be inappropriate in a newspaper column intended for general readers. In this case, you might provide specific examples of cafeteria foods containing additives—"Those deliciously smoky cold cuts are loaded with nitrates and nitrites, both known to cause cancer in laboratory animals"—and suggest ways to eat more healthily: "Pass by the deli counter and fill up instead on vegetarian pizza and fruit juices."

When analyzing your audience, ask yourself the following questions.

☑ ANALYZING YOUR AUDIENCE: A CHECKLIST

❑ What are my readers' age, sex, and educational level?
❑ What are their political, religious, and other beliefs?
❑ What interests and needs motivate my audience?
❑ How much do my readers already know about my subject?
❑ Do they have any misconceptions?
❑ What biases do they have about me, my subject, my opinion?
❑ How do my readers expect me to relate to them?
❑ What values do I share with my readers that will help me communicate with them?

Tone.   Just as a voice projects a range of feelings, writing can convey one or more *tones*, or emotional states: enthusiasm, anger, resignation, and so on. Tone is integral to meaning; it permeates writing and reflects your attitude toward yourself, your purpose, your subject, and your readers. How do you project tone? You pay close attention to sentence structure and word choice.

1. Use appropriate sentence structure.   *Sentence structure* refers to the way sentences are shaped. Although the two paragraphs that follow deal with exactly the same subject, note how differences in sentence structure create sharply dissimilar tones:

> During the 1960s, many inner-city minorities considered the police an occupying force and an oppressive agent of control. As a result, violence against police grew in poorer neighborhoods, as did the number of residents killed by police.

> An occupying force. An agent of control. An oppressor. That's how many inner-city minorities in the '60s viewed the police. Violence against police soared. Police killings of residents mounted.

Informative in its approach, the first paragraph projects a neutral, almost dispassionate tone. The sentences are fairly long, and clear transitions ("During the 1960s"; "As a result") mark the progression of thought. But the second paragraph, with its dramatic, almost alarmist tone, seems intended to elicit a strong emotional response; its short sentences, fragments, and abrupt transitions reflect the turbulence of those earlier times.

2. Choose effective words.   *Word choice* also plays a role in establishing the tone of an essay. Words have *denotations,* neutral dictionary meanings, as well as *connotations,* emotional associations that go beyond the literal meaning. The word *beach,* for instance, is defined in the dictionary as "a nearly level stretch of pebbles and sand beside a body of water." This definition, however, doesn't capture individual responses to the word. For some, *beach* suggests warmth and relaxation; for others, it calls up images of hospital waste and sewage washed up on a once-clean stretch of shoreline.

Since tone and meaning are tightly bound, you must be sensitive to the emotional nuances of words. In a respectful essay about police officers, you wouldn't refer to *cops, narcs,* or *flatfoots;* such terms convey a contempt inconsistent with the tone intended. Your words must also convey tone clearly. Suppose you're writing a satirical piece criticizing a local beauty pageant. Dubbing the participants "livestock on view" leaves no question about your tone. But if you simply referred to the participants as "attractive young women," readers might be unsure of your attitude. Remember, readers can't read your mind, only your paper.

Discover Your Essay's Limited Subject

Because too broad a subject can result in a diffuse, rambling essay, be sure to restrict your general subject before starting to write. The following examples show the difference between general subjects that are too broad for an essay and limited subjects that are appropriate and workable. The examples, of course, represent only a few among many possibilities.

General Subject	Less General	Limited
Education	Computers in education	Computers in elementary school arithmetic classes
	High school education	High school electives
Transportation	Low-cost travel	Hitchhiking
	Getting around a metropolitan area	The transit system in a nearby city
Work	Planning for a career	College internships
	Women in the work force	Women's success as managers

How do you move from a general to a narrow subject? Imagine that you're asked to prepare a straightforward, informative essay for your writing class. Reprinted below is writing assignment 2 from page 12. The assignment, prompted by Ellen Goodman's essay "Family Counterculture," is an extension of the journal-writing assignment on page 7.

> Goodman implies that, in some ways, today's world is hostile to children. Do you agree? Drawing upon but not limiting yourself to the material in your pre-reading journal, write an essay in which you support or reject this viewpoint.

Two techniques—*questioning* and *brainstorming*—can help you limit such a general assignment. While these techniques encourage you to roam freely over a subject, they also help restrict the discussion by revealing which aspects of the subject interest you most.

1. Question the general subject.   One way to narrow a subject is to ask a series of *who, how, why, where, when,* and *what* questions. The following example shows how Harriet Davids, the mother of two young teenagers, used this technique to limit the Goodman assignment.

You may recall that, before reading Goodman's essay, Harriet had used her journal to explore TV's effect on children (see page 16). After reading "Family Counterculture," Harriet concluded that she essentially agreed with Goodman; like Goodman, she felt that parents nowadays are indeed forced to raise their kids in an "increasingly hostile environment." She was pleased that the writing assignment gave her an opportunity to expand preliminary ideas she had jotted down in her journal.

Harriet soon realized that she had to narrow the Goodman assignment. She started by asking a number of pointed questions about the general topic. As she proceeded, she was aware that the same questions could have led to different limited subjects—just as other questions would have.

General Subject: We live in a world that is difficult, even hostile to children.

Question	Limited Subject
<u>Who</u> is to blame for the difficult conditions under which children grow up?	Parents' casual attitude toward child-rearing
<u>How</u> have schools contributed to the problems children face?	Not enough counseling programs for kids in distress
<u>Why</u> do children feel frightened?	Divorce
<u>Where</u> do kids go to escape?	Television, which makes the world seem even more dangerous

(Continued)

Question	Limited Subject
<u>When</u> are children most vulnerable?	The special problems of adolescents
<u>What</u> dangers or fears should parents discuss with their children?	AIDS, drugs, alcohol, war, terrorism

2. Brainstorm the general subject.   Another way to focus on a limited subject is to list quickly everything about the general topic that pops into your mind. Just jot down brief words, phrases, and abbreviations to capture your free-floating thoughts. Writing in complete sentences will slow you down. Don't try to organize or censor your ideas. Even the most fleeting, random, or seemingly outrageous thoughts can be productive. An example of brainstorming appears on page 21.

Questioning and brainstorming can suggest many possible limited subjects. To identify especially promising ones, reread your material. What arouses your interest, anger, or curiosity? What themes seem to dominate and cut to the heart of the matter? Star or circle ideas with potential.

After marking the material, write several phrases or sentences summarizing the most promising limited subjects. Here are just a few that emerged from Harriet Davids's prewriting for the Goodman assignment:

- TV partly to blame for children having such a hard time
- Relocation stressful to children
- Schools also at fault
- The special problems that parents face raising children today

Harriet decided to write on the last of these limited subjects—the special problems that parents face raising children today.

Generate Raw Material About Your Limited Subject

When a limited subject strikes you as having possibilities, use these techniques to see if you have enough interesting things to say about the subject to write an effective essay.

1. Freewrite on your limited subject.   *Freewriting* means jotting down in rough sentences or phrases everything that comes to mind. To capture this continuous stream of thought, write nonstop for ten minutes or more. Don't censor anything; put down whatever pops into your head. Don't reread, edit, or pay attention to organization, spelling, or grammar. If your mind goes blank, repeat words until another thought emerges.

Here is part of the freewriting that Harriet Davids generated about her limited subject, "The special problems that parents face raising children today":

Parents today have tough problems to face. Lots of dangers. The Internet first and foremost. Also crimes of violence against kids. Parents also have to keep up with cost of living, everything costs more, kids want and expect more. Television? Another thing is *Playboy, Penthouse*. Sexy ads and videos on TV, movies deal with sex. Kids grow up too fast, too fast. Kids grow up too fast, too fast. Drugs and alcohol. Witness real-life violence on TV, like terrorist attacks and school shootings. Little kids can't handle knowing too much at an early age. Both parents at work much of the day. Finding good day care a real problem. Lots of latchkey kids. Another problem is getting kids to do homework, lots of other things to do. Especially like going to the mall or chatting with friends online! When I was young, we did homework after dinner, no excuses accepted by my parents.

2. Brainstorm your limited subject.   Let your mind wander freely, as you did when using brainstorming to narrow your subject. This time, list every idea, fact, and example that occurs to you about your limited subject. Use brief words and phrases. For now, don't worry whether ideas fit together or whether the points listed make sense.

To gather additional material on her limited subject for the Goodman as- signment ("The special problems that parents face raising children today"), Harriet Davids brainstormed the following list:

- Trying to raise kids when both parents work
- Prices of everything outrageous, even when both parents work
- Commercials make everyone want *more* of everything
- Clothes so important
- Day care not always the answer—cases of abuse
- Day care very expensive
- Sex everywhere—TV, movies, magazines, Internet
- Sexy clothes on little kids. Absurd!
- Sexual abuse of kids
- Violence on TV, especially images of real-life terrorist attacks and school shootings—scary for kids!
- Violence against kids when parents abuse drugs
- Meth, "Ecstasy," alcohol, heroin, cocaine, AIDS
- Schools have to teach kids about these things
- Schools doing too much—not as good as they used to be
- Not enough homework assigned—kids unprepared
- Distractions from homework—Internet, TV, cellphones, MP3s, computer games

3. Use group brainstorming.   Brainstorming can also be conducted as a group activity. Thrashing out ideas with other people stretches the imagination, revealing possibilities you may not have considered on your own.

Group brainstorming doesn't have to be conducted in a formal classroom situation. You can bounce ideas around with friends and family anywhere—over lunch, at the student center, and so on.

4. Map out the limited subject.   If you're the kind of person who doodles while thinking, you may want to try *mapping*, sometimes called *diagramming* or *clustering*. Like other prewriting techniques, mapping proceeds rapidly and encourages the free flow of ideas. Begin by expressing your limited subject in a crisp phrase and placing it in the center of a blank sheet of paper. As ideas come to you, put them along lines or in boxes or circles around the limited subject. Draw arrows and lines to show the relationships among ideas. Don't stop there, however. Focus on each idea; as subpoints and details come to you, connect them to their source idea, again using boxes, lines, circles, or arrows to clarify how everything relates.

5. Use the patterns of development.   Throughout this book, we show how writers use various patterns of development (narration, process analysis, definition, and so on), singly or in combination, to develop and organize their ideas. Because each pattern has its own distinctive logic, the patterns encourage you, when you prewrite, to think about a subject in different ways, causing insights to surface that might otherwise remain submerged.

The patterns of development are discussed in detail in Chapters 3–11. The following chart shows the way each pattern can generate raw material for a limited subject.

Limited Subject: The special problems that parents face raising children today.

Pattern	Purpose	Raw Material
Description	To detail what a person, place, or object is like	Detail the sights and sounds of a glitzy mall that attracts kids
Narration	To relate an event	Recount what happened when neighbors tried to forbid their kids from going online
Exemplification	To provide specific instances or examples	Offer examples of family arguments. Will permission be given to go to a party where alcohol will be served? Can parents outlaw certain websites?
Division-classification	To divide something into parts or to group related things in categories	Identify components of a TV commercial that distorts kids' values

(Continued)

		Classify the kinds of commercials that make it difficult to teach kids values
Process analysis	To explain how something happens or how something is done	Explain step by step how family life can disintegrate when parents have to work all the time to make ends meet
Comparison-contrast	To point out similarities and/or dissimilarities	Contrast families today with those of a generation ago
Cause-effect	To analyze reasons and consequences	Explain why parents are not around to be with their kids: Industry's failure to provide day care and its inflexibility about granting time off for parents with sick kids
		Explain the consequences of absentee parents: Kids feel unloved; they spend hours on the Internet, they turn to TV for role models, they're undisciplined; they take on adult responsibility too early
Definition	To explain the meaning of a term or concept	What is meant by "tough love"?
Argumentation-persuasion	To win people over to a point of view	Convince parents that they must work with schools to develop programs that make kids feel safer and more secure

(For more on ways to use the patterns of development in different phases of the writing process, see pages 32–33, 40–41, and 573–575.)

Conduct research.   Depending on your topic, you may find it helpful to visit the library and/or to go online to identify books and articles about your limited subject. At this point, you don't need to read closely the material you find. Just skim and perhaps take a few brief notes on ideas and points that could be useful.

In researching the Goodman assignment, for instance, Harriet Davids could look under such headings and subheadings as the following:

Day care
Drug abuse
Family

Parent-child relationship
    Child abuse
    Children of divorced parents
    Children of working mothers
School and home

Organize the Raw Material

On pages 43–45, we talk about the more formal outline you may need later on in the writing process. However, a *scratch outline* or *scratch list* can be an effective strategy for imposing order on the tentative ideas generated during prewriting.

Reread your exploratory thoughts about the limited subject. Cross out anything not appropriate for your purpose, audience, and tone; add points that didn't originally occur to you. Star or circle compelling items that warrant further development. Then draw arrows between related items, your goal being to group such material under a common heading. Finally, determine what seems to be the best order for those headings.

By giving you a sense of the way your free-form material might fit together, a scratch outline makes the writing process more manageable. You're less likely to feel overwhelmed once you actually start writing because you'll already have some idea about how to shape your material into a meaningful statement. Remember, though, the scratch outline can, and most likely will, be modified along the way.

The following scratch outline shows how Harriet Davids began to shape her brainstorming (page 24) into a more organized format. Note the way she eliminated some items (for example, the points about outrageous prices and about real-life TV violence), added others (for example, the places to go that distract from homework), and grouped the brainstormed items under four main headings, with the appropriate details listed underneath. (If you'd like to see Harriet's more formal outline and her first draft, turn to pages 43–45 and 57–59.)

Limited Subject: The special problems that parents face raising children today.

1. Day care for two-career families
   - Expensive
   - Before-school problems
   - After-school problems

2. Distractions from homework
   - Internet, televisions, cellphones, MP3s
   - Places to go—malls, movies, fast-food restaurants

3. Sexually explicit materials
   - Internet
   - Television shows
   - Movies
   - Magazines

4. Life-threatening dangers
   - Drugs
   - Drinking
   - AIDS
   - Violence against children (by sitters, in day care, etc.)

The prewriting strategies just described provide a solid foundation for the next stages of your work. But invention and imaginative exploration don't end when prewriting is completed. As you'll see, remaining open to new ideas is crucial during all phases of the writing process.

Activities: Prewrite

1. Number the items in each set from 1 (*broadest subject*) to 5 (*most limited subject*):

Set A	Set B
Abortion	Business majors
Controversial social issue	Students' majors
Cutting state abortion funds	College students
Federal funding of abortions	Kinds of students on campus
Social issues	Why many students major in business

2. Which of the following topics are too broad for an essay of two to five typewritten pages: soap operas' appeal to college students; day care; trying to "kick" the junk-food habit; male and female relationships; international terrorism?

3. Use the techniques indicated in parentheses to limit each general topic listed below. Then, identify a specific purpose, audience, and tone for the one limited subject you consider most interesting. Next, with the help of the patterns of development, generate raw material about that limited subject. (You may find it helpful to work with others when developing this material.) Finally, shape your raw material into a scratch outline—crossing out, combining, and adding ideas as needed. (Save your scratch outline so you can work with it further after reading about the next stage in the writing process.)

   Friendship (*journal writing*)
   Malls (*mapping*)
   Leisure (*freewriting*)
   Television (*brainstorming*)
   Required courses (*group brainstorming*)
   Manners (*questioning*)

STAGE 2: IDENTIFY THE THESIS

The process of prewriting—discovering a limited subject and generating ideas about it—prepares you for the next stage in writing an essay: identifying the paper's *thesis,* or controlling idea. Presenting your opinion on a subject, the thesis should focus on an interesting and significant issue, one that engages your energies and merits your consideration. You may think of the thesis as the essay's hub—the central point around which all the other material revolves. Your thesis determines what does and does not belong in the essay. The thesis, especially when it occurs early in an essay, also helps focus the reader on the piece's central point.

Sometimes the thesis emerges early in the prewriting stage. Often, though, you'll need to do some work to determine your thesis. For some topics, you may need to do some library research. For others, the best way to identify a promising thesis is to look through your prewriting and ask yourself questions such as these: "What statement does all this prewriting support? What aspect of the limited subject is covered in most detail? What is the focus of the most provocative material?"

 For a look at the process of finding the thesis within prewriting material, glance back at the scratch outline (page 26–27) that Harriet Davids prepared for the limited subject "The special problems that parents face raising children today." Harriet devised the following thesis to capture the focus of this prewriting: "Being a parent today is much more difficult than it was a generation ago." (The full outline for Harriet's paper appears on pages 43–45; the first draft on pages 57–59; the final draft on pages 66–68.)

Writing an Effective Thesis

Generally expressed in one or two sentences, a thesis statement often has two parts. One part presents the *limited subject;* the other gives your *point of view,* or *attitude,* about that subject. Here are some examples of moving from general subject to limited subject to thesis statement. In each thesis statement, the limited subject is underlined once and the attitude twice.

General Subject	Limited Subject	Thesis
Education	Computers in elementary school arithmetic classes	Computer programs in arithmetic can individualize instruction more effectively than the average elementary school teacher can.

(Continued)

Transportation	A metropolitan transit system	Although the <u>city's transit system</u> still has problems, it <u>has become safer and more efficient in the last two years.</u>
Work	College internships	<u>College internships provide valuable opportunities to students uncertain about what to do after graduation.</u>
Our anti-child world	Special problems that parents face raising children today	<u>Being a parent today</u> <u>is much more difficult than it was a generation ago.</u>

(*Reminder:* The last thesis statement is Harriet Davids's, devised for the essay she planned to write for the assignment on page 12. Harriet's prewriting appears on pages 23 and 27, and her first draft on pages 57–59.)

Avoiding Thesis Pitfalls

Because identifying your thesis statement is an important step in writing a sharply focused essay, you need to avoid three common problems that lead to an ineffective thesis.

Don't make an announcement.   Some writers use the thesis statement merely to announce the limited subject of their paper and forget to indicate their attitude toward the subject. Such statements are announcements of intent, not thesis statements.

Compare the following three announcements with the thesis statements beside them.

Announcements	Thesis Statements
My essay will discuss whether a student pub should exist on campus.	This college should not allow a student pub on campus.
Handgun legislation is the subject of this paper.	Banning handguns is the first step toward controlling crime in the United States.
I want to discuss cable television.	Cable television has not delivered on its promise to provide an alternative to network programming.

Don't make a factual statement.   Your thesis and thus your essay should focus on an issue capable of being developed. If a fact is used as a thesis, you have no place to go; a fact generally doesn't invite much discussion. Notice the difference between these factual statements and thesis statements:

Factual Statements	Thesis Statements
Many businesses pollute the environment.	Tax penalties should be levied against businesses that pollute the environment.
Nowadays, many movies are violent.	Movie violence provides a healthy outlet for aggression.
The population of the United States is growing older.	The aging of the U.S. population will eventually create a crisis in the delivery of health-care services.

Don't make a broad statement.   Avoid stating your thesis in vague, general, or sweeping terms. Broad statements make it difficult for readers to grasp your essay's point. Moreover, if you start with a broad thesis, you're saddled with the impossible task of trying to develop a book-length idea in an essay that runs only several pages.

The following examples contrast statements that are too broad with thesis statements that are focused effectively.

Broad Statements	Thesis Statements
Nowadays, high school education is often meaningless.	High school diplomas have been devalued by grade inflation.
Newspapers cater to the taste of the American public.	The success of *USA Today* indicates that people want newspapers that are easy to read and entertaining.
The computer revolution is not all that we have been led to believe it is.	Home computers are still an impractical purchase for many people.

The thesis is often stated near the beginning, but it may be delayed, especially if you need to provide background information before it can be understood. Sometimes the thesis is reiterated—with fresh words—in the essay's conclusion or elsewhere. You may even leave the thesis unstated, relying on strong evidence to convey the essay's central idea.

One final point: Once you start writing your first draft, some feelings, thoughts, and examples may emerge that qualify, even contradict, your initial thesis. Don't resist these new ideas; they frequently move you toward a clearer statement of your main point. Remember, though, your essay must have a thesis. Without this central concept, you have no reason for writing.

Activities: Identify the Thesis

1. For each of the following limited subjects, four possible thesis statements are given. Indicate whether each is an announcement (*A*), a factual statement (*FS*), too broad a statement (*TB*), or an effective thesis (*OK*). Then, for each effective thesis, identify a possible purpose, audience, and tone.

   Limited Subject: The ethics of treating severely handicapped infants

   Some babies born with severe handicaps have been allowed to die.

   There are many serious issues involved in the treatment of handicapped newborns.

   The government should pass legislation requiring medical treatment for handicapped newborns.

   This essay will analyze the controversy surrounding the treatment of severely handicapped babies who would die without medical care.

   Limited Subject: Privacy and computerized records

   Computers raise some significant and crucial questions for all of us.

   Computerized records keep track of consumer spending habits, credit records, travel patterns, and other personal information.

   Computerized records have turned our private lives into public property.

   In this paper, the relationship between computerized records and the right to privacy will be discussed.

2. Each of the following sets lists the key points in an essay. Using the information provided, prepare a possible thesis for each essay.

   Set A
   - One evidence of this growing conservatism is the reemerging popularity of fraternities and sororities.
   - Beauty contests, ROTC training, and corporate recruiting—once rejected by students on many campuses—are again popular.
   - Most important, many students no longer choose risky careers that enable them to contribute to society but select, instead, safe fields with money-making potential.

   Set B
   - We do not know how engineering new forms of life might affect the earth's delicate ecological balance.
   - Another danger of genetic research is its potential for unleashing new forms of disease.
   - Even beneficial attempts to eliminate genetic defects could contribute to the dangerous idea that only perfect individuals are entitled to live.

3. Following are four pairs of general and limited subjects. Generate an appropriate thesis statement for each pair. Select one thesis, and determine which

pattern of development would support it most effectively. Use that pattern to draft a paragraph developing the thesis. (Save the paragraph so you can work with it further after reading about the next stage in the writing process.)

General Subject	Limited Subject
Psychology	The power struggles in a classroom
Health	Doctors' attitudes toward patients
U.S. politics	Television's coverage of presidential campaigns
Work	Minimum-wage jobs for young people

4. Return to the scratch outline you prepared for activity 3 on page 27. After examining the outline, identify a thesis that conveys the central idea behind most of the raw material. Then, ask others to evaluate your thesis in light of the material in the outline. Finally, keeping the thesis—as well as your purpose, audience, and tone—in mind, refine the scratch outline by deleting inappropriate items, adding relevant ones, and indicating where more material is needed. (Save your refined scratch outline and thesis so you can work with them further after reading about the next stage in the writing process.)

STAGE 3: SUPPORT THE THESIS WITH EVIDENCE

Supporting material grounds your essay, showing readers you have good reason for feeling as you do about your subject. Your evidence also adds interest and color to your writing. In college essays of five hundred to fifteen hundred words, you usually need at least three major points of evidence to develop your thesis. These major points—each focusing on related but separate aspects of the thesis—eventually become the supporting paragraphs in the body of the essay.

What Is Evidence?

By *evidence,* we mean a number of different kinds of support. *Examples* are just one option. To develop your thesis, you might also include *reasons, facts, details, statistics, anecdotes,* and *quotations from experts.* Imagine you're writing an essay with the thesis "People normally unconcerned about the environment can be galvanized to constructive action if they feel personally affected by an environmental problem." You could support this thesis with any combination of the following types of evidence:

- *Examples* of successful recycling efforts in several neighborhoods.
- *Reasons* why people got involved in a neighborhood recycling effort.
- *Facts* about other residents' efforts to preserve the quality of their well water.

- *Details* about the steps that people can take to get involved in environmental issues.
- *Statistics* showing the number of Americans concerned about the environment.
- An *anecdote* about your involvement in environmental efforts.
- A *quotation* from a well-known scientist about the impact that citizens can have on environmental legislation.

Where Do You Find Evidence?

Where do you find the examples, anecdotes, details, and other types of evidence needed to support your thesis? As you saw when you followed Harriet Davids's strategies for gathering material for an essay (pages 22–26), a good deal of evidence is generated during the prewriting stage. In this phase of the writing process, you tap into your personal experiences, draw upon other people's observations, perhaps interview a person with special knowledge about your subject. The library, with its abundant material, is another rich source of supporting evidence. In addition, the various patterns of development are a valuable source of evidence.

How the Patterns of Development Help Generate Evidence

On pages 23–24, we discussed the way patterns of development help generate material about a limited subject. The same patterns also help develop support for a thesis. The following chart shows how three patterns can generate evidence for this thesis: "To those who haven't done it, babysitting looks easy. In practice, though, babysitting can be difficult, frightening, even dangerous."

Pattern	Evidence Generated
Division-classification	A typical babysitting evening divided into stages: playing with the kids; putting them to bed; dealing with their nighttime fears once they're in bed
	Kids' nighttime fears classified by type: monsters under their beds; bad dreams; being abandoned by their parents
Process analysis	Step-by-step account of what a babysitter should do if a child becomes ill or injured
Comparison-contrast	Contrast between two babysitters: one well-prepared, the other unprepared

(For more on ways to use the patterns of development in different phases of the writing process, see pages 23–24, 40–41, and 573–575.)

Characteristics of Evidence

No matter how it is generated, all types of supporting evidence share the characteristics described in the following sections. You should keep these characteristics in mind as you review your thesis and scratch outline. That way, you can make the changes needed to strengthen the evidence gathered earlier. As you'll see shortly, Harriet Davids focused on many of these issues as she worked with the evidence she collected during the prewriting phase.

The evidence is relevant and unified.   All the evidence in an essay must clearly support the thesis. It makes no difference how riveting material might be; if it doesn't *relate directly* to the essay's central point, the material should be eliminated. Irrelevant material can weaken your position by implying that no relevant support exists. It also distracts readers from your controlling idea, thus disrupting the paper's overall unity.

The following paragraph, from an essay on changes in Americans' television-viewing habits, focuses on people's reasons for switching from network to cable television. As you'll see, the paragraph lacks unity because it contains points (underlined) unrelated to its main idea. Specifically, the comments about cable's foul language should be deleted. Although these observations bring up interesting points, they shift the paragraph's focus from reasons to objections. If the writer wants to present a balanced view of the pros and cons of cable and network television, these points *should* be covered, but in *another paragraph*.

Nonunified Support

Many people consider cable TV an improvement over network television. For one thing, viewers usually prefer the movies on cable. Unlike network films, cable movies are often only months old, they have not been edited by censors, and they are not interrupted by commercials. Growing numbers of people also feel that cable specials are superior to the ones the networks grind out. Cable viewers may enjoy such pop stars as Billy Joel, Mariah Carey, or Chris Rock in concert, whereas the networks continue to broadcast tired variety shows and boring awards ceremonies. There is, however, one problem with cable comedians. The foul language many of them use makes it hard to watch these cable specials with children. The networks, in contrast, generally present "clean" shows that parents and children can watch together. Then, too, cable TV offers viewers more flexibility since it schedules shows at various times over the month. People working night shifts or attending evening classes can see movies in the afternoon, and viewers missing the first twenty minutes of a show can always catch them later. It's not surprising that cable viewership is growing while network ratings have taken a plunge.

Early in the writing process, Harriet Davids was aware of the importance of relevant evidence. Take a moment to compare Harriet's brainstorming (page 23) and her scratch outline (page 26–27). Even though Harriet hadn't identified her thesis when she prepared the scratch outline, she realized she should delete a number of items from her brainstorming—for example, the second item and third-to-last item ("prices of everything outrageous" and "schools doing too much"). Harriet eliminated these points because they weren't consistent with the focus of her limited subject.

The evidence is specific.   When evidence is vague and general, readers lose interest in what you're saying, become skeptical of your ideas' validity, and feel puzzled about your meaning. In contrast, *specific, concrete evidence* provides sharp *word pictures* that engage your readers, persuade them that your thinking is sound, and clarify meaning.

Consider, for example, the differences between the following two sentences: "The young man had trouble lifting the box out of an old car" and "Joe, only twenty years old but severely weakened by a recent bout with the flu, struggled to lift the heavy wooden crate out of the rusty, dented Chevrolet." The first sentence, filled with generalities, is fuzzy and imprecise while the second sentence, filled with specifics, is crisp and clear.

As the preceding sentences illustrate, three strategies can be used, singly or in combination, to make writing specific. First, you can provide answers to *who, which, what,* and similar *questions.* (The question "How does the car look?" prompts a change in which "an old car" becomes "a rusty, dented Chevrolet.") Second, you can use *vigorous verbs* ("had trouble lifting" becomes "struggled to lift"). Finally, you can replace *vague, abstract* nouns with *vivid, concrete* nouns or phrases ("the young man" becomes "Joe, only twenty years old but severely weakened by a recent bout with the flu").

Following are two versions of a paragraph from an essay about trends in the business community. Although both paragraphs focus on one such trend—flexible working hours—note how the first version's bland language fails to engage the reader and how its vague generalities leave the meaning unclear. What, for example, is meant by the term "flex-time scheduling"? The second paragraph answers this question (as well as several others) with clear specifics; it also uses strong, energetic language. As a result, the second paragraph is more informative and more interesting than the first.

Nonspecific Support

More and more companies have begun to realize that flex-time scheduling offers advantages. Several companies outside Boston have tried flex-time scheduling and are pleased with the way the system reduces the difficulties their employees face getting to work. Studies show that flex-time scheduling also increases productivity, reduces on-the-job conflict, and minimizes work-related accidents.

Specific Support

More and more companies have begun to realize that flex-time scheduling offers advantages over a rigid 9-to-5 routine. Along suburban Boston's Route 128, such companies as Compugraphics and Consolidated Paper now permit employees to schedule their arrival any time between 6 A.M. and 11 A.M. The corporations report that the number of rush-hour jams and accidents has fallen dramatically. As a result, employees no longer arrive at work weighed down by tension induced by choking clouds of exhaust fumes and the blaring horns of gridlocked drivers. Studies sponsored by the journal *Business Quarterly* show that this more mellow state of mind benefits corporations. Traffic-stressed employees begin their workday anxious and exasperated, still grinding their teeth at their fellow commuters, their frustration often spilling over into their performance at work. By contrast, stress-free employees work more productively and take fewer days off. They are more tolerant of coworkers and customers, and less likely to balloon minor irritations into major confrontations. Perhaps most importantly, employees arriving at work relatively free of stress can focus their attention on working safely. They rack up significantly fewer on-the-job accidents, such as falls and injuries resulting from careless handling of dangerous equipment. Flex-time improves employee well-being, and as well-being rises, so do company profits.

At this point, it will be helpful to compare once again Harriet Davids's brainstorming (page 23) and her scratch outline (page 26–27). Note the way she added new details in the outline to make her evidence more specific. For example, to the item "Distractions from homework," she added the new examples "malls," "movies," and "fast-food restaurants." And, as you'll see when you read Harriet's first and final drafts (pages 58–59 and 66–68), she added many more vigorous specifics during later stages of the writing process.

The evidence is adequate.   Readers won't automatically accept your thesis; you need to provide *enough specific evidence* to support your viewpoint. On occasion, a single extended example will suffice. Generally, though, you'll need various kinds of evidence: facts, examples, reasons, personal observations, expert opinion, and so on.

Following are two versions of a paragraph from a paper showing how difficult it is to get personal, attentive service nowadays at gas stations, supermarkets, and department stores. Both paragraphs focus on the problem at gas stations, but one paragraph is much more effective. As you'll see, the first paragraph starts with good, specific support, yet fails to provide enough of it. The second paragraph offers additional examples, descriptive details, and dialogue—all of which make the writing stronger and more convincing.

Inadequate Support

Gas stations are a good example of this impersonal attitude. At many stations, attendants have even stopped pumping gas. Motorists pull up to a combination convenience store and gas island where an attendant is enclosed in a glass booth with a tray for taking money. The driver must get out of the car, pump the gas, and walk over to the booth to pay. That's a real inconvenience, especially when compared with the way service stations used to be run.

Adequate Support

Gas stations are a good example of this impersonal attitude. At many stations, attendants have even stopped pumping gas. Motorists pull up to a combination convenience store and gas island where an attendant is enclosed in a glass booth with a tray for taking money. The driver must get out of the car, pump the gas, and walk over to the booth to pay. Even at stations that still have "pump jockeys," employees seldom ask, "Check your oil?" or wash windshields, although they may grudgingly point out the location of the bucket and squeegee. And customers with a balky engine or a nonfunctioning heater are usually out of luck. Why? Many gas stations have eliminated on-duty mechanics. The skillful mechanic who could replace a belt or fix a tire in a few minutes has been replaced by a teenager in a jumpsuit who doesn't know a carburetor from a charge card and couldn't care less.

Now take a final look at Harriet Davids's scratch outline (page 26–27). Harriet realized she needed more than one block of supporting material to develop her limited subject; that's why she identified four separate blocks of evidence (day care, homework distractions, sexual material, and dangers). When Harriet prepared her first and final drafts (pages 58–59 and 66–68), she decided to eliminate the material about day care. But she added so many more specific and dramatic details that her evidence was more than sufficient.

The evidence is accurate.   When you have a strong belief and want readers to see things your way, you may be tempted to overstate or downplay facts, disregard information, misquote, or make up details. Suppose you plan to write an essay making the point that dormitory security is lax. You begin supporting your thesis by narrating the time you were nearly mugged in your dorm hallway. Realizing the essay would be more persuasive if you also mentioned other episodes, you decide to invent some material. Perhaps you describe several supposed burglaries on your dorm floor or exaggerate the amount of time it took campus security to respond to an emergency call from a residence hall. Yes, you've supported your point—but at the expense of truth.

The evidence is representative.   Using representative evidence means that you rely on the typical, the usual, to show that your point is valid. Contrary to the maxim, exceptions don't prove the rule. Perhaps you plan to write an essay contending that the value of seat belts has been exaggerated. To support your position, you mention a friend who survived a head-on collision without wearing a seat belt. Such an example isn't representative because the facts and figures on accidents suggest your friend's survival was a fluke.

Borrowed evidence is documented.   If you include evidence from outside sources (books, articles, interviews), you need to acknowledge where that information comes from. If you don't, readers may consider your evidence nothing more than your point of view, or they may regard as dishonest your failure to cite your indebtedness to others for ideas that obviously aren't your own.

For help in documenting sources in brief, informal papers, turn to page 481. For information on acknowledging sources in longer, more formal papers, refer to Appendix A (pages 606–637).

Strong supporting evidence is at the heart of effective writing. Without it, essays lack energy and fail to convey the writer's perspective. Such lifeless writing is more apt to put readers to sleep than to engage their interest and convince them that the points being made are valid. Taking the time to accumulate solid supporting material is, then, a critical step in the writing process.

Activities: Support the Thesis with Evidence

1. Each of the following sets includes a thesis statement and four points of support. In each set, identify the one point that is off target.

    Set A

    Thesis: Colleges should put less emphasis on sports.

    Encourages grade fixing
    Creates a strong following among former graduates
    Distracts from real goals of education
    Causes extensive and expensive injuries

    Set B

    Thesis: The United States is becoming a homogenized country.
    Regional accents vanishing
    Chain stores blanket country
    Americans proud of their ethnic identities
    Metropolitan areas almost indistinguishable from one another

2. For each of the following thesis statements, develop three points of relevant support. Then use the patterns of development to generate evidence for each point of support.

    Thesis: The trend toward disposable, throwaway products has gone too far.

Thesis: The local (or college) library fails to meet the needs of those it is supposed to serve.

Thesis: Television portrays men as incompetent creatures.

3. Choose one of the following thesis statements. Then identify an appropriate purpose, audience, and tone for an essay with this thesis. Using freewriting, mapping, or the questioning technique, generate at least three supporting points for the thesis. Last, write a paragraph about one of the points, making sure your evidence reflects the characteristics discussed in these pages. Alternatively, you may go ahead and prepare the first draft of an essay having the selected thesis. (If you choose the second option, you may want to turn to page 57 to see a diagram showing how to organize a first draft.) Save whatever you prepare so you can work with it further after reading about the next stage in the writing process.

   • Winning the lottery may not always be a blessing.
   • All of us can take steps to reduce the country's trash crisis.
   • Drug education programs in public schools are (or are not) effective.

4. Select one of the following thesis statements. Then determine your purpose, audience, and tone for an essay with this thesis. Next, use the patterns of development to generate at least three supporting points for the thesis. Finally, write a paragraph about one of the points, making sure that your evidence demonstrates the characteristics discussed in these pages. Alternatively, you may go ahead and prepare a first draft of an essay having the thesis selected. (If you choose the latter option, you may want to turn to page 57 to see a diagram showing how to organize a first draft.) Save whatever you prepare so you can work with it further after reading about the next stage in the writing process.

   • Teenagers should (or should not) be able to obtain birth control devices without their parents' permission.
   • The college's system for awarding student loans needs to be overhauled.
   • E-mail has changed for the worse (or the better) the way Americans communicate with each other.

5. Retrieve the paragraph you wrote in response to activity 3 on page 31–32. Keeping in mind the characteristics of effective evidence discussed in pages 34–38, make whatever changes are needed to strengthen the paragraph. (Save the paragraph so you can work with it further after reading about the next stage in the writing process.)

6. Look at the thesis and refined scratch outline you prepared in response to activity 4 on page 31–32. Where do you see gaps in the support for your thesis? By brainstorming with others, generate material to fill these gaps. If some of the new points generated suggest that you should modify your thesis, make the appropriate changes now. (Save this material so you can work with it further after reading about the next stage in the writing process.)

STAGE 4: ORGANIZE THE EVIDENCE

After you've generated supporting evidence, you're ready to *organize* that material. Even highly compelling evidence won't illustrate the validity of your thesis or achieve your purpose if readers have to plow through a maze of chaotic evidence. Some writers can move quickly from generating support to writing a clearly structured first draft. (They usually say they have sequenced their ideas in their heads.) Most, however, need to spend some time sorting out their thoughts on paper before starting the first draft; otherwise, they tend to lose their way in a tangle of ideas.

When moving to the organizing stage, you should have in front of you your scratch outline (see pages 26–27) and thesis plus any supporting material you've accumulated. To find a logical framework for all this material, you'll need to

- Determine which pattern of development is implied in your evidence.
- Select one of four basic approaches for organizing your evidence.
- Outline your evidence.

Use the Patterns of Development

Each pattern of development (see pages 23–26) has its own internal logic that makes it appropriate for some writing purposes but not for others. Once you see which pattern (or combination of patterns) is implied by your purpose, you can block out your paper's general structure. Imagine that you're writing an essay *explaining why* some students drop out of college during the first semester. You might organize the essay around a three-part discussion of the key *causes* contributing to the difficulty that students have adjusting to college: (1) they miss friends and family, (2) they take inappropriate courses, and (3) they experience conflicts with roommates. As you can see, your choice of pattern of development significantly influences your essay's content and organization.

Some essays follow a single pattern, but most blend them, with a predominant pattern providing the piece's organizational framework. In our example essay, you might include a brief *description* of an overwhelmed first-year college student; you might *define* the psychological term "separation anxiety"; you might end the paper by briefly explaining a *process* for making students' adjustment to college easier. Still, the essay's overall organizational pattern would be *cause-effect* since the paper's primary purpose is to explain why students drop out of college. (For more information on the way patterns often blend in writing, see Chapter 12, "Combining the Patterns.")

Although writers often combine the patterns of development, writing an essay organized according to a single pattern can help you understand a particular pattern's unique demands. Keep in mind, though, that most writing begins not with a specific pattern but with a specific *purpose*. The pattern or combination of patterns evolves out of that purpose.

Select an Organizational Approach

No matter which pattern(s) of development you select, you need to know four general approaches for organizing supporting evidence—chronological, spatial, emphatic, and simple-to-complex.

Chronological approach. When an essay is organized *chronologically*, supporting material is arranged in a clear time sequence, usually starting with what happened first and ending with what happened last. Occasionally, chronological sequences can be rearranged to create flashback or flashforward effects, two techniques discussed in Chapter 4 on narration. Essays using narration (for example, an experience with prejudice) or process analysis (for instance, how to deliver an effective speech) are most likely to be organized chronologically. The paper on public speaking might use a time sequence to present its points: how to prepare a few days before the presentation is due; what to do right before the speech; what to concentrate on during the speech itself. (For examples of chronologically arranged student essays, turn to pages 136 and 292.)

Spatial approach. When you arrange supporting evidence *spatially*, you discuss details as they occur in space, or from certain locations. This strategy is particularly appropriate for description. Imagine that you plan to write an essay describing the happy times you spent as a child playing by a towering old oak tree in the neighborhood park. Using spatial organization, you start by describing the rich animal life (the plump earthworms, swarming anthills, and numerous animal tracks) you observed while hunkered down *at the base* of the tree. Next, you re-create the contented feeling you experienced sitting on a branch *in the middle* of the tree. Finally, you end by describing the glorious view of the world you had *from the top* of the tree.

Although spatial arrangement is flexible (you could, for instance, start with a description from the top of the tree), you should always proceed systematically. And once you select a particular spatial order, you should usually maintain that sequence throughout the essay; otherwise, readers may get lost along the way. (A spatially arranged student essay appears on page 80.)

Emphatic approach. In *emphatic* order, the most compelling evidence is saved for last. This arrangement is based on the psychological principle that people remember best what they experience last. Emphatic order has built-in momentum because it starts with the least important point and builds to the most significant. This method is especially effective in argumentation-persuasion essays, in papers developed through examples, and in pieces involving comparison-contrast, division-classification, or causal analysis.

Consider an essay analyzing the negative effect that workaholic parents can have on their children. The paper might start with a brief discussion of relatively minor effects such as the family's eating mostly frozen or takeout foods. Paragraphs on more serious effects might follow: children get no parental help with homework; they try to resolve personal problems without parental advice. Finally, the essay might close with a detailed discussion of the most significant effect—children's lack of self-esteem because they feel unimportant in their parents' lives. (The student essays on pages 182, 346, and 437 all use an emphatic arrangement.)

Simple-to-complex approach.   A final way to organize an essay is to proceed from relatively *simple* concepts to more *complex* ones. By starting with easy-to-grasp, generally accepted evidence, you establish rapport with your readers and assure them that the essay is firmly grounded in shared experience. In contrast, if you open with difficult or highly technical material, you risk confusing and alienating your audience.

Assume you plan to write a paper arguing that your college has endangered students' health by not making an all-out effort to remove asbestos from dormitories and classroom buildings. It probably wouldn't be a good idea to begin with a medically sophisticated explanation of precisely how asbestos damages lung tissue. Instead, you might start with an observation that is likely to be familiar to your readers—one that is part of their everyday experience. You could, for example, open with a description of asbestos—as readers might see it—wrapped around air ducts and furnaces or used as electrical insulation and fireproofing material. Having provided a basic, easy-to-visualize description, you could then go on to explain the complicated process by which asbestos can cause chronic lung inflammation. (See page 393 for an example of a student essay using the simple-to-complex arrangement.)

Depending on your purpose, any one of these four organizational approaches might be appropriate. For example, assume that you planned to write an essay developing Harriet Davids's thesis: "Being a parent today is much more difficult than it was a generation ago." To emphasize that the various stages in children's lives present parents with different difficulties, you'd probably select a *chronological* sequence. To show that the challenges that parents face vary depending on whether children are at home, at school, or in the world at large, you'd probably choose a *spatial* sequence. To stress the range of problems that parents face (from less to more serious), you'd probably use an *emphatic* sequence. To illustrate today's confusing array of theories for raising children, you might take a *simple-to-complex* approach, moving from the basic to the most sophisticated theories.

Prepare an Outline

Having an outline—a skeletal version of your paper—*before* you begin the first draft makes the writing process much more manageable. The outline helps you organize your thoughts beforehand, and it guides your writing as you work on the draft. Even though ideas continue to evolve during the draft, an outline clarifies how ideas fit together, which points are major, which should come first, and so on. An outline may also reveal places where evidence is weak, underscoring the need, perhaps, for more prewriting.

Some people prepare highly structured outlines; others make only a few informal jottings. Sometimes outlining will go quickly, with points falling easily into place; at other times you'll have to work hard to figure out how points are related. If that happens, be glad you caught the problem while outlining rather than while writing the first draft.

To prepare an effective outline, you should reread and evaluate your scratch outline and thesis as well as any other evidence you've generated since the prewriting stage. Then decide which pattern of development (description, cause-effect, and so on) seems to be suggested by your evidence. Also determine whether your evidence lends itself to a chronological, a spatial, an emphatic, or a simple-to-complex order. Having done all that, you're ready to identify and sequence your main and supporting points.

The amount of detail in an outline will vary according to the paper's length and the instructor's requirements. A scratch outline (like the one on page 26–27) is often sufficient, but for longer papers, you'll probably need a more detailed and formal outline. In such cases, the suggestions in the accompanying checklist will help you develop a sound plan. Feel free to modify these guidelines to suit your needs.

☑ OUTLINING: A CHECKLIST

❑ Write your purpose, audience, tone, and thesis at the top.

❑ Below the thesis, enter the pattern of development you've chosen.

❑ Record the organizational approach you've selected.

❑ Delete from your supporting material anything that doesn't develop the thesis or that isn't appropriate for your purpose, audience, and tone.

❑ Add any new points or material. Group related items together. Give each group a heading that represents a main topic in support of your thesis.

❑ Label these main topics with roman numerals (I, II, III, and so on). Let the order of the numerals indicate the best sequence.

- ❏ Identify subtopics and group them under the appropriate main topics. Indent and label these subtopics with capital letters (A, B, C, and so on). Let the order of the letters indicate the best sequence.

- ❏ Identify supporting points (often, reasons and examples) and group them under the appropriate subtopics. Indent and label these supporting points with arabic numbers (1, 2, 3, and so on). Let the numbers indicate the best sequence.

- ❏ Identify specific details (secondary examples, facts, statistics, expert opinions, quotations) and group them under the appropriate supporting points. Indent and label these specific details with lowercase letters (a, b, c, and so on). Let the letters indicate the best sequence.

- ❏ Examine your outline, looking for places where evidence is weak. Where appropriate, add new evidence.

- ❏ Double-check that all main topics, subtopics, supporting points, and specific details develop some aspect of the thesis. Also confirm that all items are arranged in the most logical order.

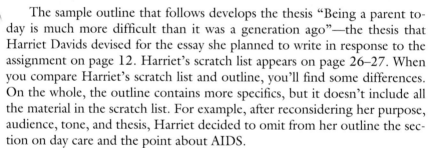

The sample outline that follows develops the thesis "Being a parent today is much more difficult than it was a generation ago"—the thesis that Harriet Davids devised for the essay she planned to write in response to the assignment on page 12. Harriet's scratch list appears on page 26–27. When you compare Harriet's scratch list and outline, you'll find some differences. On the whole, the outline contains more specifics, but it doesn't include all the material in the scratch list. For example, after reconsidering her purpose, audience, tone, and thesis, Harriet decided to omit from her outline the section on day care and the point about AIDS.

The plan shown below is called a *topic outline* because it uses phrases, or topics, for each entry. For a lengthier or more complex paper, a *sentence outline* would be more appropriate.

Purpose: To inform

Audience: Instructor as well as class members, most of whom are 18–20 years old

Tone: Serious and straightforward

Thesis: Being a parent today is much more difficult than it was a generation ago.

Pattern of development: Exemplification

Organizational approach: Emphatic order

I. Distractions from homework
  A. At home
    1. MP3 players

2. Computers—Internet, computer games
3. Television
   B. Outside home
      1. Malls
      2. Movie theaters
      3. Fast-food restaurants
II. Sexually explicit materials
   A. Internet
      1. Easy-to-access adult chat rooms
      2. Easy-to-access pornographic websites
   B. In print and in movies
      1. Sex magazines
         a. *Playboy*
         b. *Penthouse*
      2. Casual sex
   C. On television
      1. Soap operas
      2. R-rated comedians
      3. R-rated movies on cable
III. Increased dangers
   A. Drugs—peer pressure
   B. Alcohol—peer pressure
   C. Violent crimes against children

(If you'd like to see the first draft that resulted from Harriet's outline, turn to pages 58–59. Hints for moving from an outline to a first draft appear on page 47.)

Before starting to write your first draft, show your outline to several people (your instructor, friends, classmates) for their reactions, especially about areas needing additional work. After making whatever changes are needed, you're in a good position to go ahead and write the first draft of your essay.

Activities: Organize the Evidence

1. The thesis statement below is followed by a scrambled list of supporting points. Prepare an outline for a potential essay, making sure to distinguish between major and secondary points.

   Thesis: Our schools, now in crisis, could be improved in several ways.

   Certification requirements for teachers
   Schedules
   Teachers
   Longer school year
   Merit pay for outstanding teachers
   Curriculum

> Better textbooks for classroom use
> Longer school days
> More challenging content in courses

2. Assume you plan to write an essay based on the following brief outline, which consists of a thesis and several points of support. Determine which pattern of development (page 40) you would probably use for the essay's overall framework. Also identify which organizational approach (pages 41–42) you would most likely adopt to sequence the points of support listed. Then, use one or more patterns of development to generate material to support those points. Having done that, review the material generated, deleting, adding, combining, and arranging ideas in logical order. Finally, make an outline for the body of the essay. (Save your outline so you can work with it further after reading about the next stage in the writing process.)

   Thesis: Friends of the opposite sex fall into one of several categories: the pal, the confidant, or the pest.

   - Frequently, an opposite-sex friend is simply a "pal."
   - Sometimes, though, a pal turns, step by step, into a confidant.
   - If a confidant begins to have romantic thoughts, he or she may become a pest, thus disrupting the friendship.

3. Retrieve the writing you prepared in response to activity 3, 4, or 5 on pages 38–39. As needed, reshape that material, applying the organizational principles discussed in these pages. Be sure, for example, that you select the approach (chronological, spatial, emphatic, or simple-to-complex) that would be most appropriate, given your main idea, purpose, audience, and tone. (Save whatever you prepare so you can work with it further after reading about the next stage in the writing process.)

4. Look again at the thesis and scratch outline you refined and elaborated in response to activity 6 on page 39. Reevaluate this material by deleting, adding, combining, and rearranging ideas as needed. Also, keeping your purpose, audience, and tone in mind, consider whether a chronological, a spatial, an emphatic, or a simple-to-complex approach will be most appropriate. Now prepare an outline of your ideas. Finally, ask at least one person to evaluate your organizational plan. (Save your outline. After reading about the next stage in the writing process, you can use it to write the essay's first draft.)

STAGE 5: WRITE THE FIRST DRAFT

Your *first draft*—a rough, provisional version of your essay—may flow quite smoothly. But don't be discouraged if it doesn't. You may find that your thesis has to be reshaped, that a point no longer fits, that you need to return to a prewriting activity to generate additional material. Such stopping and starting is to be expected. Writing the first draft is a process of discovery, involving the continual clarification and refining of ideas.

How to Proceed

There's no single right way to prepare a first draft. Some writers rely heavily on their scratch lists or outlines; others glance at them only occasionally. Some people write in longhand; others use a computer.

However you choose to proceed, consider the suggestions in the following checklist when moving from an outline or scratch list to a first draft.

☑ TURNING OUTLINE INTO FIRST DRAFT: A CHECKLIST

❑ Make the outline's *main topics* (I, II, III) the *topic sentences* of the essay's supporting paragraphs. (Topic sentences are discussed later, on page 48.)

❑ Make the outline's *subtopics* (A, B, C) the *subpoints* in each paragraph.

❑ Make the outline's *supporting points* (1, 2, 3) the key *examples* and *reasons* in each paragraph.

❑ Make the outline's *specific details* (a, b, c) the *secondary examples, facts, statistics, expert opinions,* and *quotations* in each paragraph.

(To see how Harriet Davids moved from outline to first draft, turn to pages 58–59.)

Although outlines and lists are valuable for guiding your work, don't be so dependent on them that you shy away from new ideas that surface during your writing of the first draft. If promising new thoughts pop up, jot them down in the margin. Then, at the appropriate point, go back and evaluate them: Do they support your thesis? Are they appropriate for your essay's purpose, audience, and tone? If so, go ahead and include the material in your draft.

It's easy to get bogged down while preparing the first draft if you try to edit as you write. Remember: A draft isn't intended to be perfect. For the time being, adopt a relaxed, noncritical attitude. Working as quickly as you can, don't stop to check spelling, correct grammar, or refine sentence structure. Save these tasks for later. One good way to help remind you that the first draft is tentative is to write in longhand using scrap paper and pencil. Writing on alternate lines also underscores your intention to revise later on, when the extra space will make it easier to add and delete material. Similarly, writing on only one side of the paper can prove helpful if, during revision, you decide to move a section to another part of the paper.

What should you do if you get stuck while writing your first draft? Stay calm and try to write something—no matter how awkward or imprecise it may seem. Just jot a reminder to yourself in the margin ("Fix this," "Redo," or "Ugh!") to finetune the section later. Or leave a blank space to hold a spot for the right words when they finally break loose. It may also help to reread—out loud is best—what you've already written. Regaining a sense of the larger context is often enough to get you moving again. You might also try talking your way through a troublesome section. By speaking aloud, you tap your natural oral fluency and put it to work in your writing.

If a section of the essay is particularly difficult, don't spend time struggling with it. Move on to an easier section, write that, and then return to the challenging part. If you're still getting nowhere, take a break. Watch television, listen to music, talk with friends. While you're relaxing, your thoughts may loosen up and untangle the knotty section.

Because you read essays from beginning to end, you may assume that writers work the same way, starting with the introduction and going straight through to the conclusion. Often, however, this isn't the case. In fact, since an introduction depends so heavily on everything that follows, it's usually best to write the introduction *after* the essay's body.

When preparing your first draft, you may find it helpful to follow this sequence:

1. Write the supporting paragraphs.
2. Connect ideas in the supporting paragraphs.
3. Write the introduction.
4. Write the conclusion.
5. Write the title.

Write the Supporting Paragraphs

Drawn from the main sections in your outline or scratch list (I, II, III, etc.), each *supporting paragraph* should develop an aspect of your essay's thesis. A strong supporting paragraph is (1) often focused by a topic sentence and (2) organized around one or more patterns of development. As you write, keep in mind that you shouldn't expect your draft paragraphs to be perfect; you'll have a chance to revise them later on.

Use topic sentences.   Frequently, a *topic sentence* functions as a kind of mini-thesis for a supporting paragraph. Generally one or two sentences in length, the topic sentence usually appears at or near the beginning of the paragraph. However, it may also appear at the end, in the middle, or—with varied wording—several times within the paragraph.

The topic sentence states the paragraph's main idea while the other sentences in the paragraph provide support for this central point in the form of examples, facts, expert opinion, and so on. Like a thesis statement, the topic sentence *signals the paragraph's subject* and frequently *indicates the writer's attitude* toward that subject. In the topic sentences that follow, the subject of the paragraph is underlined once and the attitude toward that subject is underlined twice:

> Some students select a particular field of study for the wrong reasons.
> The ocean dumping of radioactive waste is a ticking time bomb.
> Several contemporary rock groups show unexpected sensitivity to social issues.
> Political candidates are sold like slickly packaged products.

As you work on the first draft, you may find yourself writing paragraphs without paying too much attention to topic sentences. That's fine, as long as you evaluate the paragraphs later on. When revising, you can provide a topic sentence for a paragraph that needs a sharper focus, recast a topic sentence for a paragraph that ended up taking an unexpected turn, even eliminate a topic sentence altogether if a paragraph's content is sufficiently unified to imply its point.

Use the patterns of development.   As you saw on page 40, an entire essay can be organized around one or more patterns of development (narration, process analysis, definition, and so forth). These patterns can also provide the organizational framework for an essay's supporting paragraphs. Assume you're writing an article for your town newspaper with the thesis "Year-round residents of an ocean community must take an active role in safeguarding the seashore environment." Your supporting paragraphs could develop this thesis through a variety of patterns, with each paragraph's topic sentence suggesting a specific pattern or combination of patterns. For example, one paragraph might start with the topic sentence "In a nearby ocean community, signs of environmental danger are everywhere" and go on to *describe* a seaside town with polluted waters, blighted trees, and diseased marine life. The next paragraph might have the topic sentence "Fortunately, not all seaside towns are plagued by such environmental problems" and continue by *contrasting* the troubled community with another, more ecologically sound shore town. A later paragraph, focused by the topic sentence "Residents can get involved in a variety of pro-environment activities," might use *division-classification* to elaborate on activities at the neighborhood, town, and municipal levels.

Connect Ideas in the Supporting Paragraphs

While writing the supporting paragraphs, you can try to smooth out the progression of ideas within and between paragraphs. In a *coherent* essay, the relationship between points is clear; readers can easily follow the development of your thoughts. (Sometimes, working on coherence causes a first draft to get bogged down; if this happens, move on, and wait until the revision stage to focus on such matters.)

The following paragraph lacks coherence for two main reasons. First, it sequences ideas improperly. (The idea about the toll attendants' being cut off from coworkers is introduced, dropped, then picked up again. References to motorists are similarly scattered throughout the paragraph.) Second, it doesn't indicate how individual ideas are related. (What, for example, is the connection between drivers who pass by without saying anything and attendants who have to work at night?)

Incoherent Support

Collecting tolls on the turnpike must be one of the loneliest jobs in the world. Each toll attendant sits in his or her booth, cut off from other attendants. Many drivers pass by each booth. None stays long enough for a brief "hello." Most don't acknowledge the attendant at all. Many toll attendants work at night, pushing them "out of synch" with the rest of the world. And sometimes the attendants have to deal with rude drivers who treat them like non-people, swearing at them for the long lines at the tollgate. Attendants also dislike how cut off they feel from their coworkers. Except for infrequent breaks, they have little chance to chat with each other and swap horror stories—small pleasures that would make their otherwise routine jobs bearable.

Coherent Support

Collecting tolls on the turnpike must be one of the loneliest jobs in the world. First of all, although many drivers pass by the attendants, none stays long enough for more than a brief "hello." Most drivers, in fact, don't acknowledge the toll collectors at all, with the exception of those rude drivers who treat the attendants like non-people, swearing at them for the long lines at the tollgate. Then, too, many toll attendants work at night, pushing them further "out of synch" with the rest of the world. Worst of all, attendants say, is how isolated they feel from their coworkers. Each attendant sits in his or her booth, cut off from other attendants. Except for infrequent breaks, they have little chance to chat with each other and swap horror stories—small pleasures that would make their otherwise routine jobs bearable.

To avoid the kinds of problems found in the incoherent paragraph, use—as the revised version does—two key strategies: (1) a clearly *chronological, spatial, emphatic* ("*Worst of all,* attendants say...") or *simple-to-complex* approach and

(2) *signal devices* ("*First of all*, although many drivers pass by...") to show how ideas are connected. To review the four organizational approaches, see pages 40–43. The following paragraphs describe signal devices.

Once you determine a logical approach for presenting your points, you need to make sure readers can follow the progression of those points. Signal devices provide readers with cues, reminding them where they have been and indicating where they are going.

Aim to include some signals—however awkward or temporary—in your first draft. If you find you *can't*, that's probably a warning that your ideas may not be arranged logically. A light touch should be your goal with such signals. Too many call attention to themselves, making the essay mechanical and plodding. In any case, here are some signaling devices to consider.

1. Transitions.   Words and phrases that ease readers from one idea to another are called transitions. The following list gives a variety of such signals.

Time
first, before, earlier, next, then, now, immediately, at the same time, simultaneously, in the meantime, meanwhile, subsequently, afterward, after, finally, later eventually

Addition (or Sequence)
moreover; also; furthermore; in addition; first,... second,... third; one ... another; and; also; too; besides; next; finally; last

Space
above, below, next to, behind

Examples
for instance, for example, to illustrate, specifically, namely

Contrast
but, however, yet, in contrast, on the contrary, although, otherwise, conversely, despite, even though, on the one (other) hand, still, whereas, nevertheless, nonetheless

Comparison
similarly, in the same way, also, likewise, too, in comparison

Cause or Effects
because, as a result, consequently, therefore, then, so, since

Summary or Conclusion
therefore, thus, in short, in conclusion

Here's an earlier paragraph from this chapter. Note how the italicized transitions show readers how ideas fit together.

> *After* you've generated supporting evidence, you're ready to organize that material. Even highly compelling evidence won't illustrate the validity of your thesis or achieve your purpose if the readers have to plow through a maze of chaotic evidence. Some writers can move quickly from generating support to writing a clearly structured first draft. (They usually say they have sequenced their ideas in their heads.) Most, *however,* need to spend some time sorting out their thoughts on paper before starting the first draft; *otherwise,* they tend to lose their way in a tangle of ideas.

2. Bridging sentences.   Although bridging sentences may be used within a paragraph, they are more often used to move readers from one paragraph to the next. Look again at the first sentence in the preceding paragraph. Note that the sentence consists of two parts: The first part reminds readers that the previous discussion focused on techniques for generating evidence; the second part tells readers that the focus will now be the organization of such evidence.

3. Repeated words, synonyms, and pronouns.   The repetition of important words maintains continuity, reassures readers that they are on the right track, and highlights key ideas. Synonyms—words similar in meaning—also provide coherence, but without unimaginative and tedious repetitions. Finally, pronouns (*he, she, it, they, this, that*) enhance coherence by causing readers to think back to the original word the pronoun replaces (antecedent). When using pronouns, however, be sure there is no ambiguity about antecedents.

Reprinted here is another paragraph from this chapter. Repeated words have been underlined once, synonyms underlined twice, and pronouns printed in italic type to illustrate how these techniques were used to integrate the paragraph's ideas.

> The process of prewriting—discovering a limited subject and generating ideas about *it*—prepares you for the next stage in writing an essay: identifying the paper's <u>thesis</u> or <u>controlling idea</u>. Presenting your opinion on a subject, the <u>thesis</u> should focus on an interesting and significant issue, *one* that engages your energies and merits your consideration. You may think of the <u>thesis</u> as the essay's <u>hub</u>—the <u>central point</u> around which all the other material revolves. Your <u>thesis</u> determines what does and does not belong in the essay. The <u>thesis</u>, especially when *it* occurs early in an essay, also helps focus the reader on the piece's central point.

Write the Introduction

Many writers don't prepare an introduction until they have started to revise; others feel more comfortable if their first draft includes in basic form all parts of the final essay. If that's how you feel, you'll probably write the introduction as you complete your first draft. No matter when you prepare it, keep in mind how crucial the introduction is to your essay's success. Specifically, the introduction serves three distinct functions: It arouses readers' interest, introduces your subject, and presents your thesis.

The length of your introduction will vary according to your paper's scope and purpose. Most essays you write, however, will be served best by a one- or two-paragraph beginning. To write an effective introduction, use any of the following methods, singly or in combination. The thesis statement in each sample introduction is underlined.

Broad Statement Narrowing to a Limited Subject

For generations, morality has been molded primarily by parents, religion, and schools. Children traditionally acquired their ideas about what is right and wrong, which goals are important in life, and how other people should be treated from these three sources collectively. But in the past few decades, a single force—television—has undermined the beneficial influence that parents, religion, and school have on children's moral development. Indeed, television often implants in children negative values about sex, work, and family life.

Brief Anecdote

At a local high school recently, students in a psychology course were given a hint of what it is like to be the parents of a newborn. Each "parent" had to carry a raw egg around at all times to symbolize the responsibilities of parenthood. The egg could not be left alone; it limited the "parents'" activities; it placed a full-time emotional burden on "Mom" and "Dad." This class exercise illustrates a common problem facing the majority of new mothers and fathers. Most people receive little preparation for the job of being parents.

Idea That Is the Opposite of the One Developed

We hear a great deal about divorce's disastrous impact on children. We are deluged with advice on ways to make divorce as painless as possible for youngsters; we listen to heartbreaking stories about the confused, grieving children of divorced parents. Little attention has been paid, however, to a different kind of effect that divorce may have on children. Children from divorced families may become skilled manipulators, playing off one parent against the other, worsening an already painful situation.

Series of Short Questions

What happens if a child is caught vandalizing school property? What happens if a child goes for a joyride in a stolen car and accidentally hits a pedestrian? Should parents be liable for their children's mistakes? Should parents have to pay what might be hundreds of thousands of dollars in damages? Adults have begun to think seriously about such questions because the laws concerning the limits of parental responsibility are changing rapidly. With unfortunate frequency, courts have begun to hold parents legally and financially accountable for their children's misdeeds.

Quotation

Educator Neil Postman believes that television has blurred the line between childhood and adulthood. According to Postman, "All the secrets that a print culture kept from children . . . are revealed all at once by media that do not, and cannot, exclude any audience." This media barrage of information, once intended only for adults, has changed childhood for the worse.

Refutation of a Common Belief

Adolescents care only about material things; their lives revolve around brand-name sneakers, designer jeans, the latest fad in electronics. They resist education, don't read, barely know who is president, mainline rock 'n' roll, experiment with drugs, and exist on a steady diet of Ring-Dings, nachos, and beer. This is what many adults, including parents, seem to believe about the young. The reality is, however, that young people today show more maturity and common sense than most adults give them credit for.

Dramatic Fact or Statistic

Seventy percent of the respondents in a poll conducted by columnist Ann Landers stated that if they could live their lives over, they would choose not to have children. This startling statistic makes one wonder what these people believed parenthood would be like. Most parents, it seems, have unrealistic expectations about their children. Parents want their children to accept their values, follow their paths, and succeed where they failed.

Introductory paragraphs sometimes end with a *plan of development:* a quick preview of the essay's major points in the order in which those points will be discussed. The plan of development may be part of the thesis (as in the first sample introduction) or it may immediately follow the thesis (as in the last sample introduction). Because the plan of development outlines the essay's organizational structure, it helps prepare the reader for the essay's progression of ideas. In a brief essay, readers can often keep track of the ideas without this extra help. In a longer paper, though, a plan of development can be an effective unifying device since it highlights the main ideas the essay will develop.

Write the Conclusion

You may have come across essays that ended with jarring abruptness because they had no conclusions at all. Other papers may have had conclusions, but they sputtered to a weak close, a sure sign that the writers had run out of steam and wanted to finish as quickly as possible. Just as satisfying closes are an important part of everyday life (we feel cheated if dinner doesn't end with dessert or if a friend leaves without saying goodbye), a strong conclusion is an important part of an effective essay.

Generally one or two paragraphs, the conclusion should give the reader a feeling of completeness and finality. One way to achieve this sense of "rounding off" is to return to an image, idea, or anecdote from the introduction. Because people tend to remember most clearly the points they read last, the conclusion is also a good place to remind readers of your thesis. You may also use the conclusion to make a final point about your subject. Be careful, though, not to open an entirely new line of thought at the essay's close.

Illustrated briefly here are several strategies for writing sound conclusions. These techniques may be used singly or in combination. The first strategy, the summary conclusion, can be especially helpful in long, complex essays since readers may appreciate a review of your points. Tacked onto a short essay, though, a summary conclusion often seems boring and mechanical.

Summary

Contrary to what many adults think, most adolescents are not only aware of the important issues of the times but also deeply concerned about them. They are sensitive to the plight of the homeless, the destruction of the environment, and the pitfalls of rampant materialism. Indeed, today's young people are not less mature and sensible than their parents were. If anything, they are more so.

Prediction

The growing tendency on the part of the judicial system to hold parents responsible for the actions of their wayward children can have a disturbing impact on all of us. Parents will feel bitter toward their own children and cynical about a system that holds them accountable for the actions of minors. Children, continuing to escape the consequences of their actions, will become even more lawless and destructive. Society cannot afford two such possibilities.

Quotation

The comic W. C. Fields is reputed to have said, "Anyone who hates children and dogs can't be all bad." Most people do not share Fields's cynicism. Viewing childhood as a time of purity, they are alarmed at the way television exposes children to the seamy side of life, stripping youngsters of their innocence and giving them a glib sophistication that is a poor substitute for wisdom.

Statistic

Granted, divorce may, in some cases, be the best thing for families torn apart by parents who battle one another. However, in longitudinal studies of children from divorced families, psychologist Judith Wallerstein found that only 10 percent of the youngsters felt relief at their parents' divorce; the remaining 90 percent felt devastated. Such statistics surely call into question parents' claims that they are divorcing for their children's sake.

Recommendation or Call for Action

It is a mistake to leave parenting to instinct. Instead, we should make parenting skills a required course in schools. In addition, a nationwide hotline should be established to help parents deal with crises. Such training and continuing support would help adults deal more effectively with many of the problems they face as parents.

Write the Title

Some writers say that they began a certain piece with only a title in mind. But for most people, writing a title is a finishing touch. Although creating a title for your paper is usually one of the last steps in writing an essay, it shouldn't be done haphazardly. It may take time to write an effective title—one that hints at the essay's thesis and snares the reader's interest.

Good titles may make use of the following techniques: repetition of sounds ("The Border on Our Backs"); questions ("What Are Friends For?"); and humor ("How to Say Nothing in 500 Words"). More often, though, titles are straightforward phrases derived from the essay's subject or thesis: "Shooting an Elephant" and "The Ways We Lie," for example.

Pull It All Together

Now that you know how to prepare a first draft, you might find it helpful to examine Figure 2.2 to see how the different parts of a draft can fit together. Keep in mind that not every essay you write will take this

FIGURE 2.2
Structure of an Essay

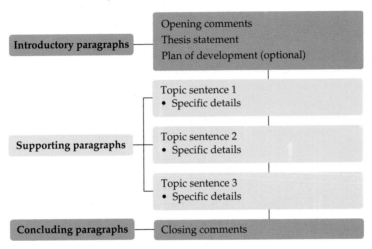

shape. As your purpose, audience, and tone change, so will your essay's structure. An introduction or conclusion, for instance, may be developed in more than one paragraph; the thesis statement may be implied or de-layed until the essay's middle or end; not all paragraphs may have topic sentences; and several supporting paragraphs may be needed to develop a single topic sentence. Even so, the basic format presented here offers a strategy for organizing a variety of writing assignments—from term pa-pers to lab reports. Once you feel comfortable with the structure, you have a foundation on which to base your variations. (This book's student and professional essays illustrate some possibilities.) Even when using a specific format, you always have room to give your spirit and imagination free play. The language you use, the details you select, the perspective you offer are uniquely yours. They are what make your essay different from everyone else's.

Sample First Draft

Here is the first draft of Harriet Davids's essay. (The assignment and prewriting for the essay appear on pages 12, 22–23, and 26.) Harriet wrote the draft in one sitting. Working at a computer, she started by typing her thesis at the top of the first page. Then, following the guidelines on page 47, she moved the material in her outline (pages 43–45) to her draft. Harriet worked rapidly; she started with the first body paragraph and wrote straight through to the last supporting paragraph.

By moving quickly, Harriet got down her essay's basic text rather easily. Once she felt she had captured in rough form what she wanted to say, she reread her draft to get a sense of how she might open and close the essay. Then she drafted her introduction and conclusion; both appear here, together with the body of the essay. The commentary following the draft will give you a clearer sense of how Harriet proceeded. (Note that the marginal annotations reflect Harriet's comments to herself about areas she needs to address when revising her first draft.)

Challenges for Today's Parents
by Harriet Davids

Thesis: Being a parent today is much more difficult than it was a generation ago.

Raising children used to be much simpler in the '50s and '60s. I remember TV images from that era showing that parenting involved simply teaching kids to clean their rooms, do

Add specifics ——— their homework, and _____.But being a parent today is much more difficult because nowadays parents have to shield/protect kids from lots of things, like distractions from schoolwork, from sexual material, from dangerous situations.

Parents have to control all the new distractions/ temptations that turn kids away from schoolwork. These days many kids have stereos, computers, and televisions in their rooms. Certainly, my girls can't resist the urge to listen to MTV and go online, especially if it's time to do homework. Unfortunately, though, kids aren't assigned much homework and what is assigned too often is busywork. And there are even more distractions outside the home. Teens no longer hang out/congregate on the corner where Dad and Mom can yell to them to come home and do homework. Instead they hang out at the mall, in movie theaters, and fast-food restaurants. Obviously, parents and school can't

Weak trans. ——— compete with all this.

Also parents have to help kids develop responsible sexual values even though sex is everywhere. Kids see sex magazines and dirty paperbacks in the corner store where they used to get candy and comic books. And instead of the artsy nude shots of

Sp? ——— the past, kids see ronchey, explicit shots in *Playboy* and *Penthouse*. And movies have sexy stuff in them today. Teachers seduce students and people treat sex casually/as a sport. Not exactly traditional values. TV is no better. Kids see soap-opera characters in bed and cable shows full of nudity by just flipping the dial. Even worse is what's on the Internet. Too easy for kids

to access chat rooms and websites dealing with adult, sometimes pornographic material. The situation has gotten so out of
hand that maybe the government should establish guidelines on
what's permissible.

Worst of all are the life-threatening dangers that parents
must help children fend off over the years. With older kids,
drugs fall into place as a main concern. Peer pressure to try
drugs is bigger to kids than their parents' warnings. Other
kinds of warnings are common when children are small. Then
parents fear violence since news shows constantly report stories of little children being abused. And when kids aren't
much older, they have to resist the pressure to drink. Alcohol
has always attracted kids, but nowadays they are drinking
more and this can be deadly, especially when drinking is combined with driving.

Most adults love their children and want to be good parents. But it's difficult because the world seems stacked
against young people. Even Holden Caufield had trouble dealing with society's confusing pressures. Parents must give
their children some freedom but not so much that the kids lose
sight of what's important.

Marginal notes (left): Awk · Wrong word · Add specifics · Redo · Sp?

Commentary

As you can see, Harriet's draft is rough. Because she knew she would
revise later on (page 60), she "zapped out" the draft in an informal, col-
loquial style. For example, she occasionally expressed her thoughts in
fragments ("Not exactly traditional values"), relied heavily on "and" as a
transition, and used slangy expressions such as "kids," "dirty paperbacks," and "lots of things." She also used slashes between alternative
word choices and left a blank space when wording just wouldn't come.
Then, as Harriet reviewed the printed copy of this rough draft, she
made handwritten marginal notes to herself: "Awk" or "Redo" to signal
awkward sentences; "Add specifics" to mark overly general statements;
"Wrong word" after an imprecise word; "Sp?" to remind herself to
check spelling in the dictionary; "Weak trans." to indicate where a
stronger signaling device was needed. (Harriet's final draft appears on
pages 66–68.)

Writing a first draft may seem like quite a challenge, but the tips offered
in these pages should help you proceed with confidence. Indeed, as you
work on the draft, you may be surprised how much you enjoy writing. After
all, this is your chance to get down on paper something you want to say.

Activities: Write the First Draft

1. Retrieve the writing you prepared in response to activity 3 on page 46. Applying the principles just presented, rework that material. If you wrote a single paragraph earlier, expand the material into a full essay draft. If you prepared an essay, strengthen what you wrote. In both cases, remember to consider your purpose, audience, and tone as you write the body of the essay as well as its introduction and conclusion. (Save your draft so you can rework it even further after reading about the next stage in the writing process.)

2. Referring to the outline you prepared in response to activity 2 or activity 4 on page 46, draft the body of your essay, making your evidence as strong as possible. As you work, keep your purpose, audience, and tone in mind. After reading what you've prepared, go ahead and draft a rough introduction, conclusion, and title. Finally, ask at least one other person to react to your draft by listing its strengths and weaknesses. (Save the draft so you can work with it further after reading about the next stage in the writing process.)

STAGE 6: REVISE THE ESSAY

By now, you've probably abandoned any preconceptions you might have had about good writers sitting down and creating a finished product in one easy step. Alexander Pope's comment that "true ease in writing comes from art, not chance" is as true today as it was more than two hundred years ago. Writing that seems effortlessly clear is often the result of sustained work, not of good luck or even inborn talent. And much of this work takes place during the final stage of the writing process when ideas, paragraphs, sentences, and words are refined and reshaped.

Professional writers—novelists, journalists, textbook authors—seldom submit a piece of writing that hasn't been revised. They recognize that rough, unpolished work doesn't do them justice. What's more, they often look forward to revising. Columnist Ellen Goodman puts it this way: "What makes me happy is rewriting. . . . It's like cleaning house, getting rid of all the junk, getting things in the right order, tightening up."

In a sense, revision occurs throughout the writing process: At some earlier stage, you may have dropped an idea, overhauled your thesis, or shifted paragraph order. What, then, is different about the rewriting that occurs in the revision stage? The answer has to do with the literal meaning of the word *revision*—to resee, or to see again. Genuine revision involves casting clear eyes on your work, viewing it as though you're a reader rather than the writer. Revision means that you go through your paper looking for trouble, ready to pick a fight with your own writing. And then you must be willing to sit down and make the changes needed for your writing to be as effective as possible.

Revision is not, as some believe, simply touch-up work—changing a sentence here or a word there, eliminating spelling errors, preparing a neat final copy. Revision means cutting deadwood, rearranging paragraphs, substituting new words for old ones, recasting sentences, improving coherence, even generating new material when appropriate. With experience, you'll learn how to streamline the process so you can focus on the most critical issues for a particular piece of writing. (For advice on correcting some common writing errors, see Appendix B on pages 638–651.)

Five Revision Strategies

Because revision is challenging, you may find yourself unsure about how to proceed. Keep in mind that there are no hard-and-fast rules about the revision process. Even so, the following pointers should help get you going if you balk at or feel overwhelmed by revising.

- *Set your draft aside for a while* before revising. When you pick up your paper again, you'll have a fresh, more objective point of view.
- *Work from printed-out material* whenever possible. Having your essay in neutral typed letters instead of in your own familiar writing helps you see the paper impartially, as if someone else had written it. Each time you make major changes, try to print out a copy of that section so that you can see it anew.
- *Read your draft aloud* as often as you can. Hearing how your writing sounds helps you pick up problems that you passed by before: places where sentences are awkward, meaning is ambiguous, words are imprecise. Even better, have another person read aloud to you what you have written. If the reader slows to a crawl over a murky paragraph or trips over a convoluted sentence, you know where you have to do some rewriting.
- *View revision as a series of steps.* Don't try to tackle all of a draft's problems at once; instead, proceed step by step, starting with the most pressing issues. Although there are bound to be occasions when you have time for only one quick pass over a draft, whenever possible, read your draft several times; each time focus on different matters and ask yourself different questions. Move from a broad view of the draft to an up-close look at its mechanics.
- *Evaluate and respond to instructor feedback.* Often, instructors collect and respond to students' first drafts. Like many students, you may be tempted to look only briefly at your instructor's comments. Perhaps you've "had it" with the essay and don't want to think about revising the paper to reflect the instructor's

remarks. But taking your instructor's comments into account when revising is often what's needed to turn a shaky first draft into a strong final draft.

When an instructor returns a final draft graded, you may think that the grade is all that counts. Remember, though: Grades are important, but comments are even more so. They can help you *improve* your writing—if not in this paper, then in the next one. If you don't understand or agree with the instructor's observations, don't hesitate to request a conference. Getting together gives both you and the instructor a chance to clarify your respective points of view.

Peer Review: An Additional Revision Strategy

Many instructors include in-class or at-home peer review as a regular part of a composition course. Peer review—the critical reading of another person's writing with the intention of suggesting changes—accomplishes several important goals. First, peer review helps you gain a more objective perspective on your work. When you write something, you're often too close to what you've prepared to evaluate it fairly; you may have trouble seeing where the writing is strong and where it needs to be strengthened. Peer review supplies the fresh, neutral perspective you need. Second, reviewing your classmates' work broadens your own composing options. You may be inspired to experiment with a technique you admired in a classmate's writing but wouldn't have thought of on your own. Finally, peer review trains you to be a better reader and critic of your *own* writing. When you get into the habit of critically reading other students' writing, you become more adept at critiquing your own.

The Peer Review/Revision Checklist on the inside front cover of this book will help focus your revision—whether you're reworking your own paper or responding to a peer's. Your instructor may have you respond to all questions on the checklist or to several selected items. What follows is a peer review worksheet that Harriet Davids's instructor prepared to help students respond to first drafts based on the assignment on page 12. Wanting students to focus on four areas (thesis statement, support for thesis statement, overall organization, and signal devices), the instructor drew upon relevant sections from the Peer Review/Revision Checklist. With this customized worksheet in hand, Harriet's classmate Frank Tejada was able to give Harriet constructive feedback on her first draft (see pages 58–59). (*Note:* Because Harriet didn't want to influence Frank's reaction, the draft she gave him didn't include her marginal notations to herself.)

Peer Review Worksheet

Essay Author's Name: <u>Harriet Davids</u> Reviewer's Name: <u>Frank Tejada</u>

1. What is the essay's thesis? Is it explicit or implied? Does the thesis focus on a limited subject and express the writer's attitude toward that subject?

   Thesis: "Being a parent today is much more difficult [than it used to be]."
   The thesis is limited and expresses a clear attitude. But the sentence the
   thesis appears in (last sentence of para. 1) is too long because it also contains the plan of development. Maybe put thesis and plan of development in
   separate sentences.

2. What are the main points supporting the thesis? List the points. Is each supporting point developed sufficiently? If not, where is more support needed?

   (1) Parents have to control kids' distractions from school.
   (2) Parents have to help kids develop responsible sexual values despite sex
   being everywhere.
   (3) Parents have to protect kids from life-threatening dangers.
   The supporting points are good and are explained pretty well,
   except for a few places. The "Unfortunately" sentence in para. 2 is irrelevant. Also, in para. 2, you use the example of your girls, but never again.
   Either include them throughout or not at all. In para. 3, the final sentence about the government guidelines opens a whole new topic; maybe
   steer away from this. The items in para. 4 seem vague and need specific
   examples. In the conclusion, omit Holden Caulfield; since he was from
   an earlier generation, this example undermines your thesis about
   parenting today.

3. What overall format (chronological, spatial, emphatic, simple-to-complex) is used to sequence the essay's main points? Does this format work? Why or why not? What organizational format is used in each supporting paragraph? Does the format work? Why or why not?

   The paper's overall emphatic organization seems good. Emphatic order also
   works in para. 3, and spatial order works well in para. 2. But the sentences
   in para. 4 need rearranging. Right now, the examples are in mixed-up chronological order, making it hard to follow. Maybe you should reorder the examples from young kids to older kids.

4. What signal devices are used to connect ideas within and between paragraphs? Are there too few signal devices or too many? Where?

The topic sentence of para. 3 needs to be a stronger bridging sentence. Also, too many "and's" in para. 3. Try "in addition" or "another" in some places. I like the "worst of all" transition to para. 4.

As you can see, Frank flagged several areas that Harriet herself also noted needed work. (Turn to pages 58–59 to see Harriet's marginal comments on her draft.) But he also commented on entirely new areas (for example, the sequence problem in paragraph 4), offering Harriet a fresh perspective on what she needed to do to polish her draft. To see which of Frank's suggestions Harriet followed, take a look at her final draft on pages 66–68 and at the "Commentary" following the essay.

Becoming a skilled peer reviewer.   Even with the help of a checklist, preparing a helpful peer review is a skill that takes time to develop. At first, you, like many students, may be too easy or too critical. Effective peer review calls for rigor and care; you should give classmates the conscientious feedback that you hope for in return. Peer review also requires tact and kindness; feedback should always be constructive and include observations about what works well in a piece of writing. People have difficulty mustering the energy to revise if they feel there's nothing worth revising.

If your instructor doesn't include peer review, you can set up peer review sessions outside of class, with classmates getting together to respond to each other's drafts. Or you may select non-classmates who are objective (not a love-struck admirer or a doting grandparent) and skilled enough to provide useful commentary.

To focus your readers' comments, you may adapt the Peer Review/ Revision Checklist on the inside front cover of this book, or you may develop your own questions. If you prepare the questions yourself, be sure to solicit *specific* observations about what does and doesn't work in your writing. If you simply ask, "How's this?" you may receive a vague comment like "It's not very effective." What you want are concrete observations and suggestions: "I'm confused because what you say in the fifth sentence contradicts what you say in the second." To promote such specific responses, ask your readers targeted (preferably written) questions like "I'm having trouble moving from my second to my third point. How can I make the transition smoother?" Such questions require more than "yes" or "no" responses; they encourage readers to dig into your writing where you sense it needs work. (If it's feasible, encourage readers to *write* their responses to your questions.)

If you and your peer reviewer(s) can't meet in person, e-mail can provide a crucial means of contact. With a couple of clicks, you can simply send each other computer files of your work. You and your reviewer(s) also need to decide exactly how to exchange comments about your drafts. You might conclude, for example, that you'll type your responses, perhaps in bold capitals, into the file itself. Or you might decide to print out the drafts and reply to the comments in writing, later exchanging the annotated drafts in person. No matter what you and your peer(s) decide, you'll probably find e-mail an invaluable tool in the writing process.

Evaluating and responding to peer review.   Accepting criticism isn't easy (even if you asked for it), and not all peer reviewers will be diplomatic. Even so, try to listen with an open mind to those giving you feedback. Take notes on their oral observations and/or have them fill out relevant sections from the Peer Review/Revision Checklist (on the inside front cover). Later, when you're ready to revise your paper, reread your notes. Which reviewer remarks seem valid? Which don't? Rank the problems and solutions that your reviewers identified, designating the most critical as number 1. Using the peer feedback, enter your own notes for revising in the margins of a clean copy of your draft. This way, you'll know exactly what changes need to be made in your draft as you proceed. Then, keeping the problems and remedies in mind, start revising. Type in your changes, or handwrite changes directly on the draft above the appropriate line. (Rework extensive sections on a separate piece of paper.) When revising, always keep in mind that you may not agree with every reviewer suggestion. That's fine. It's *your* paper, and it's *your* decision to implement or reject the suggestions made by your peers.

STAGE 7: EDIT AND PROOFREAD

Your essay is not finished until you have dealt with errors in grammar, punctuation, and spelling.

If you are using a computer,

- Use your computer's spelling check program to identify and correct misspelled words.
- Read the screen slowly, looking for wrong words (such as "there" when "their" is meant), errors in proper names, and errors in grammar.
- Format the essay using your instructor's guidelines, and print a copy.
- Proofread the printed paper slowly to catch typos and other mistakes.

If you find just a few errors in the printed paper, you may correct them by hand in dark ink. But if a page starts to look messy, you will need to print a clean, corrected copy to include in your final paper.

STUDENT ESSAY

In this chapter, we've taken you through the various stages in the writing process. You've seen how Harriet Davids used prewriting (pages 22–23 and 26–27) and outlining (pages 44–45) to arrive at her first draft (pages 58–59). You've also seen how Harriet's peer reviewer, Frank Tejada, critiqued her first draft (pages 63–64). In the following pages, you'll look at Harriet's final draft—the paper she submitted to her instructor.

Harriet, a thirty-eight-year-old college student and mother of two teenagers, wanted to write an informative paper with a straightforward, serious tone. While preparing her essay, she kept in mind that her audience would include her course instructor as well as her classmates, many of them considerably younger than she. This is the assignment that prompted Harriet's essay:

> Goodman implies that, in some ways, today's world is hostile to children. Do you agree? Drawing upon but not limiting yourself to the material in your pre-reading journal, write an essay in which you support or reject this viewpoint.

Harriet's essay is annotated so that you can see how it illustrates the essay format described on page 57. As you read her essay, try to determine how well it reflects the principles of effective writing. The commentary following the paper will help you look at the essay more closely and give you some sense of the way Harriet went about revising her first draft.

Challenges for Today's Parents

By Harriet Davids

Introduction   Reruns of situation comedies from the 1950s and early   1
1960s dramatize the kinds of problems that parents used to have with their children. On classic television shows such as Leave It to Beaver, the Cleavers scold their son Beaver for not washing his hands before dinner; on Ozzie and Harriet, the Nelsons dock little Ricky's allowance because he keeps forgetting to clean his room. But times have

Thesis —————— changed dramatically. Being a parent today is much more

Plan of
development —————— difficult than it was a generation ago. Parents nowadays must protect their children from a growing number of distractions, from sexually explicit material, and from life-threatening situations.

First supporting paragraph

Topic sentence

Today's parents must try, first of all, to control all the new distractions that tempt children away from school-work. At home, a child may have a room furnished with an MP3 player, television, and computer. Not many young people can resist the urge to listen to music, watch TV, go online, or play computer games and IM their friends—especially if it's time to do schoolwork. Outside the home, the distractions are even more alluring. Children no longer "hang out" on a neighborhood corner within earshot of Mom or Dad's reminder to come in and do homework. Instead, they congregate in vast shopping malls, movie theaters, and gleaming fast-food restaurants. Parents and school assignments have obvious difficulty competing with such enticing alternatives.   2

Second supporting paragraph

Topic sentence with link to previous paragraph

Besides dealing with these distractions, parents have to shield their children from a flood of sexually explicit materials. Today, children can find pornographic websites and chat rooms on the Internet with relative ease. With the click of a mouse, they can be transported, intentionally or unintentionally, to a barrage of explicit images and conversations. Easily obtainable copies of sex magazines can be found at most convenience stores, many times alongside the candy. Children will not see the fuzzily photographed nudes that a previous generation did but will encounter the hard-core raunchiness of *Playboy* or *Penthouse*. Moreover, the movies young people view often focus on highly sexual situations. It is difficult to teach children traditional values when films show young people treating sex as a casual sport. Unfortunately, television, with its often heavily sexual content, is no better. With just a flick of the channel, children can see sexed-up music videos, watch reality-TV stars cavorting in bed, or watch cable programs where nudity is common.   3

Third supporting paragraph

Topic sentence with emphasis signal

Most disturbing to parents today, however, is the increase in life-threatening dangers that face young people. When children are small, parents fear that their youngsters may be victims of violence. Every news program seems to carry a report about a school shooting or child predator who has been released from prison, only to repeat an act of violence against a minor. When children are older, parents begin to worry about their kids' use of drugs. Peer pressure to experiment with drugs is often stronger than parents' warnings. This pressure to experiment can be fatal. Finally, even if young people escape the hazards associated with drugs, they must still resist the pressure to drink. Although   4 alcohol has always held an attraction for teenagers, reports indicate that they are drinking more than ever before. As many parents know, the consequences of this attraction can be deadly—especially when drinking is combined with driving.

Conclusion

Within a generation, the world as a place to raise children has changed dramatically. One wonders how yesterday's parents would have dealt with today's problems. Could the Nelsons have shielded little Ricky from sexually explicit material on the Internet? Could the Cleavers have protected Beaver from drugs and alcohol? Parents must be aware of all these distractions and dangers yet be willing to give their children the freedom they need to become responsible adults. This is not an easy task.

References to TV shows recall introduction

5

COMMENTARY

Introduction and thesis.   The opening paragraph attracts readers' interest by recalling several vintage television shows that have almost become part of our cultural heritage. Harriet begins with these examples from the past because they offer such a sharp contrast to the present, thus underscoring the idea expressed in her *thesis:* "Being a parent today is much more difficult than it was a generation ago." Opening in this way, with material that serves as a striking contrast to what follows, is a common and effective strategy. Note, too, that Harriet's thesis states the paper's subject (being a parent) as well as her attitude toward the subject (the job is more demanding than it was years ago).

Plan of development.   Harriet follows her thesis with a *plan of development* that anticipates the three major points to be covered in the essay's supporting paragraphs. When revising her first draft, Harriet followed peer reviewer Frank Tejada's recommendation (page 63–64) to put her thesis and plan of development in separate sentences. Unfortunately, though, her plan of development ends up being somewhat mechanical, with the major points being trotted past the reader in one long, awkward sentence. To deal with the problem, Harriet could have rewritten the sentence or eliminated the plan of development altogether, ending the introduction with her thesis.

Patterns of development.   Although Harriet develops her thesis primarily through *examples,* she also draws on two other patterns of development. The whole paper implies a *contrast* between the way life and parenting are now and the way they used to be. The essay also contains an element of *causal analysis* since all the factors that Harriet cites affect children and the way they are raised.

Purpose, audience, and tone.   Given the essay's *purpose* and *audience,* Harriet adopts a serious *tone,* providing no-nonsense evidence to support her thesis. But assume she had been asked by her daughters' school newspaper to write a humorous column about the trials and tribulations that parents face raising children. Aiming for a different tone, purpose, and audience, Harriet would have taken another approach. Drawing on her personal experience, she might have confessed how she survives her daughters' nearly nonstop use of the computer, as well as the constant thumping sounds that emanate from the ear buds of their MP3s: She cuts off the electricity and hides the ear buds. This material—with its personalized perspective, exaggeration, and light tone—would be appropriate.

Organization.   Structuring the essay around a series of *relevant* and *specific examples,* Harriet uses *emphatic order* to sequence the paper's three main points: that a growing number of distractions, sexually explicit materials, and life-threatening situations make parenting difficult nowadays. The third supporting paragraph begins with the words "Most disturbing to parents today . . . ," signaling that Harriet feels particular concern about the physical dangers children face. Moreover, she uses basic organizational strategies to sequence the supporting examples within each paragraph. The details in the first supporting paragraph are organized *spatially,* starting with distractions at home and moving to those outside the home. The second supporting paragraph arranges examples *emphatically.* Harriet starts with sexually explicit material on the Internet and ends with the "heavily sexual content" on TV. Note that Harriet followed Frank's peer review advice (page 63–64) about omitting her first-draft observation that kids don't get enough homework—or that they get too much busywork. The third and final supporting paragraph is organized *chronologically;* it begins by discussing dangers to small children and concludes by talking about teenagers. Again, Frank's advice—to use a clearer time sequence in this paragraph (page 63–64)—was invaluable when Harriet was revising.

The essay also displays Harriet's familiarity with other kinds of organizational strategies. Each supporting paragraph opens with a *topic sentence.* Further, *signal devices* are used throughout the paper to show how ideas are related to one another: *transitions* ("Instead, they congregate in vast shopping malls"; "Moreover, the movies young people attend often focus on highly sexual situations"); *repetition* ("sexual situations" and "sexual content"); *synonyms* ("distractions...enticing alternatives" and "life-threatening...fatal"); *pronouns* ("young people...they"); and *bridging sentences* ("Besides dealing with these distractions, parents have to shield their children from a flood of sexually explicit material").

Two minor problems.   Harriet's efforts to write a well-organized essay result in a somewhat predictable structure. It might have been better had she rewritten one of the paragraphs, perhaps embedding the topic sentence in the middle of the paragraph or saving it for the end. Similarly, Harriet's signal devices are a little heavy-handed. Even so, an essay with a sharp focus and clear signals is preferable to one with a confusing or inaccessible structure. As she gains more experience, Harriet can work on making the structure of her essays more subtle.

Conclusion.   Following Frank's suggestion, Harriet dropped from the final paragraph the first draft's problematic reference to Holden Caulfield (page 63). Having done that, she's able to bring the essay to a satisfying *close* by reminding readers of the paper's central idea and three main points. The final paragraph also extends the essay's scope by introducing a new but related issue: that parents have to strike a balance between their need to provide limitations and their children's need for freedom. Besides eliminating the distracting reference to Holden Caulfield, she deleted the shopworn opening sentence ("Most adults love their children...") and added references to the vintage TV shows mentioned in the introduction: ("Could the Nelsons...? Could the Cleavers...?"). These questions help unify Harriet's paper and bring it to a rounded close.

These are just a few of the changes Harriet made when reworking her essay. Realizing that writing is a process, she left herself enough time to revise—and to carefully consider Frank Tejada's comments. Early in her composition course, Harriet learned that attention to the various stages in the writing process yields satisfying results, for writer and reader alike.

Activity: Revise the Essay

Return to the draft you wrote in response to either activity 1 or activity 2 on page 60. Also look at any written feedback you received on the draft. To identify any further problems in the draft, get together with several people (classmates, friends, or family members) and request that one of them read the draft aloud to you. Then ask your audience focused questions about the areas you sense need work, or use the checklist on the inside front cover to focus the feedback. In either case, summarize and rank the comments on a feedback chart or in marginal annotations. Then, using the comments as a guide, go ahead and revise the draft. Either type a new version or do your revising by hand, perhaps on a photocopy of the draft. Don't forget to proofread closely before submitting the paper to your instructor.

Rudi Von Briel/PhotoEdit, Inc.

DESCRIPTION

WHAT IS DESCRIPTION?

All of us respond in a strong way to sensory stimulation. The sweet perfume of a candy shop takes us back to childhood; the blank white walls of the campus infirmary remind us of long vigils at a hospital where a grandmother lay dying; the screech of a subway car sets our nerves on edge.

Without any sensory stimulation, we sink into a less-than-human state. Neglected babies, left alone with no human touch, no colors, no lullabies, become withdrawn and unresponsive. And prisoners dread solitary confinement, knowing that the sensory deprivation can be unbearable, even to the point of madness.

Because sensory impressions are so potent, descriptive writing has a unique power and appeal. *Description* can be defined as the expression, in vivid language, of what the five senses experience. A richly rendered description freezes a subject in time, evoking sights, smells, sounds, textures, and tastes in such a way that readers become one with the writer's world.

HOW DESCRIPTION FITS YOUR
PURPOSE AND AUDIENCE

Description can be a supportive technique that develops part of an essay, or it can be the dominant technique used throughout an essay. Here are some examples of the way description can help you meet the objective of an essay developed chiefly through another pattern of development:

- In a *causal analysis* showing the *consequences* of pet overpopulation, you might describe the desperate appearance of a pack of starving stray dogs.
- In an *argumentation-persuasion* essay urging more rigorous handgun control, you might start with a description of a violent family confrontation that ended in murder.
- In a *process analysis* explaining the pleasure of making ice cream at home, you might describe the beauty of an old-fashioned, hand-cranked ice-cream maker.
- In a *narrative essay* recounting a day in the life of a street musician, you might describe the musician's energy and the joyous appreciation of passersby.

In each case, the essay's overall purpose would affect the amount of description needed.

Your readers also influence how much description to include. As you write, ask yourself, "What do my particular readers need to know to understand and experience keenly what I'm describing? What descriptive details will they enjoy most?" Your answers to these and similar questions will help you tailor your description to specific readers. Consider an article intended for professional horticulturists; its purpose is to explain a new technique for controlling spider mites. Because of readers' expertise, there would be little need for a lengthy description of the insects. Written for a college newspaper, however, the article would probably provide a detailed description of the mites so student gardeners could distinguish between the pesky parasites and flecks of dust.

While your purpose and audience define *how much* to describe, you have great freedom deciding *what* to describe. Description is especially suited to objects (your car or desk, for example), but you can also describe a person, an animal, a place, a time, and a phenomenon or concept. You might write an effective description of a friend who runs marathons (person), a pair of ducks that return each year to a neighbor's pond (animals), the kitchen of a fast-food restaurant (place), a period when you were unemployed (time), the "fight or flight" response to danger (phenomenon or concept).

Description can be divided into two types: *objective* and *subjective*. In an objective description, you describe the subject in a straightforward and literal way, without revealing your attitude or feelings. Reporters, as well as technical and scientific writers, specialize in objective description;

their jobs depend on their ability to detail experiences without emotional bias. For example, a reporter may write an unemotional account of a township meeting that ended in a fistfight. Or a marine biologist may write a factual report describing the way sea mammals are killed by the plastic refuse (sandwich wrappings, straws, fishing lines) that humans throw into the ocean.

In contrast, when writing a subjective description, you convey a highly personal view of your subject and seek to elicit a strong emotional response from your readers. Such subjective descriptions often take the form of reflective pieces or character studies. For example, in an essay describing the rich plant life in an inner-city garden, you might reflect on people's longing to connect with the soil and express admiration for the gardeners' hard work—an admiration you'd like readers to share. Or, in a character study of your grandfather, you might describe his stern appearance and gentle behavior, hoping that the contradiction will move readers as much as it moves you.

The *tone* of a subjective description is determined by your purpose, your attitude toward the subject, and the reader response you wish to evoke. Consider an essay about a dynamic woman who runs a center for disturbed children. If you want readers to admire the woman, your tone will be serious and appreciative. But if you want to criticize her high-pressure tactics and management style, your tone will be disapproving and severe.

The language of a descriptive piece also depends, to a great extent, on whether your purpose is primarily objective or subjective. If the description is objective, the language is straightforward, precise, and factual. Such *denotative* language consists of neutral dictionary meanings. To describe as dispassionately as possible fans' violent behavior at a football game, you might write about the "large crowd" and its "mass movement onto the field." But for a subjective piece that inspires outrage in readers, you might write about the "swelling mob" and its "rowdy stampede onto the field." In the latter case, the language you used would be *connotative* and emotionally charged so that readers would share your feelings.

Subjective and objective descriptions often overlap. Sometimes a single sentence contains both objective and subjective elements: "Although his hands were large and misshapen by arthritis, they were gentle to the touch, inspiring confidence and trust." Other times, part of an essay may provide a factual description (the physical appearance of a summer cabin your family rented), while another part of the essay may be highly subjective (how you felt in the cabin, sitting in front of a fire on a rainy day).

At this point, you have a good sense of the way writers use description to achieve their purpose and to connect with their readers. Now take a moment to look closely at the photograph at the beginning of this chapter. Imagine you're writing a column, accompanied by the photo, for the local newspaper. Your purpose is to encourage businesspeople to support the city's mural arts program. Jot down some phrases you might use to *describe* the mural and its impact on the community.

SUGGESTIONS FOR USING DESCRIPTION IN AN ESSAY

The suggestions here and in Figure 3.1 on page 76 will be helpful whether you use description as a dominant or a supportive pattern of development.

1. Focus a descriptive essay around a dominant impression.   Like other kinds of writing, a descriptive essay must have a thesis, or main point. In a descriptive essay with a subjective slant, the thesis usually centers on the *dominant impression* you have about your subject. Suppose you decide to write an essay on your ninth-grade history teacher, Ms. Hazzard. You want the paper to convey how unconventional and flamboyant she was. The essay could, of course, focus on a different dominant impression—how insensitive she could be to students, for example. What's important is that you establish—early in the paper—the dominant impression you intend to convey. Although descriptive essays often imply, rather than explicitly state, the dominant impression, that impression should be unmistakable.

2. Select the details to include.   The power of description hinges on your ability to select from all possible details only those that support the dominant impression. All others, no matter how vivid or interesting, must be left out. If you're describing how flamboyant Ms. Hazzard could be, the details in the following paragraph would be appropriate.

A large-boned woman, Ms. Hazzard wore her bright red hair piled on top of her head, where it perched precariously. By the end of class, wayward strands of hair tumbled down and fell into eyes fringed by

FIGURE 3.1
Development Diagram: Writing a Description Essay

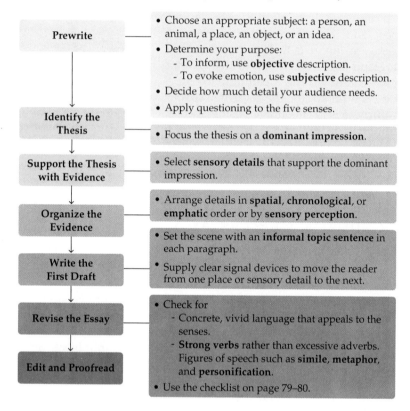

Prewrite
- Choose an appropriate subject: a person, an animal, a place, an object, or an idea.
- Determine your purpose:
  - To inform, use **objective** description.
  - To evoke emotion, use **subjective** description.
- Decide how much detail your audience needs.
- Apply questioning to the five senses.

Identify the Thesis
- Focus the thesis on a **dominant impression**.

Support the Thesis with Evidence
- Select **sensory details** that support the dominant impression.

Organize the Evidence
- Arrange details in **spatial, chronological,** or **emphatic** order or by **sensory perception**.

Write the First Draft
- Set the scene with an **informal topic sentence** in each paragraph.
- Supply clear signal devices to move the reader from one place or sensory detail to the next.

Revise the Essay
- Check for
  - Concrete, vivid language that appeals to the senses.
  - **Strong verbs** rather than excessive adverbs.
  - Figures of speech such as **simile, metaphor,** and **personification**.

Edit and Proofread
- Use the checklist on page 79–80.

spiky false eyelashes. Ms. Hazzard's nails, filed into crisp points, were painted either bloody burgundy or neon pink. Plastic bangle bracelets, also either burgundy or pink, clattered up and down her ample arms as she scrawled on the board the historical dates that had, she claimed, "changed the world."

Such details—the heavy eye makeup, stiletto nails, gaudy bracelets—contribute to the impression of a flamboyant, unusual person. Even if you remembered times that Ms. Hazzard seemed perfectly conventional and understated, most likely you wouldn't describe those times since they contradict the dominant impression.

You must also be selective in the *number of details* you include. Having a dominant impression helps you eliminate many details gathered during prewriting, but there still will be choices to make. For example, it would be inappropriate to describe in exhaustive detail everything in a messy room:

> The brown desk, made of a grained plastic laminate, is directly under a small window covered by a torn yellow-and-gold plaid curtain. In the left corner of the desk are four crumbled balls of blue-lined yellow paper, three red markers, two fine-point blue pens, an ink eraser, and four letters, two bearing special wildlife stamps. A green down-filled vest and a red cable-knit sweater are thrown over the back of the bright blue metal bridge chair pushed under the desk. Under the chair is an oval braided rug, its once brilliant blues and greens spotted by old coffee stains.

Readers will be reluctant to wade through such undifferentiated specifics. Even more important, such excessive detailing dilutes the focus of the essay. You end up with a seemingly endless list of specifics rather than with a carefully crafted picture in words. In this regard, sculptors and writers are similar—what they take away is as important as what they leave in.

Perhaps you're wondering how to generate the details that support your dominant impression. As you can imagine, you have to develop heightened powers of observation and recall. To sharpen these key faculties, it can be helpful to make up a chart with separate columns for each of the five senses. If you can observe your subject directly, enter in the appropriate columns what you see, hear, taste, and so on. If you're attempting to remember something from the past, try to recollect details under each of these sense headings. Ask yourself questions ("How did it smell? What did I hear?") and list each memory recaptured. You'll be surprised how this simple technique can tune you in to your experiences and help uncover the specific details needed to develop your dominant impression.

3. Organize the descriptive details.   Select the organizational pattern (or combination of patterns) that best supports your dominant impression. The paragraphs in a descriptive essay are usually sequenced *spatially* (from top to bottom, interior to exterior, near to far) or *chronologically* (as the subject is experienced in time). But the paragraphs can also be ordered *emphatically* (ending with your subject's most striking elements) or by *sensory impression* (first smell, then taste, then touch, and so on).

You might, for instance, use a *spatial* pattern to organize a description of a large city as you viewed it from the air, a taxi, and a subway car. A description of your first day on a new job might move *chronologically*, starting with how you felt the first hour on the job and proceeding through the rest of the day. In a paper describing a bout with the flu, you might arrange details *emphatically*, beginning with a description of your low-level aches and pains and concluding with an account of your raging fever. An essay about a neighborhood garbage dump, euphemistically called an "ecology landfill" by its owners, could be organized by *sensory impressions:* the sights of the dump, its smells, its sounds. Regardless of the organizational pattern you use, provide enough *signal devices* (for example, *about, next, worst of all*) so that readers can follow the description easily.

Finally, although descriptive essays don't always have conventional topic sentences, each descriptive paragraph should have a clear focus. Often this focus is indicated by a sentence early in the paragraph that names the scene, object, or individual to be described. Such a sentence functions as a kind of *informal topic sentence;* the paragraph's descriptive details then develop that topic sentence.

4. Use vivid sensory language and varied sentence structure.   The connotative language typical of subjective description should be richly evocative. The words you select must etch in readers' minds the same picture that you have in yours. For this reason, rather than relying on vague generalities, you must use language that involves readers' senses. Consider the difference between the following paired descriptions.

Vague	Vivid
The food was unappetizing.	The stew congealed into an oval pool of milky-brown fat.
The toothpaste was refreshing.	The toothpaste, tasting minty sweet, felt good against slippery teeth, free finally from braces.
Filled with passengers and baggage, the car moved slowly down the road.	Burdened with its load of clamoring children and well-worn suitcases, the car labored down down the interstate on bald tires and worn shocks, emitting puffs of blue exhaust and an occasional backfire.

Unlike the *concrete, sensory-packed* sentences on the right, the sentences on the left fail to create vivid word pictures that engage readers. While all good writing blends abstract and concrete language, descriptive writing demands an abundance of specific sensory language.

Keep in mind, too, that *verbs pack more of a wallop* than adverbs. The following sentence has to rely on adverbs (italicized) because its verbs are so weak: "She walked *casually* into the room and *deliberately* tried not to pay much attention to their stares." Rewritten, so that verbs (italicized), not adverbs, do the bulk of the work, the sentence becomes more powerful: "She *strolled* into the room and *ignored* their stares."

Figures of speech—nonliteral, imaginative comparisons between two basically dissimilar things—are another way to enliven descriptive writing. *Similes* use the words *like* or *as* when comparing; *metaphors* state or imply that two things being compared are alike; and *personification* attributes human characteristics to inanimate things.

The examples that follow show how effective figurative language can be in descriptive writing.

> Moving as jerkily as a marionette on strings, the old man picked himself up off the sidewalk and staggered down the street. (*simile*)
>
> Stalking their prey, the hall monitors remained hidden in the corridors, motionless and ready to spring on any unsuspecting student who dared to sneak into class late. (*metaphor*)
>
> The scoop of vanilla ice cream, plain and unadorned, cried out for hot-fudge sauce and a sprinkling of sliced pecans. (*personification*)

Finally, when writing descriptive passages, you need to *vary sentence structure*. Don't use the same subject-verb pattern in all sentences. The second example above, for instance, could have been written as follows: "The hall monitors stalked their prey. They hid in the corridors. They remained motionless and ready to spring on any unsuspecting student who tried to sneak into class late." But the sentence is richer and more interesting when the descriptive elements are embedded, eliminating what would otherwise have been a clipped and predictable subject-verb pattern.

REVISION STRATEGIES

Once you have a draft of the essay, you're ready to revise. The following checklist will help you and those giving you feedback apply to description some of the revision techniques discussed on pages 60–62.

☑ DESCRIPTION: A REVISION/PEER REVIEW CHECKLIST

Revise Overall Meaning and Structure

❏ What dominant impression does the essay convey? Is the dominant impression stated or implied? Where? Should it be made more obvious or more subtle?

❏ Is the essay primarily objective or subjective? Should the essay be more emotionally charged or less so?

❏ Which descriptive details don't support the dominant impression? Should they be deleted, or should the dominant impression be adjusted to encompass the details?

Revise Paragraph Development

❏ How are the essay's descriptive paragraphs organized—spatially, chronologically, emphatically, or by sensory impression? Would another organizational pattern be more effective? Which one(s)?

❏ Which paragraphs lack a distinctive focus?

❏ Which descriptive paragraphs are mere lists of sensory impressions?

❏ Which descriptive paragraphs fail to engage the reader's senses? How could they be made more concrete?

Revise Sentences and Words

❏ What signal devices guide readers through the description? Are there enough signals? Too many?

❏ Where should sentence structure be varied to make it less predictable?

❏ Which sentences should include more sensory images?

❏ Which flat verbs should be replaced with vigorous verbs?

❏ Where should there be more or fewer adjectives?

❏ Do any figures of speech seem contrived or trite? Which ones?

STUDENT ESSAY

The following student essay was written by Marie Martinez in response to this assignment:

> The essay "Life, Death and Spring" is an evocative piece about a spot that had special meaning for Gary Kamiya. Write an essay about a place that holds rich significance for you, centering the description on a dominant impression.

While reading Marie's paper, try to determine how well it applies the principles of description. The annotations on Marie's paper and the commentary following it will help you look at the essay more closely.

Salt Marsh
by Marie Martinez

Introduction   In one of his journals, Thoreau told of the difficulty he had 1
escaping the obligations and cares of society: "It sometimes
happens that I cannot easily shake off the village. The thought
of some work will run in my head and I am not where my body
is—I am out of my senses. In my walks I . . . return to my
senses." All of us feel out of our senses at times. Overwhelmed

Dominant impression (thesis)

by problems or everyday annoyances, we lose touch with sensory pleasures as we spend our days in noisy cities and stuffy classrooms. Just as Thoreau walked in the woods to return to his senses, I have a special place where I return to mine: the salt marsh behind my grandparents' house.

Informal topic sentence: Definition paragraph

My grandparents live on the East Coast, a mile or so 2 inland from the sea. Between the ocean and the mainland is a wide fringe of salt marsh. A salt marsh is not a swamp, but an expanse of dark, spongy soil threaded with saltwater creeks and clothed in a kind of grass called salt meadow hay. All the water in the marsh rises and falls daily with the ocean tides, an endless cycle that changes the look of the marsh—partly flooded or mostly dry—as the day progresses.

Informal topic sentence: First paragraph in a four-part spatial sequence

Heading out to the marsh from my grandparents' house, 3 I follow a short path through the woods. As I walk along, a sharp smell of salt mixed with the rich aroma of peaty soil fills my nostrils. I am always amazed by the way the path changes with the seasons. Sometimes I walk in the brilliant green of spring, sometimes in the tawny gold of autumn, sometimes in the grayish tan of winter. No matter the season, the grass

Simile

flanking the trail is often flattened into swirls, like thick Van Gogh brush strokes that curve and recurve in circular patterns. No people come here. The peacefulness heals me like a soothing drug.

Informal topic sentence: Second paragraph in the spatial sequence

After a few minutes, the trail suddenly opens up to a view 4 that calms me no matter how upset or discouraged I might be: a line of tall waving reeds bordering and nearly hiding the salt marsh creek. To get to the creek, I part the reeds.

Informal topic sentence: Third paragraph in the spatial sequence

The creek is a narrow body of water no more than fifteen 5 feet wide, and it ebbs and flows as the ocean currents sweep toward the land or rush back toward the sea. The creek winds in a sinuous pattern so that I cannot see its beginning or end, the places where it trickles into the marsh or spills into the open ocean. Little brown birds dip in and out of the reeds on the far shore of the creek, making a special "tweep-tweep" sound peculiar to the marsh. When I stand at low tide on the shore of the creek, I am on a miniature cliff, for the bank of the creek falls abruptly and steeply into the water. Below me, green grasses wave and shimmer under the water while tiny minnows flash their silvery sides as they dart through the underwater tangles.

Informal topic sentence: Last paragraph in the spatial sequence

The creek water is often much warmer than the ocean, so 6 I can swim there in three seasons. Sitting on the edge of the creek, I scoop some water into my hand, rub my face and neck, then ease into the water. Where the creek is shallow, my feet

Simile

sink into a foot of muck that feels like mashed potatoes mixed with motor oil. But once I become accustomed to it, I enjoy squishing the slimy mud through my toes. Sometimes I feel brushing past my legs the blue crabs that live in the creek. Other times, I hear the splash of a turtle or an otter as it slips from the shore into the water. Otherwise, it is silent. The salty water is buoyant and lifts my spirits as I stroke through it to reach the middle of the creek. There in the center, I float weightlessly, surrounded by tall reeds that reduce the world to water and sky. I am at peace.

Conclusion

The salt marsh is not the kind of dramatic landscape 7 found on picture postcards. There are no soaring mountains, sandy beaches, or lush valleys. The marsh is a flat world that some consider dull and uninviting. I am glad most people do not respond to the marsh's subtle beauty because that means Echo of idea in introduction I can be alone there. Just as the rising tide sweeps over the marsh, floating debris out to the ocean, the marsh washes away my concerns and restores me to my senses.

COMMENTARY

The dominant impression.   Marie responded to the assignment by writing a moving tribute to a place having special meaning for her—the salt marsh near her grandparents' home. Like most descriptive pieces, Marie's essay is organized around a *dominant impression:* the marsh's peaceful solitude and gentle, natural beauty. The essay's introduction provides a context for the dominant impression by comparing the pleasure Marie experiences in the marsh to the happiness Thoreau felt in his walks around Walden Pond.

Combining patterns of development.   Before developing the essay's dominant impression, Marie uses the second paragraph to *define* a salt marsh. An *objective description,* the definition clarifies that a salt marsh—with its spongy soil, haylike grass, and ebbing tides—is not to be confused with a swamp. Because Marie offers such a factual definition, readers have the background needed to enjoy the personalized view that follows.

Besides the definition paragraph and the comparison in the opening paragraph, the essay contains a strong element of *causal analysis:* Throughout, Marie describes the marsh's effect on her.

Sensory language.   At times, Marie develops the essay's dominant impression explicitly, as when she writes "No people come here" (paragraph 3) and "I am at peace" (6). But Marie generally uses the more subtle techniques characteristic of *subjective description* to convey the dominant impression. First of all, she fills the essay with strong *connotative language,* rich with *sensory images.* The third paragraph describes what she smells (the "sharp smell of salt mixed with the rich aroma of peaty soil") and what she sees ("brilliant green," "tawny gold," and "grayish tan"). In the fifth paragraph, she tells us that she hears the chirping sounds of small birds. And the sixth paragraph includes vigorous descriptions of how the marsh feels to Marie's touch. She splashes water on her face and neck; she digs her toes into the mud at the bottom of the creek; she delights in the delicate brushing of crabs against her legs.

Figurative language, vigorous verbs, and varied sentence structure.   You might also have noted that *figurative language, energetic verbs,* and *varied sentence patterns* contribute to the essay's descriptive power. Marie develops a *simile* in the third paragraph when she compares the flattened swirls of swamp grass to the brush strokes in a painting by Van Gogh. Later she uses another simile when she writes that the creek's thick mud feels "like mashed potatoes mixed with motor oil." Moreover, throughout the essay, she uses lively verbs ("shimmer," "flash") to capture the marsh's magical quality. Similarly, Marie enhances descriptive passages by varying the length of her sentences. Long, fairly elaborate sentences are interspersed with short, dramatic statements. In the third paragraph, for example, the long sentence describing the circular swirls of swamp grass is followed by the brief statement "No people come here." And the sixth paragraph uses two short sentences ("Otherwise, it is silent" and "I am at peace") to punctuate the paragraph's longer sentences.

Organization.   We can follow Marie's journey through the marsh because she uses an easy-to-follow combination of *spatial, chronological,* and *emphatic* patterns to sequence her experience. The essay relies primarily on a spatial arrangement since the four body paragraphs focus on the different spots that Marie reaches: first, the path behind her grandparents' house (paragraph 3); then the area bordering the creek (4); next, her view of the creek (5); last, the creek itself (6). Each stage of her walk is signaled by an *informal topic sentence* near the start of each paragraph. Furthermore, *signal devices* (marked by italics here) indicate not only her location but also the chronological passage of time: "*As* I walk along, a sharp smell . . . fills my nostrils" (3); "*After* a few minutes, the trail suddenly opens up . . ." (4); "*Below* me, green grasses wave . . ." (5). And to call attention to the creek's serene beauty, Marie saves for last the description of the peace she feels while floating in the creek.

An inappropriate figure of speech.   Although the four body paragraphs focus on the distinctive qualities of each location, Marie runs into a minor problem in the third paragraph. Take a moment to reread that paragraph's last sentence. Comparing the peace of the marsh to the effect of a "soothing drug" is jarring. The effectiveness of Marie's essay hinges on her ability to create a picture of a pure, natural world. A reference to drugs is inappropriate. Now, reread the paragraph aloud, stopping after "No people come here." Note how much more in keeping with the essay's dominant impression the paragraph is when the reference to drugs is omitted.

Conclusion.   The concluding paragraph brings the essay to a graceful close. The powerful *simile* found in the last sentence contains an implied reference to Thoreau and to Marie's earlier statement about the joy to be found in special places having restorative powers. Such an allusion echoes, with good effect, the paper's opening comments.

Revising the first draft.   When Marie met with some classmates during a peer review session, the students agreed that Marie's first draft was strong and moving. But they also said that they had difficulty following her route through the marsh; they found her third paragraph especially confusing. Marie kept track of her classmates' comments on a separate piece of paper and then entered them, numbered in order of importance, in the margin of her first draft. Following is the first-draft version of Marie's third paragraph.

Original Version of the Third Paragraph

As I head out to the marsh from the house, I follow a short trail through the woods. A smell of salt mixed with the aroma of soil fills my nostrils. The end of the trail suddenly opens up to a view that calms me no matter how upset or discouraged I might be: a line of tall waving reeds bordering the salt marsh creek. Civilization seems far away as I walk the path of flattened grass and finally reach my goal, the salt marsh creek hidden behind the tall waving reeds. The path changes with the seasons; sometimes I walk in the brilliant green of spring, sometimes in the tawny gold of autumn, sometimes in the quiet grayish tan of winter. In some areas, the grass is flattened into swirls that make the marsh resemble one of those paintings by Van Gogh. No people come here. The peacefulness heals me like a soothing drug. The path stops at the line of tall waving reeds, standing upright at the border of the creek. I part the reeds to get to the creek.

When Marie looked more carefully at the paragraph, she agreed it was confusing. For one thing, the paragraph's third and fourth sentences indicated that she had come to the path's end and had reached the reeds bordering the creek. In the following sentences, however, she was on the path again. Then, at the end, she was back at the creek, as if she had just arrived there. Marie resolved this confusion by breaking the single paragraph into two separate ones—the first describing the walk along the path, the second describing her arrival at the creek. This restructuring, especially when combined with clearer transitions, eliminated the confusion.

While revising her essay, Marie also intensified the sensory images in her original paragraph. She changed the "smell of salt and soil" to the "sharp smell of salt mixed with the rich aroma of peaty soil." And when she added the phrase "thick Van Gogh brush strokes that curve and recurve in circular patterns," she made the comparison between the marsh grass and a Van Gogh painting more vivid.

These are just some of the changes Marie made while rewriting her paper. Her skillful revisions provided the polish needed to make an already strong essay even more evocative.

Activities: Description

Prewriting Activities

1. Imagine you're writing two essays: One explains the *process* by which students get "burned out"; the other *argues* that being a spendthrift is better (or worse) than being frugal. Jot down ways you might use description in each essay.

2. Go to a place on campus where students congregate. In preparation for an *objective* description of this place, make notes of various sights, sounds, smells, and textures, as well as the overall "feel" of the place. Then, in preparation for a *subjective* description, observe and take notes on another sheet of paper. Compare the two sets of material. What differences do you see in word choice and selection of details?

Revising Activities

3. Revise each of the following sentence sets twice. The first time, create an unmis-takable mood; the second time, create a sharply contrasting mood. To convey atmosphere, vary sentence structure, use vigorous verbs, provide rich sensory details, and pay special attention to words' connotations.

   a. The card players sat around the table. The table was old. The players were, too.
   b. A long line formed outside the movie theater. People didn't want to miss the show. The movie had received a lot of attention recently.
   c. A girl walked down the street in her first pair of high heels. This was a new experience for her.

4. The following descriptive paragraph is from the first draft of an essay showing that personal growth may result when romanticized notions and reality collide. How effective is the paragraph in illustrating the essay's thesis? Which details are pow-erful? Which could be more concrete? Which should be deleted? Where should sentence structure be more varied? How could the description be made more coherent? Revise the paragraph, correcting any problems you discover and adding whatever sensory details are needed to enliven the description. Feel free to break the paragraph into two or more separate ones.

As a child, I was intrigued by stories about the farm in Harrison County, Maine, where my father spent his teens. Being raised on a farm seemed more interesting than growing up in the suburbs. So about a year ago, I decided to see for myself what the farm was like. I got there by driving on Route 334, a surprisingly easy-to-drive, four-lane highway that had recently been built with matching state and federal funds. I turned into the dirt road leading to the farm and got out of my car. It had been washed and waxed for the occasion. Then I headed for a dirt-colored barn. Its roof was full of huge, rotted holes. As I rounded the bushes, I saw the house. It too was dirt-colored. Its paint must have worn off decades ago. A couple of dead-looking old cars were sprawled in front of the barn. They were dented and windowless. Also by the barn was an ancient refrigerator, crushed like a discarded accordion. The porch steps to the house were slanted and wobbly. Through the open windows came a stale smell and the sound of television. Looking in the front door screen, I could see two chickens jumping around inside. Everything looked dirty both inside and out. Secretly grateful that no one answered my knock, I bolted down the stairs, got into my clean, shiny car, and drove away.

Maya Angelou

Born Marguerite Johnson in 1928, Maya Angelou spent her childhood in Stamps, Arkansas, with her brother, Bailey, and her grandmother, "Momma." Although her youth was difficult—she was raped at age eight and became a mother at sixteen—Angelou somehow managed to thrive. Multi-talented, she later worked as a professional dancer, starred in an off-Broadway play, appeared in the television miniseries *Roots,* served as a coordinator for the Southern Christian Leadership Conference, and wrote several well-received volumes of poetry—among them *Oh Pray My Wings Are Gonna Fit Me Well* (1975) and *And Still I Rise* (1996). She has also written essay collections, such as *Even the Stars Look Lonesome* (1997), and children's books, including *My Painted House, My Friendly Chicken, and Me* (1994), and *Kofi and His Magic* (1996). A professor at Wake Forest University since 1981, Angelou delivered at the 1993 presidential inauguration a stirring poem written for the occasion. The recipient of numerous honorary doctorates, Angelou is best known for her series of six autobiographical books, starting with *I Know Why the Caged Bird Sings* (1970) and concluding with *A Song Flung Up to Heaven* (2002). The following essay is taken from *I Know Why the Caged Bird Sings.*

For ideas about how this description essay is organized, see Figure 3.2 on page 92.

Pre-Reading Journal Entry

Growing up isn't easy. In your journal, list several challenges you've had to face in your life. In each case, was there someone who served as a "lifeline," providing you with crucial guidance and support? Who was that individual? How did this person steer you through the difficulty?

Sister Flowers

For nearly a year [after I was raped], I sopped around the house, the Store, the school and the church, like an old biscuit, dirty and inedible. Then I met, or rather got to know, the lady who threw me my first life line. 1

Mrs. Bertha Flowers was the aristocrat of Black Stamps. She had the grace of control to appear warm in the coldest weather, and on the Arkansas summer days it seemed she had a private breeze which swirled around, cooling her. She was thin without the taut look of wiry people, and her printed voile dresses and flowered hats were as right for her as denim overalls for a farmer. She was our side's answer to the richest white woman in town. 2

Her skin was a rich black that would have peeled like a plum if snagged, but then no one would have thought of getting close enough to Mrs. Flowers to ruffle her dress, let alone snag her skin. She didn't encourage familiarity. She wore gloves too. 3

I don't think I ever saw Mrs. Flowers laugh, but she smiled often. A slow   4
widening of her thin black lips to show even, small white teeth, then the slow
effortless closing. When she chose to smile on me, I always wanted to thank
her. The action was so graceful and inclusively benign.

She was one of the few gentlewomen I have ever known, and has   5
remained throughout my life the measure of what a human being can be.

Momma had a strange relationship with her. Most often when she passed   6
on the road in front of the Store, she spoke to Momma in that soft yet carrying voice, "Good day, Mrs. Henderson." Momma responded with "How
you, Sister Flowers?"

Mrs. Flowers didn't belong to our church, nor was she Momma's famil-   7
iar. Why on earth did she insist on calling her Sister Flowers? Shame made
me want to hide my face. Mrs. Flowers deserved better than to be called
Sister. Then, Momma left out the verb. Why not ask, "How *are* you,
Mrs. Flowers?" With the unbalanced passion of the young, I hated her for
showing her ignorance to Mrs. Flowers. It didn't occur to me for many years
that they were as alike as sisters, separated only by formal education.

Although I was upset, neither of the women was in the least shaken by   8
what I thought an unceremonious greeting. Mrs. Flowers would continue
her easy gait up the hill to her little bungalow, and Momma kept on shelling
peas or doing whatever had brought her to the front porch.

Occasionally, though, Mrs. Flowers would drift off the road and down   9
to the Store and Momma would say to me, "Sister, you go on and play." As
she left I would hear the beginning of an intimate conversation. Momma
persistently using the wrong verb, or none at all.

"Brother and Sister Wilcox is sho'ly the meanest—" "Is," Momma?   10
"Is"? Oh, please, not "is," Momma, for two or more. But they talked, and
from the side of the building where I waited for the ground to open up and
swallow me, I heard the soft-voiced Mrs. Flowers and the textured voice of
my grandmother merging and melting. They were interrupted from time to
time by giggles that must have come from Mrs. Flowers (Momma never gig-
gled in her life). Then she was gone.

She appealed to me because she was like people I had never met per-   11
sonally. Like women in English novels who walked the moors (whatever
they were) with their loyal dogs racing at a respectful distance. Like the
women who sat in front of roaring fireplaces, drinking tea incessantly from
silver trays full of scones and crumpets. Women who walked over the
"heath" and read morocco-bound books and had two last names divided by
a hyphen. It would be safe to say that she made me proud to be Negro, just
by being herself.

She acted just as refined as whitefolks in the movies and books and she   12
was more beautiful, for none of them could have come near that warm color
without looking gray by comparison.

It was fortunate that I never saw her in the company of powhitefolks. 13
For since they tend to think of their whiteness as an evenizer, I'm certain
that I would have had to hear her spoken to commonly as Bertha, and my
image of her would have been shattered like the unmendable Humpty-
Dumpty.

One summer afternoon, sweet-milk fresh in my memory, she stopped 14
at the Store to buy provisions. Another Negro woman of her health and
age would have been expected to carry the paper sacks home in one hand,
but Momma said, "Sister Flowers, I'll send Bailey up to your house with
these things."

She smiled that slow dragging smile, "Thank you, Mrs. Henderson. 15
I'd prefer Marguerite, though." My name was beautiful when she said
it. "I've been meaning to talk to her, anyway." They gave each other age-
group looks.

Momma said, "Well, that's all right then. Sister, go and change your 16
dress. You going to Sister Flowers's."

The chifforobe was a maze. What on earth did one put on to go to 17
Mrs. Flowers's house? I knew I shouldn't put on a Sunday dress. It might be
sacrilegious. Certainly not a house dress, since I was already wearing a fresh
one. I chose a school dress, naturally. It was formal without suggesting that
going to Mrs. Flowers's house was equivalent to attending church.

I trusted myself back into the Store. 18

"Now, don't you look nice." I had chosen the right thing, for once.... 19

There was a little path beside the rocky road, and Mrs. Flowers walked 20
in front swinging her arms and picking her way over the stones.

She said, without turning her head, to me, "I hear you're doing very 21
good school work, Marguerite, but that it's all written. The teachers report
that they have trouble getting you to talk in class." We passed the triangular
farm on our left and the path widened to allow us to walk together. I hung
back in the separate unasked and unanswerable questions.

"Come and walk along with me, Marguerite." I couldn't have refused 22
even if I wanted to. She pronounced my name so nicely. Or more correctly, she
spoke each word with such clarity that I was certain a foreigner who didn't
understand English could have understood her.

"Now no one is going to make you talk—possibly no one can. But bear 23
in mind, language is man's way of communicating with his fellow man and
it is language alone which separates him from the lower animals." That was
a totally new idea to me, and I would need time to think about it.

"Your grandmother says you read a lot. Every chance you get. That's good, 24
but not good enough. Words mean more than what is set down on paper. It
takes the human voice to infuse them with the shades of deeper meaning."

I memorized the part about the human voice infusing words. It seemed 25
so valid and poetic.

She said she was going to give me some books and that I not only must   26
read them, I must read them aloud. She suggested that I try to make a sentence sound in as many different ways as possible.

"I'll accept no excuse if you return a book to me that has been badly   27
handled." My imagination boggled at the punishment I would deserve if
in fact I did abuse a book of Mrs. Flowers's. Death would be too kind
and brief.

The odors in the house surprised me. Somehow I had never connected   28
Mrs. Flowers with food or eating or any other common experience of common people. There must have been an outhouse, too, but my mind never
recorded it.

The sweet scent of vanilla had met us as she opened the door.   29

"I made tea cookies this morning. You see, I had planned to invite you   30
for cookies and lemonade so we could have this little chat. The lemonade is
in the icebox."

It followed that Mrs. Flowers would have ice on an ordinary day, when   31
most families in our town bought ice late on Saturdays only a few times during the summer to be used in the wooden ice-cream freezers.

She took the bags from me and disappeared through the kitchen door.   32
I looked around the room that I had never in my wildest fantasies imagined
I would see. Browned photographs leered or threatened from the walls and
the white, freshly done curtains pushed against themselves and against the
wind. I wanted to gobble up the room entire and take it to Bailey, who
would help me analyze and enjoy it.

"Have a seat, Marguerite. Over there by the table." She carried a platter   33
covered with a tea towel. Although she warned that she hadn't tried her
hand at baking sweets for some time, I was certain that like everything else
about her the cookies would be perfect.

They were flat round wafers, slightly browned on the edges and butter-   34
yellow in the center. With the cold lemonade they were sufficient for childhood's lifelong diet. Remembering my manners, I took nice little lady-like
bites off the edges. She said she had made them expressly for me and that
she had a few in the kitchen that I could take home to my brother. So I
jammed one whole cake in my mouth and the rough crumbs scratched the
insides of my jaws, and if I hadn't had to swallow, it would have been a
dream come true.

As I ate she began the first of what we later called "my lessons in liv-   35
ing." She said that I must always be intolerant of ignorance but understanding of illiteracy. That some people, unable to go to school, were
more educated and even more intelligent than college professors. She
encouraged me to listen carefully to what country people called mother
wit. That in those homely sayings was couched the collective wisdom of
generations.

When I finished the cookies she brushed off the table and brought a thick, small book from the bookcase. I had read *A Tale of Two Cities* and found it up to my standards as a romantic novel. She opened the first page and I heard poetry for the first time in my life. 36

"It was the best of times and the worst of times..." Her voice slid in and curved down through and over the words. She was nearly singing. I wanted to look at the pages. Were they the same that I had read? Or were there notes, music, lined on the pages, as in a hymn book? Her sounds began cascading gently. I knew from listening to a thousand preachers that she was nearing the end of her reading, and I hadn't really heard, heard to understand, a single word. 37

"How do you like that?" 38

It occurred to me that she expected a response. The sweet vanilla flavor was still on my tongue and her reading was a wonder in my ears. I had to speak. 39

I said, "Yes, ma'am." It was the least I could do, but it was the most also. 40

"There's one more thing. Take this book of poems and memorize one for me. Next time you pay me a visit, I want you to recite." 41

I have tried often to search behind the sophistication of years for the enchantment I so easily found in those gifts. The essence escapes but its aura remains. To be allowed, no, invited, into the private lives of strangers, and to share their joys and fears, was a chance to exchange the Southern bitter worm-wood for a cup of mead with Beowulf[1] or a hot cup of tea and milk with Oliver Twist.[2] When I said aloud, "It is a far, far better thing that I do, than I have ever done..."[3] tears of love filled my eyes at my selflessness. 42

On that first day, I ran down the hill and into the road (few cars ever came along it) and had the good sense to stop running before I reached the Store. 43

I was liked, and what a difference it made. I was respected not as Mrs. Henderson's grandchild or Bailey's sister but for just being Marguerite Johnson. 44

Childhood's logic never asks to be proved (all conclusions are absolute). I didn't question why Mrs. Flowers had singled me out for attention, nor did it occur to me that Momma might have asked her to give me a little talking to. All I cared about was that she had made tea cookies for *me* and read to *me* from her favorite book. It was enough to prove that she liked me. 45

---

[1]The hero of an Old English epic poem dating from the eighth century (editors' note).

[2]The main character in Charles Dickens's novel *Oliver Twist* (1837) (editors' note).

[3]The last words of Sydney Carton, the selfless hero of Charles Dickens's novel *A Tale of Two Cities* (1859) (editors' note).

FIGURE 3.2
Essay Structure Diagram: "Sister Flowers" by Maya Angelou

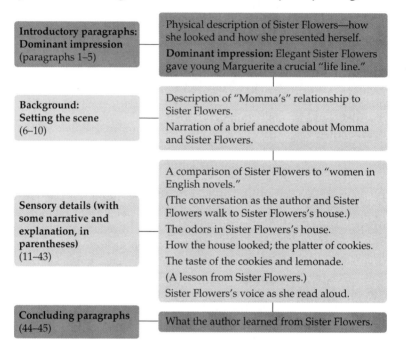

Questions for Close Reading

1. What is the selection's thesis (or dominant impression)? Locate the sentence(s) in which Angelou states her main idea. If she doesn't state the thesis explicitly, express it in your own words.
2. Angelou states that Mrs. Flowers "has remained throughout my life the measure of what a human being can be" (paragraph 5). What does Angelou admire about Mrs. Flowers?
3. Why is young Angelou so ashamed of Momma when Mrs. Flowers is around? How do Momma and Mrs. Flowers behave with each other?
4. What are the "lessons in living" that Angelou receives from Mrs. Flowers during their first visit? How do you think these lessons might have subsequently influenced Angelou?
5. Refer to your dictionary as needed to define the following words used in the selection: *taut* (paragraph 2), *voile* (2), *benign* (4), *unceremonious* (8), *gait* (8), *moors* (11), *incessantly* (11), *scones* (11), *crumpets* (11), *heath* (11), *chifforobe* (17), *sacrilegious* (17), *infuse* (24), *couched* (35), and *aura* (42).

Questions About the Writer's Craft

1. **The pattern.** Reread the essay, focusing on the descriptive passages first of Mrs. Flowers and then of Angelou's visit to Mrs. Flowers's house. To what senses does Angelou appeal in these passages? What method of organization (see pages 41–42) does she use to order these sensory details?

2. To enrich the description of her eventful encounter with Mrs. Flowers, Angelou draws upon figures of speech (see page 78). Consider, for example, the similes in paragraphs 1 and 11. How do these figures of speech contribute to the essay's dominant impression?

3. **Other patterns.** Because Angelou's description has a strong *narrative* component, it isn't surprising that there's a considerable amount of dialogue in the selection. For example, in paragraphs 7 and 10, Angelou quotes Momma's incorrect grammar. She then provides an imagined conversation in which the young Angelou scolds Momma and corrects her speech. What do these imagined scoldings of Momma reveal about young Angelou? How do they relate to Mrs. Flowers's subsequent "lessons in life"?

4. Although it's not the focus of this selection, the issue of race remains in the background of Angelou's portrait of Mrs. Flowers. Where in the selection does Angelou imply that race was a fact of life in her town? How does this specter of racism help Angelou underscore the significance of her encounter with Mrs. Flowers?

Writing Assignments Using Description as a Pattern of Development

1. At one time or another, just about all of us have met someone who taught us to see ourselves more clearly and helped us understand what we wanted from life. Write an essay describing such a person. Focus on the individual's personal qualities, as a way of depicting the role he or she played in your life. Be sure not to limit yourself to an objective description. Subjective description, filled with lively language and figures of speech, will serve you well as you provide a portrait of this special person.

2. Thrilled by the spectacle of Mrs. Flowers's interesting home, Angelou says she wanted to "gobble up the room entire" and share it with her brother. Write an essay describing in detail a place that vividly survives in your memory. You may describe a setting that you visited only once or a familiar setting that holds a special place in your heart. Before you write, list the qualities and sensory impressions you associate with this special place; then refine the list so that all details support your dominant impression. You may want to read Gary Kamiya's "Life, Death and Spring" (page 111) to see how a professional writer evokes the qualities of a special place in his life.

Writing Assignments Combining Patterns of Development

3. When the young Angelou discovers, thanks to Mrs. Flowers, the thrill of acceptance, she experiences a kind of *epiphany*—a moment of enlightenment. Write an essay about an event in your life that represented a kind of epiphany. You might

write about a positive discovery, such as when you realized you had a special talent for something, or about a negative discovery, such as when you realized that a beloved family member had a serious flaw. To make the point that the moment was a turning point in your life, start by *describing* what kind of person you were before the discovery. Then *narrate* the actual incident, using vivid details and dialogue to make the event come alive. End by discussing the importance of this epiphany in your life. For additional accounts of personal epiphanies, you might read Audre Lorde's "The Fourth of July" (page 142), Langston Hughes's "Salvation" (page 160), and Beth Johnson's "Bombs Bursting in Air" (page 215).

4. Think of an activity that engages you completely, one that provides—as reading does for Angelou—an opportunity for growth and expansion. Possibilities include reading, writing, playing an instrument, doing crafts, dancing, hiking, playing a sport, cooking, or traveling. Write an essay in which you *argue* the merits of your chosen pastime. Assume that some of your readers are highly skeptical. To win them over, you'll need to provide convincing *examples* that demonstrate the pleasure and benefits you have discovered in the activity.

Writing Assignment Using a Journal Entry as a Starting Point

5. Write an essay about a time when someone threw you a much-needed "lifeline" at a challenging time. Review your pre-reading journal entry, selecting *one* time when a person's encouragement and support made a great difference in your life. Be sure to describe the challenge you faced before recounting the specific details of the person's help. Dialogue and descriptive details will help you recreate the power of the experience. You should consider reading "Showing What Is Possible" (page 405), in which Jacques D'Amboise shows how a "wise" teacher made a world of difference in his life.

Gordon Parks

The son of deeply religious tenant farmers, Gordon Parks (1912–2006) grew up in Kansas knowing both the comforts of familial love and the torments of poverty and racism. Sent as a teenager to live with his sister in Minnesota after his mother's death, Parks was thrown out on his own in a frigid winter by his brother-in-law. To support himself, Parks worked as a janitor in a flophouse and as a piano player in a bordello. These and other odd jobs gave Parks the means to buy his first camera. Fascinated by photographic images, Parks studied the masters and eventually developed his own powers as a photographer. So evocative were his photographic studies that both *Life* and *Vogue* brought him on staff, the first black photographer to be hired by the two magazines. Parks's prodigious creativity has found expression in filmmaking (*Shaft* in 1971), musical composition (both classical and jazz), fiction, nonfiction, and poetry (titles include *The Learning Tree, A Choice of Weapons, To Smile in Autumn, Arias in Silence, Glimpses Toward Infinity, A Star for Noon,* and *The Sun Stalker,* published, respectively, in 1986, 1987, 1988, 1994, 1996, 2000, and 2003.). But it is Parks's photographic essays, covering five decades of American life, that brought him the most acclaim. In the following essay, taken from his 1990 autobiography, *Voices in the Mirror,* Parks tells the story behind one of his most memorable photographic works—that of a twelve-year-old boy and his family, living in the slums of Rio de Janeiro.

Pre-Reading Journal Entry

The problem of poverty has provoked a wide array of proposed solutions. One controversial proposal argues that the government should pay poor women financial incentives to use birth control. What do you think of this proposal? Why is such a policy controversial? Use your journal to explore your thinking on this issue.

Flavio's Home

I've never lost my fierce grudge against poverty. It is the most savage of 1 all human afflictions, claiming victims who can't mobilize their efforts against it, who often lack strength to digest what little food they scrounge up to survive. It keeps growing, multiplying, spreading like a cancer. In my wanderings I attack it wherever I can—in barrios, slums and favelas.

Catacumba was the name of the favela[1] where I found Flavio da Silva. It 2 was wickedly hot. The noon sun baked the mud-rot of the wet mountainside. Garbage and human excrement clogged the open sewers snaking down the slopes. José Gallo, a *Life* reporter, and I rested in the shade of a jacaranda tree halfway up Rio de Janeiro's most infamous deathtrap. Below and

---

[1]Slums on the outskirts of Rio de Janeiro, Brazil, inhabited by seven hundred thousand people (editors' note).

above us were a maze of shacks, but in the distance alongside the beach stood the gleaming white homes of the rich.

Breathing hard, balancing a tin of water on his head, a small boy climbed   3
toward us. He was miserably thin, naked but for filthy denim shorts. His legs resembled sticks covered with skin and screwed into his feet. Death was all over him, in his sunken eyes, cheeks and jaundiced coloring. He stopped for breath, coughing, his chest heaving as water slopped over his bony shoulders. Then jerking sideways like a mechanical toy, he smiled a smile I will never forget. Turning, he went on up the mountainside.

The detailed *Life* assignment in my back pocket was to find an impover-   4
ished father with a family, to examine his earnings, political leanings, religion, friends, dreams and frustrations. I had been sent to do an essay on poverty. This frail boy bent under his load said more to me about poverty than a dozen poor fathers. I touched Gallo, and we got up and followed the boy to where he entered a shack near the top of the mountainside. It was a leaning crumpled place of old plankings with a rusted tin roof. From inside we heard the babblings of several children. José knocked. The door opened and the boy stood smiling with a bawling naked baby in his arms.

Still smiling, he whacked the baby's rump, invited us in and offered us a   5
box to sit on. The only other recognizable furniture was a sagging bed and a broken baby's crib. Flavio was twelve, and with Gallo acting as interpreter, he introduced his younger brothers and sisters: "Mario, the bad one; Baptista, the good one; Albia, Isabel and the baby Zacarias." Two other girls burst into the shack, screaming and pounding on one another. Flavio jumped in and parted them. "Shut up, you two." He pointed at the older girl. "That's Maria, the nasty one." She spit in his face. He smacked her and pointed to the smaller sister. "That's Luzia. She thinks she's pretty."

Having finished the introductions, he went to build a fire under the   6
stove—a rusted, bent top of an old gas range resting on several bricks. Beneath it was a piece of tin that caught the hot coals. The shack was about six by ten feet. Its grimy walls were a patchwork of misshapen boards with large gaps between them, revealing other shacks below stilted against the slopes. The floor, rotting under layers of grease and dirt, caught shafts of light slanting down through spaces in the roof. A large hole in the far corner served as a toilet. Beneath that hole was the sloping mountainside. Pockets of poverty in New York's Harlem, on Chicago's south side, in Puerto Rico's infamous El Fungito seemed pale by comparison. None of them had prepared me for this one in the favela of Catacumba.

Flavio washed rice in a large dishpan, then washed Zacarias's feet in the   7
same water. But even that dirty water wasn't to be wasted. He tossed in a chunk of lye soap and ordered each child to wash up. When they were finished he splashed the water over the dirty floor, and, dropping to his knees, he scrubbed the planks until the black suds sank in. Just before sundown he

put beans on the stove to warm, then left, saying he would be back shortly. "Don't let them burn," he cautioned Maria. "If they do and Poppa beats me, you'll get it later." Maria, happy to get at the licking spoon, switched over and began to stir the beans. Then slyly she dipped out a spoonful and swallowed them. Luzia eyed her. "I see you. I'm going to tell on you for stealing our supper."

Maria's eyes flashed anger. "You do and I'll beat you, you little bitch." 8
Luzia threw a stick at Maria and fled out the door. Zacarias dropped off to sleep. Mario, the bad one, slouched in a corner and sucked his thumb. Isabel and Albia sat on the floor clinging to each other with a strange tenderness. Isabel held onto Albia's hair and Albia clutched at Isabel's neck. They appeared frozen in an act of quiet violence.

Flavio returned with wood, dumped it beside the stove and sat down to 9 rest for a few minutes, then went down the mountain for more water. It was dark when he finally came back, his body sagging from exhaustion. No longer smiling, he suddenly had the look of an old man and by now we could see that he kept the family going. In the closed torment of that pitiful shack, he was waging a hopeless battle against starvation. The da Silva children were living in a coffin.

When at last the parents came in, Gallo and I seemed to be part of 10 the family. Flavio had already told them we were there. "Gordunn Americano!" Luzia said, pointing at me. José, the father, viewed us with skepticism. Nair, his pregnant wife, seemed tired beyond speaking. Hardly acknowledging our presence, she picked up Zacarias, placed him on her shoulder and gently patted his behind. Flavio scurried about like a frightened rat, his silence plainly expressing the fear he held of his father. Impatiently, José da Silva waited for Flavio to serve dinner. He sat in the center of the bed with his legs crossed beneath him, frowning, waiting. There were only three tin plates. Flavio filled them with black beans and rice, then placed them before his father. José da Silva tasted them, chewed for several moments, then nodded his approval for the others to start. Only he and Nair had spoons; the children ate with their fingers. Flavio ate off the top of a coffee can. Afraid to offer us food, he edged his rice and beans toward us, gesturing for us to take some. We refused. He smiled, knowing we understood.

Later, when we got down to the difficult business of obtaining permis- 11 sion from José da Silva to photograph his family, he hemmed and hawed, wallowing in the pleasant authority of the decision maker. He finally gave in, but his manner told us that he expected something in return. As we were saying good night Flavio began to cough violently. For a few moments his lungs seemed to be tearing apart. I wanted to get away as quickly as possible. It was cowardly of me, but the bluish cast of his skin beneath the sweat, the choking and spitting were suddenly unbearable.

Gallo and I moved cautiously down through the darkness trying not to   12
appear as strangers. The Catacumba was no place for strangers after sundown. Desperate criminals hid out there. To hunt them out, the police came
in packs, but only in daylight. Gallo cautioned me. "If you get caught up
here after dark it's best to stay at the da Silvas' until morning." As we drove
toward the city the large white buildings of the rich loomed up. The world
behind us seemed like a bad dream. I had already decided to get the boy
Flavio to a doctor, and as quickly as possible.

The plush lobby of my hotel on the Copacabana waterfront was crammed   13
with people in formal attire. With the stink of the favela in my clothes, I hur-
ried to the elevator hoping no passengers would be aboard. But as the door
was closing a beautiful girl in a white lace gown stepped in. I moved as far
away as possible. Her escort entered behind her, swept her into his arms and
they indulged in a kiss that lasted until they exited on the next floor. Neither
of them seemed to realize that I was there. The room I returned to seemed
to be oversized; the da Silva shack would have fit into one corner of it. The
steak dinner I had would have fed the da Silvas for three days.

Billowing clouds blanketed Mount Corcovado as we approached the   14
favela the following morning. Suddenly the sun burst through, silhouetting
Cristo Redentor, the towering sculpture of Christ with arms extended, its
back turned against the slopes of Catacumba. The square at the entrance to
the favela bustled with hundreds of favelados. Long lines waited at the sole
water spigot. Others waited at the only toilet on the entire mountainside.
Women, unable to pay for soap, beat dirt from their wash at laundry tubs.
Men, burdened with lumber, picks and shovels and tools important to their
existence threaded their way through the noisy throngs. Dogs snarled,
barked and fought. Woodsmoke mixed with the stench of rotting things. In
the mist curling over the higher paths, columns of favelados climbed like ants
with wood and water cans on their heads.

We came upon Nair bent over her tub of wash. She wiped away sweat   15
with her apron and managed a smile. We asked for her husband and she pointed to a tiny shack off to her right. This was José's store, where he sold
kerosene and bleach. He was sitting on a box, dozing. Sensing our presence,
he awoke and commenced complaining about his back. "It kills me. The
doctors don't help because I have no money. Always talk and a little pink pill
that does no good. Ah, what is to become of me?" A woman came to buy
bleach. He filled her bottle. She dropped a few coins and as she walked away
his eyes stayed on her backside until she was out of sight. Then he was complaining about his back again.

"How much do you earn a day?" Gallo asked.   16
"Seventy-five cents. On a good day maybe a dollar."   17
"Why aren't the kids in school?"   18

"I don't have money for the clothes they need to go to school." 19

"Has Flavio seen a doctor?" 20

He pointed to a one-story wooden building. "That's the clinic right 21
there. They're mad because I built my store in front of their place. I won't
tear it down so they won't help my kids. Talk, talk, talk and pink pills." We
bid him good-bye and started climbing, following mud trails, jutting rock,
slime-filled holes and shack after shack propped against the slopes on shaky
pilings. We sidestepped a dead cat covered with maggots. I held my breath
for an instant, only to inhale the stench of human excrement and garbage.
Bare feet and legs with open sores climbed above us—evils of the terrible soil
they trod every day, and there were seven hundred thousand or more afflict-
ed people in favelas around Rio alone. Touching me, Gallo pointed to Flavio
climbing ahead of us carrying firewood. He stopped to glance at a man
descending with a small coffin on his shoulder. A woman and a small child
followed him. When I lifted my camera, grumbling erupted from a group of
men sharing beer beneath a tree.

"They're threatening," Gallo said. "Keep moving. They fear cameras. 22
Think they're evil eyes bringing bad luck." Turning to watch the funeral
procession, Flavio caught sight of us and waited. When we took the wood
from him he protested, saying he was used to carrying it. He gave in when
I hung my camera around his neck. Then, beaming, he climbed on ahead
of us.

The fog had lifted and in the crisp morning light the shack looked more 23
squalid. Inside the kids seemed even noisier. Flavio smiled and spoke above
their racket. "Someday I want to live in a real house on a real street with
good pots and pans and a bed with sheets." He lit the fire to warm leftovers
from the night before. Stale rice and beans—for breakfast and supper. No
lunch; midday eating was out of the question. Smoke rose and curled up
through the ceiling's cracks. An air current forced it back, filling the place
and Flavio's lungs with fumes. A coughing spasm doubled him up, turned
his skin blue under viscous sweat. I handed him a cup of water, but he waved
it away. His stomach tightened as he dropped to his knees. His veins
throbbed as if they would burst. Frustrated, we could only watch; there was
nothing we could do to help. Strangely, none of his brothers or sisters
appeared to notice. None of them stopped doing whatever they were doing.
Perhaps they had seen it too often. After five interminable minutes it was
over, and he got to his feet, smiling as though it had all been a joke. "Maria,
it's time for Zacarias to be washed!"

"But there's rice in the pan!" 24

"Dump it in another pan—and don't spill water!" 25

Maria picked up Zacarias, who screamed, not wanting to be washed. 26
Irritated, Maria gave him a solid smack on his bare bottom. Flavio stepped over
and gave her the same, then a free-for-all started with Flavio, Maria and

Mario slinging fists at one another. Mario got one in the eye and fled the shack calling Flavio a dirty son-of-a-bitch. Zacarias wound up on the floor sucking his thumb and escaping his washing. The black bean and rice breakfast helped to get things back to normal. Now it was time to get Flavio to the doctor.

The clinic was crowded with patients—mothers and children covered with open sores, a paralytic teenager, a man with an ear in a state of decay, an aged blind couple holding hands in doubled darkness. Throughout the place came wailings of hunger and hurt. Flavio sat nervously between Gallo and me. "What will the doctor do to me?" he kept asking. 27

"We'll see. We'll wait and see." 28

In all, there were over fifty people. Finally, after two hours, it was Flavio's turn and he broke out in a sweat, though he smiled at the nurse as he passed through the door to the doctor's office. The nurse ignored it; in this place of misery, smiles were unexpected. 29

The doctor, a large, beady-eyed man with a crew cut, had an air of impatience. Hardly acknowledging our presence, he began to examine the frightened Flavio. "Open your mouth. Say 'Ah.' Jump up and down. Breathe out. Take off those pants. Bend over. Stand up. Cough. Cough louder. Louder." He did it all with such cold efficiency. Then he spoke to us in English so Flavio wouldn't understand. "This little chap has just about had it." My heart sank. Flavio was smiling, happy to be over with the examination. He was handed a bottle of cough medicine and a small box of pink pills, then asked to step outside and wait. 30

"This the da Silva kid?" 31

"Yes." 32

"What's your interest in him?" 33

"We want to help in some way." 34

"I'm afraid you're too late. He's wasted with bronchial asthma, malnutrition and, I suspect, tuberculosis. His heart, lungs and teeth are all bad." He paused and wearily rubbed his forehead. "All that at the ripe old age of twelve. And these hills are packed with other kids just as bad off. Last year ten thousand died from dysentery alone. But what can we do? You saw what's waiting outside. It's like this every day. There's hardly enough money to buy aspirin. A few wealthy people who care help keep us going." He was quiet for a moment. "Maybe the right climate, the right diet, and constant medical care might..." He stopped and shook his head. "Naw. That poor lad's finished. He might last another year—maybe not." We thanked him and left. 35

"What did he say?" Flavio asked as we scaled the hill. 36

"Everything's going to be all right, Flav. There's nothing to worry about." 37

It had clouded over again by the time we reached the top. The rain swept in, clearing the mountain of Corcovado. The huge Christ figure loomed up 38 again with clouds swirling around it. And to it I said a quick prayer for the boy walking beside us. He smiled as if he had read my thoughts. "Papa says 'El Cristo' has turned his back on the favela."

"You're going to be all right, Flavio."   39

"I'm not scared of death. It's my brothers and sisters I worry about. 40 What would they do?"

"You'll be all right, Flavio."[2]   41

---

[2]Parks's photo-essay on Flavio generated an unprecedented response from *Life* readers. Indeed, they sent so much money to the da Silvas that the family was able to leave the *favela* for better living conditions. Parks brought Flavio to the United States for medical treatment, and the boy's health was restored. However, Flavio's story didn't have an unqualifiedly happy ending. Although he overcame his illness and later married and had a family, Flavio continuously fantasized about returning to the United States, convinced that only by returning to America could he improve his life. His obsession eventually eroded the promise of his life in Brazil (editors' note).

Questions for Close Reading

1. What is the selection's thesis (or dominant impression)? Locate the sentence(s) in which Parks states his main idea. If he doesn't state the thesis explicitly, express it in your own words.
2. What is Flavio's family like? Why does Flavio have so much responsibility in the household?
3. What are some of the distinctive characteristics of Flavio's neighborhood and home?
4. What seems to be the basis of Flavio's fear of giving food to Parks and Gallo? What did Parks and Gallo understand that led them to refuse?
5. Refer to your dictionary as needed to define the following words used in the selection: *barrios* (paragraph 1), *jacaranda* (2), *jaundiced* (3), and *spigot* (14).

Questions About the Writer's Craft

1. **The pattern.** Without stating it explicitly, Parks conveys a dominant impression about Flavio. What is that impression? What details create it?
2. **Other patterns.** When relating how Flavio performs numerous household tasks, Parks describes several *processes*. How do these step-by-step explanations reinforce Parks's dominant impression of Flavio?
3. Parks provides numerous sensory specifics to depict Flavio's home. Look closely, for example, at the description in paragraph 6. Which words and phrases convey strong sensory images? How does Parks use transitions to help the reader move from one sensory image to another?
4. Paragraph 13 includes a scene that occurs in Parks's hotel. What's the effect of this scene? What does it contribute to the essay that the most detailed description of the *favela* could not?

Writing Assignments Using Description as a Pattern of Development

1. Parks paints a wrenching portrait of a person who remains vibrant and hopeful even though he is suffering greatly—from physical illness, poverty, overwork, and worry. Write a description about someone you know who has shown courage or other positive qualities during a time of personal trouble. Include, as Parks does, plentiful details about the person's appearance and behavior so that you don't have to state directly what you admire about the person. Maya Angelou's "Sister Flowers" (page 87) shows how one writer conveys the special quality of an admirable individual.

2. Parks presents an unforgettable description of the *favela* and the living conditions there. Write an essay about a region, city, neighborhood, or building that also projects an overwhelming negative feeling. Include only those details that convey your dominant impression, and provide—as Parks does—vivid sensory language to convey your attitude toward your subject.

Writing Assignments Combining Patterns of Development

3. The doctor reports that a few wealthy people contribute to the clinic, but the reader can tell from the scene in Parks's hotel that most people are insensitive to those less fortunate. Write an essay *describing* a specific situation that you feel reflects people's tendency to ignore the difficulties of others. Analyze why people distance themselves from the problem; then present specific *steps* that could be taken to sensitize them to the situation. John M. Darley and Bibb Latané's "When Will People Help in a Crisis?" (page 416), and Mark Twain's "The Damned Human Race" (page 525) will provide some perspective on the way people harden themselves to the pain of others.

4. Although Parks celebrates Flavio's generosity of spirit, the writer also *illustrates* the brutalizing effect of an impoverished environment. Prepare an essay in which you also show that setting, architecture, even furnishings can influence mood and behavior. You may, as Parks does, focus on the corrosive effect of a negative environment, or you may write about the nurturing effect of a positive environment. Either way, provide vivid *descriptive* details of the environment you're considering. Possible subjects include a park in the middle of a city, a bus terminal, and a college library.

Writing Assignment Using a Journal Entry as a Starting Point

5. Write an essay explaining why you think impoverished women should—or should not—be paid financial incentives to practice birth control. To help define your position, review your pre-reading journal entry, and interview classmates, friends, and family members to get their opinions. Consider supplementing this informal research with material gathered in the library and/or on the Internet. Weigh all the evidence carefully before formulating your position.

David Helvarg

David Helvarg is a journalist and environmental activist. Born in 1951, he started his career as a freelance journalist and then became a war correspondent. Today he writes primarily about politics, AIDS, and marine life. Helvarg is also the founder and president of Blue Frontier Campaign, a marine conservation lobbying group that was inspired by his book about the world's oceans, *Blue Frontier*. Helvarg's lobbying on environmental issues grows out of his experiences covering war, political conflict, and marine biology. This article, about the aftermath of Hurricane Katrina, which devastated New Orleans and the Gulf Coast in 2005, is excerpted from the September/October 2005 issue of *Multinational Monitor*, a magazine that examines multinational corporations and also covers issues relating to the environment and development.

Pre-Reading Journal Entry

Although humans have shaped the environment in many ways, we are still at the mercy of nature at times. Recall a hurricane, tornado, thunderstorm, windstorm, mudslide, earthquake, volcanic eruption, tsunami, drought, flood, or other natural event that affected you and your community. What was the event? What was the experience like? Use your journal to answer these questions.

The Storm This Time

Urban Floodplain

I arrive in Baton Rouge with a planeload of relief workers, FEMA functionaries and crew cut contractors, all working their cell phones and BlackBerrys. After renting a car and making my way through the daily traffic jam (Baton Rouge's population has exploded since the storm) I head south on Interstate 10, tuning into the United Radio Broadcasters of New Orleans, a consortium of local stations playing 24/7 information and call-in reports on Katrina's aftermath.

A police spokesperson assures listeners there are still 20 to 30 roadblocks around New Orleans and 11,000 guardsmen in the city. The mayor wants to open the city back up to residents but the approach of Hurricane Rita has forced him to postpone his plan.

Around the New Orleans airport in Jefferson Parish, I begin to see box stores, warehouses and motels with their roofs ripped off or caved in, downed trees and broken street signs, house roofs covered in blue tarps and high-rises with glass windows popped out like broken eyes. I hit a traffic jam and follow an SUV across the median strip to an exit where I stop to take a picture of a small office complex with its second story front and roof gone. Rain-soaked cardboard boxes fill the exposed floor above a CPA's office.

I talk to a carpet-store owner removing samples. He helps me locate where we are on a map. I get a call from a contact at the New Orleans Aquarium. They lost most of their fish when the pumps failed but managed to evacuate the penguins and sea otters to Monterey. I get on a wide boulevard that leads to a roadblock where a police officer checks my press identification. "This is only for emergency vehicles, but go ahead," she says.

I drive into Lakeview, one of the large sections of the city that sat under-   4
water for two weeks and will likely have to be bulldozed. It reminds me of war zones I've been in after heavy street fighting. There are trees and power poles down, electric lines hanging, metal sheets and street signs on mud-caked pavement, smashed cars, boats on sidewalks and torn-open houses, all colored in sepia tones of gray and brown. Unable to drive far in the debris chocked streets, I get out of my car, half expecting the sweet, rotting smell of death. Instead, I'm confronted with an equally noxious odor. It's what I'll come to think of as the smell of a dead city, like dried cow pies and mold with a stinging chemical aftertaste. Fine yellow dust starts rising up from under my boots and infiltrating the car. I retreat. The I-10 exit is barricad-ed, forcing me north again. I do a U-turn at a major roadblock and get chased down by some angry cops. I explain that I'm just following another cop's helpful directions and soon find myself speeding along a near-empty freeway bridge approaching downtown.

The rusted ruined roof of the Superdome inspires me to choose an exit   5
and, after getting turned around at a friendly National Guard checkpoint, I'm soon in the deserted streets of the central business district, checking out the rubble piles and empty highrises. A big wind-damaged 'Doubletree' hotel sign reads D UL EE. The French Quarter is still intact with even a few bars open for soldiers, FBI agents and fire fighters. On Canal Street, it looks like a Woodstock for first responders with Red Cross and media satellite trucks, tents and RVs pulled up on the central streetcar median by the Sheraton. Red-bereted troops from the 82nd Airborne cruise by in open-sided trucks, M-4s at the ready in case the undead should appear at sunset. Uptown, some boats lie in the middle of the street, along with cars crushed by a falling wall and a pharmacy trashed by looters. Further on are the smashed homes and muddied boulevards and still-flooded underpasses and cemeteries, abandoned cars and broken levees of an eerily hollow city.

In the coming days. I'll travel across this new urban landscape, tracing   6
the brown floodwater line that marks tens of thousands of homes, schools, offices, banks, churches, grocery stores and other ruined structures, includ-ing the main sewage plant. I'll cross paths with animal rescue crews, military patrols, utility crews from New York and Pennsylvania, and body recovery search teams with K-9 dogs using orange spray paint to mark the doors of still unexamined buildings, writing the date and adding a zero for no bodies or numbers where bodies have been found. . . .

New Orleans house showing flood line and searcher's graffiti. The zero indicates that no bodies were found in the house. (©*David Helvarg*)

Life After Katrina

I put up with an AP colleague in the less damaged Algiers Point section   7
of the city just across the Mississippi from where the helicopter assault ship Iwo Jima and Carnival Cruise Line ship Ecstasy are being used to house city employees and relief workers. Blackhawk helicopters fly overhead at sunset while a Red Cross truck down the street offers hot food to the handful of residents still here.

Back in Lakeview, I encounter Bob Chick. Bob snuck past the check-   8
points to see if he can salvage anything from his green Cajun Cottage near where the 17th Street floodwall breached.

He hasn't had much luck, "just some tools that might be OK," he says. "I   9
left all my photos on top of a chest of drawers thinking the water wouldn't get that high. They say if you have more than five inches of water in your house for five days it's a loss. We had eight feet for two weeks." He's found one of his cats dead but thinks the other two might have escaped. He invites me to look inside. From the door it's a jumble of furniture, including a sofa, table, twisted carpet, lamps and wooden pieces all covered in black and gray gunk, reeking of mold and rotted cat food. I try not to breathe too deeply. "I had a collection of Jazz Fest T shirts going back to '79 but they're gone." He's wearing a mask, rubber boots and gloves, but still manages to give an expressive shrug of resignation

Bob Chick examines his flood-ruined house in the Lakeview section of New Orleans. (©*David Helvarg*)

when I take his picture. "I lived in this house 16 years. We'd have been fine if the levee hadn't broke. We'd be moving back right now."...

A Disappeared Town

I catch a ride along the west bank of the Mississippi in Plaquemines   10
Parish south of New Orleans with deputy Sheriff Ken Harvey. This is where towns of several thousand, like Empire and Buras, got washed away and some oil tank farms ruptured. Where the road's cut by water, we drive up on the eroded levee and keep going. There are boats on the land, and houses in the water or washed onto the road or turned into woodpiles. At one point where the levee broke and the water poured through, there's nothing but a field where Diamond, an unincorporated town of about 300 including many trailer-park residents, stood. Those folks never seem to catch a break.

I take a picture of an antebellum white mansion in the water along with a   11
floating pickup, a larger truck hanging off a tree, a semi-trailer cab under the bottom of an uplifted house, a speedboat through a picture window, the Buras water tower collapsed next to a wrecked store, shrimp boats on the levee, on the road and in the bushes with military patrols passing by. We stop and stare in awe at a 200-foot barge tossed atop the levee like a bath toy on a tub rim.

Approaching the Empire Bridge, I note the white church facing north   12
towards us is still intact and suggest that's a hopeful sign. "It used to face the
road," Ken points out....

Unfortunately, as I drive east through Mississippi and Alabama I find   13
most of [the] coastal trees and wetlands festooned with plastic like Tibetan
prayer flags (as if monks were praying over dead turtles and seabirds). In
Biloxi, along with smashed casinos, historic homes and neighborhoods, I
find miles of beachfront covered in plastic buckets and insulation, mattress-
es, furniture, chunks of drywall and Styrofoam pellets that the seabirds are
eyeing as potential snack food. I wave down a truck marked "Department of
Natural Resources," but the guys inside are from Indiana.

I feel like an eco-geek being more concerned about the gulls and wet-   14
lands than the lost revenue from the casinos that everyone else seems to be
obsessing on. The waterside wing of the new Hard Rock Casino is now a
smashed tangle of twisted girders and concrete. I pull over by an 8,000 ton,
600-foot-long casino barge that was pushed half a mile by the storm, land-
ing on Beach Drive. Somewhere underneath its barnacle-encrusted black
hull is a historic mansion. Nearby, the Grand Casino barge has taken out
much of the stately facade of the six story yellow brick Biloxi Yacht Club
before grounding next to it. Another barge landed on the Holiday Inn,
where more than 25 people may have been trying to ride out the hurricane.
No one's been able to do a body-recovery there yet.

Because Southern Baptist and other religious conservatives objected to   15
"land-based" gambling in Mississippi, much of Biloxi's wetlands were torn
up to make way for these floating casinos.

I talk with Phil Sturgeon, a Harrah's security agent hanging out with   16
some cops from Winter Park, Florida. He's in jeans and a gray shirt with a
toothbrush and pen sticking out the pocket. He tells me the storm surge
crested at about 35 feet, at least five feet higher than Camille in '69.

In Waveland, I drive over twisted railroad tracks where the eye of Katrina   17
passed into neighborhoods of jagged wooden debris. A middle-aged couple
is trying to clear the drive to the lot where their home once stood. A surfboard leans up against one of the live oaks that seem to have fared better
then the houses in between them.

"Are you an adjuster," the woman asks.   18

"No, a reporter."   19

"Good, because we don't like adjusters. Nationwide was not on our side."   20

Apparently they've been offered $1,700 on their $422,000 home.   21

"At least you've got your surfboard," I tell John, her husband, "Oh,   22
that's not my surfboard," he grins, pointing around. "And that's not my
boat, and that's not my Corvette (buried to its hood in the rubble), and
that's not our roof. We think it might belong to the house at the end of
the street."...

Starting Again

I'm back in New Orleans on Canal Street, where the Salvation Army offers   23
me cold water, a baloney sandwich (I decline) and a fruit cocktail. It's been
a long day with the Army Corps of Engineers, who've leased helicopters
that are dropping 3,000 and 7,000 pound sandbags on the latest breach in
the Industrial Canal which has reflooded the Lower Ninth Ward. I enter
the Sheraton after getting cleared by muscular Blackwater Security guys in
tan and khaki tee shirts and shorts with Glocks on their hips. Another one
sits by the elevators checking room IDs. I wonder if being a professional
mercenary is good training for concierge duty. I sit by the Pelican bar in
the lobby looking out the big three-story glass window at the media RVs
and SUVs on the street—feeling as if I've been in this hotel before in
various war zones and Third World capitals like Managua, Tegucigalpa,
and Suva.

The Gulf region is now very much like a war zone, only with fewer   24
deaths (about 1,200 bodies recovered at the time of my visit) and far more
extensive damage. It also offers many of the same ironies and bizarre
moments. Unity Radio announces that if you're going to tonight's Louisiana
State University football game in Baton Rouge you can return after curfew
provided you show your game stubs to the deputies at the roadblocks.

Three years ago I made a decision. I'd lost a key person in my life and   25
was trying to decide what to do next. I was considering either going back to
war reporting, as George Bush was clearly planning a pre-emptive invasion
of Iraq, or turning from journalism to ocean advocacy.... Finally, I decided
that while we'll probably always have wars, we may not always have living
reefs, wild fish or protective coastal wetlands.

What we know we are going to have are more environmental disasters   26
like the Hurricane Season of '05 linked to fossil-fuel-fired climate change
and bad coastal policies driven by saltwater special interests.

Still, destruction on a biblical scale also offers Noah-like opportunities   27
for restoration after the flood. There are practical solutions to the dangers we
confront, along with models of how to live safely by the sea. Things can be
done right in terms of building wisely along the coasts, and advancing social
and environmental equity. But it will take a new wave of citizen activism to
avoid repetition of old mistakes, with even more dire consequences.

Questions for Close Reading

1. What is the selection's thesis? Locate the sentence(s) in which Helvarg states his
   main idea. If he doesn't state his thesis explicitly, express it in your own words.
2. Helvarg uses headings to divide his essay into sections. What is the subject of the
   section entitled "Urban Floodplain"? How does this section frame the remainder
   of the essay?

3. Most of the details in Helvarg's essay focus on the destruction caused by the hurricane and the recovery effort. However, he does give a description of an activity that shows life going on as normal. What is it? Why does Helvarg include this description?
4. Some words are so new they are not yet in dictionaries. Helvarg uses such a word when he describes himself as an "eco-geek" in paragraph 14. Given the context, and the meanings of the root *eco* and the word *geek,* how would you define this word?
5. Refer to your dictionary as needed to define the following words used in the selection: *consortium* (paragraph 1), *infiltrating* (4), *Woodstock* (5), *salvage* (8), *ruptured* (10), *antebellum* (11), *festooned* (13), *storm surge* (16), *adjuster* (18), and *mercenary* (23).

Questions About the Writer's Craft

1. **The pattern.** How does Helvarg organize his points in this essay? What transitional words and phrases does he use to keep the reader oriented as his essay progresses?
2. Most of the description in this essay focuses on visual details, but Helvarg also describes some other sensations. Find the passages in which Helvarg describes something other than the sights of the post-Katrina landscape, and evaluate their vividness. What do these passages contribute to the essay?
3. In paragraphs 4 and 24, to what does Helvarg compare the post-Katrina Gulf Coast? How does this analogy help the reader envision the destruction? How does it help express the dominant impression of the essay?
4. Helvarg took the photographs that accompany this essay. Compare the photograph of the marked door on page 105 with the author's description of it in paragraph 6. Does this photograph add to the description in the essay, or is the author's description so vivid that the photograph is unnecessary? Now compare the photograph of Bob Chick on page 106 with the author's description of him in paragraph 9. Does this photograph add to the description of Bob in the essay, or is the author's description so vivid that the photograph is unnecessary? If you were writing this essay, would you include the photographs? If so, how would they affect the way you wrote the essay?

Writing Assignments Using Description as a Pattern of Development

1. One reason Helvarg's essay has such an impact is that destruction of the normal Gulf Coast environment was sudden as well as devastating. Not all environmental destruction is so dramatic, however. Find something in your own environment— your home, neighborhood, city, or region—that has been damaged or destroyed by gradual overuse or neglect. For example, your home may have a shabby room, or part of your yard may be overgrown. Or your neighborhood may have a run-down playground or park, or roads full of potholes, or an abandoned building. Select a location that has been neglected or overused, and write an essay in which you describe this damaged environment.

2. Although severe weather, like Hurricane Katrina, provides good subject matter for description, so does more common, less destructive weather. Think of a day on which the weather was important to you but turned out badly. For example, you might have planned an outdoor event and it rained, or you might have scheduled a trip and it snowed, or you might have worn great new clothes and been too hot or too cold. Write an essay in which you describe this uncooperative weather. Use sensory details and figures of speech to convey your feelings about this day.

Writing Assignments Combining Patterns of Development

3. In "The Storm This Time," the environmental devastation was caused by a natural event. However, much destruction of the environment is caused by people rather than by weather or other natural disasters. Select a place you know that has changed for the worse through human use. For example, you might choose an industrial site, a polluted river or lake, or a park. *Compare* and *contrast* the place as it once was and as it is now. Provide vivid *descriptions* of how the place has changed. Before you start, you can read about a place that humans have polluted in Rachel Carson's "A Fable for Tomorrow" on page 359.

4. The Gulf Coast has a lot of experience with hurricanes; Katrina was just the most destructive one in recent years. Other areas are prone to other types of natural disasters. Research the destructive weather and other natural events that your area typically experiences. Good places to start are the websites of the Federal Emergency Management Agency (www.fema.gov) and the National Oceanic and Atmospheric Administration (www.noaa.gov). Then write an essay in which you *classify* the natural disasters that occur in your area and *describe* each type, giving specific *examples* where possible.

Writing Assignment Using a Journal Entry as a Starting Point

5. Review your pre-reading journal entry about the natural disaster or event that you experienced. Write an essay in which you *describe* its aftermath. How did it *affect* you and others in your community? How did the event change your attitude toward nature? How did it *affect* the way you prepare for future natural emergencies? You might first read Joan Didion's "The Santa Ana" (page 600), an essay about a recurring hot wind that affects southern California.

Gary Kamiya

Gary Kamiya was born in Oakland, California, in 1953. He was educated at Yale University and the University of California at Berkeley, where he was awarded the Mark Schorer Citation as the outstanding undergraduate in English literature. After receiving a master's degree from Berkeley, he worked as a freelance writer for publications including *ArtForum* and *Sports Illustrated* before becoming an editor and culture writer at *The San Francisco Examiner.* Kamiya cofounded the website *Salon.com,* where he was executive editor for many years and is now a columnist. His essays have appeared in Harvard University Press's *A New Literary History of America*, the essay and photography collection *What Matters,* and other books. He lives in San Francisco with his wife—the novelist Kate Moses—and their two children. This essay was published on *Salon.com* on April 22, 2008.

Pre-Reading Journal Entry

All of us have places that we cherish, perhaps because they are beautiful, or perhaps because they play a big role in our lives. Think about the special places in your life, whether they are rooms, landscapes, buildings, or childhood hiding spots. What are some of these places? What are they like? Why are they important to you? Use your journal to answer these questions.

Life, Death and Spring

The stench hit us right after we climbed up the dug-out steps in the bank, by the bend in the stream where the mountain lion and I surprised each other four years ago. It had to be something pretty big. I walked through the little meadow toward the lake, gingerly following my nose. After 30 yards or so I saw it. A small, delicate white skull, like an overgrown rodent's, with a surprisingly thick spine, 2 or 3 feet long. Nothing else—no body or legs. A deer. Almost all the flesh was gone, but there was still enough left to raise a powerful stink. We walked on through the young grass, where in a few weeks the lupine and sweet pea would cover the ground with their exuberant bluish-purple and pink and white blossoms.

I'd driven with my mother up to our family ranch in the Sierra foothills to join my brother, uncle, cousin and some other clan members for a work weekend. We were going to clear brush along the edge of the big meadow, hauling out fallen wood, clearing pine needles and debris and cutting down the cedars and yellow pines that were crowding a magnificent avenue of oaks. If weather permitted, we were going to ignite the piles of brush that were evenly spaced out in the meadow. We were looking forward to this atavistic ritual, heaping branches onto the pyres,

1

2

consuming last year's dead matter, leaning on our McLeods[1] and watching the orange tongues twisting and leaping upward in the cool April air.

But mostly I was looking for spring.   3

San Francisco, where I live, doesn't really have seasons. Yes, we have   4
an Indian summer in September and October, a week or two of 80 degree
days that overheats our delicate constitutions and causes all the fans in the
hardware stores to immediately disappear. It rains a lot in the winter
months. And around the time school gets out in June, the summer fog
starts rolling in, a giant cotton-candy wave breaking in slow motion over
Twin Peaks at 4 p.m. But aside from those minor markers, the seasons are
pretty indistinguishable. Most Februaries I can sunbathe on my deck, and
I frequently shiver in July. The temperature rarely goes below 50 in the
day, or above 70. This city belongs to the sea, not the land, and the sea's
seasons are inscrutable.

And I don't really see the signs of spring that are there. When you live   5
in a city, the world is blocked from view. Too many buildings, too many
people, too many street lights changing mechanically, too many thoughts
changing just as mechanically. Even the moon, that harbinger of mystery,
feels like an impostor.

You can exist without spring, but it cramps your soul. It's good to have   6
a place where you can go to watch the world get old and young, live and die.
Mine is the ranch.

It lies a shade under 4,000 feet in Calaveras County, which means   7
"skulls" and which an unknown journalist, writing under the peculiar,
Mississippi-redolent pseudonym "Mark Twain," made famous when he
penned a story[2] about a celebrated jumping frog that some wag stuffed full
of birdshot. Calaveras is gold country, but the ranch is too high for prospecting. The property was a double homestead spread, 320 acres, first worked in
1882 by a driven German-American pioneer and his wife who together
cleared 25 forested acres for a meadow, using a mule team to pull the stumps
out of the ground. He then erected an astonishingly grandiloquent structure
at the edge of the meadow, a 55-foot-high asymmetrical barn that may still
be the tallest building in the county. The hay from the meadow wouldn't
even fill a fifth of this vast structure. He must have built it so high just
because he could. The German is long gone but his barn still stands, a great
gray monument to his sublime orneriness.

One infamous day, we almost lost the whole place. On Sept. 10, 2001,   8
a devastating forest fire roared up out of the Stanislaus River canyon to the
east. When the flames crowned the trees on the other side of the ridge and

[1]A firefighting tool with a hoe-like blade on one side and a rake-like blade on the other
(editors' note).
[2]"The Celebrated Jumping Frog of Calaveras County" (editors' note).

were visible from the meadow, my mother and my uncles simultaneously decided to tell the firemen, "Save the barn before the houses." Hundreds of firemen from all over the state made their stand, fighting tree to tree on the steep ridge. The meadow looked like a war zone, filled with dozens of fire trucks. We were the last line of defense for the town of Arnold. The battle wasn't won until bombers swept in low and dumped borate[3] on the inferno. It was the last day the big planes could have saved us: The next day all civil aviation in the United States was grounded. My uncle's partner called from New York the next day early in the morning. First she asked, "Is the ranch still there?" Then she said, "Turn on your television."

My grandparents bought the ranch in 1943 for next to nothing. Land in the middle of nowhere wasn't worth anything then. It comprises a long, narrow valley watered by a creek and most of the two ridges on each side. It lies in what naturalists call the Yellow Pine Forest, also known as the Mixed Coniferous Forest or the Transition Zone, located between the oak woodland of the lower foothills and the higher lodgepole-red fir forest. Yellow pine (also known as Ponderosa) is the dominant tree. Incense cedar, white fir and John Muir's[4] favorite conifer, the sugar pine, the tallest pine in the world, share the woods with slender-trunked maples and stands of dogwoods, which in May dress up in dazzling white. The royalty of our trees, though, are the black oaks. They are greatly outnumbered by conifers at this elevation, but if the world keeps getting hotter and drier, they will become the dominant species. And if there are any human beings left on the earth then, they will probably enjoy them.

The German also planted 20 or so acres of apple trees in three orchards. The old trees still bear fruit, rare and delicious varietals—King Davids and Spitzenbergs and Winter Bananas and Black Johns—but they are rapidly dying off. My grandfather, a truck driver who later opened the first gas station in Angel's Camp, maintained the ranch as a gentleman farmer, pruning and irrigating and harvesting. But he died 24 years ago, none of the rest of us have time or inclination, and anyway the trees are nearing the end. Every year, snow in the winter and ravenous climbing bears in the fall crack a few more big branches off the old trees. Their gnarled remaining limbs look like twisted gray hands outstretched to the sky, waving a very long goodbye.

The day we left San Francisco for the ranch was scorching hot for April, and the unseasonable heat carried through the Central Valley and all the way through the oak foothills to the ranch. But the winter rains and snows were not long past, and everything was still green, that deep, fragile green that you wish could last forever, but that fades almost as you look at it.

9

10

11

[3]Fire retardant and suppressant (editors' note).
[4]John Muir (1838–1914), a preservationist who helped save Western wilderness areas and influenced the modern environmental movement (editors' note).

April is unpredictable, edgy—the turning month. The apple trees had   12
barely begun to leaf out, the ferns had not yet started their scarily fast
growth, and only a few modest wildflowers had begun to appear—five-spots
and red-flowered gooseberries and tiny exquisite white stars that none of us
knew the names of. We plunged into the creek-side trail that my cousin, my
uncle Bob and I hacked out of the woods a dozen years ago. Winter had
been here and left chaos and destruction, and no one had cleaned up after
it. Black-tongued trilliums and crimson snow plants, eerie post-winter
arrivals, had pushed through the pine needles. A big yellow pine had fallen
across the trail and an even larger cedar had fallen below the spillway of the
big lake. Chain-saw work. All of the big trees on this steep bank were in danger, more of them falling every year as erosion exposed their roots.

Years ago Bob had put up a wooden bench by a gentle bend downstream   13
on the creek, a place where he could sit and take in the Sierra summer before
heading back to Manhattan and his life as a college professor. Then he found
out he had pancreatic cancer and died a few weeks later. The winter after his
death, a cedar by the stream came down and smashed right through the center of the bench. Bob's ashes and my aunt Wendy's are buried on the ranch,
along with their parents'. When my time comes, mine will join them.

The ranch exists on the boundary of wilderness and the familiar, and you   14
make your negotiations between them. Walking down to the big lake, I saw
a familiar form slowly rouse itself on the bank and creak arthritically into the
air, at first barely able to get moving, but with each ponderous flap of its
heavy wings gaining disconcerting chunks of altitude and speed. We rushed
down to the water and got there just in time to see it in full flight, our great
blue heron, now soaring high above the far end of the lake. Two herons used
to live on the lake. Years ago one of them vanished and never returned, and
for a couple of years the remaining heron was rarely seen. When he began to
return regularly, it felt like a benediction.

Not for the frogs, though. For them, he's Heron the Impaler. He stands   15
motionless in the shallow water, waiting for a frog to come within reach, and
then strikes with incredible speed, driving his heavy pointed beak right
through the frog's body. He then leaves the indigestible bits on the raft for
us to clean up.

It's the Great Chain of Killing. We love the fat bullfrogs that the heron   16
kills. They're musical croakers, an indicator species[5] and a link with the
romance of Mark Twain. But these old friends are the implacable destroyers
of our equally beloved orange and blue dragonflies. And the dragonflies are
like mini Apache gunships, swerving with insane precision to devour the tiny

[5]A species that defines a trait or characteristic of an environment, such as climate, pollution,
disease, and so on. Changes in an indicator species often warn biologists that the environment
is changing (editors' note).

insects that dance above the surface of the lake. In the Sierra foothills, you begin to see that beauty is just a surface effect—below it, jaws are always about to snap shut.

One animal stands at the top of the killing chain: the mountain lion. 17
One afternoon in August I was walking along the creek-side trail when I heard a crunching noise. I looked up to see an enormous male mountain lion staring right at me, about 20 yards away on the other side of the stream. These supreme predators are normally soundless, but I was coming from upwind and walking quietly, and he was thirsty and had to make his way through a maze of fallen branches to drink, and even he couldn't avoid breaking some branches. We stared at each other for a second or two. For the first time in my life I was put emphatically and finally in my species place. If this 250-pound predator, so muscular, lethal and coiled that he might as well have weighed 400, decided he wanted to take me, there would be nothing I could do about it.

The experience was so alien, so unfathomable, that it was hard to believe 18
it even while it was happening. We stared at each other. Then he turned and bounded with massive hydraulic power up the bank, knocking aside little trees and disappearing in seconds. With shaking hands, I went looking for the biggest stick I could find. It was not a relaxing walk back to the cabin.

The heron settled into one of his favorite perches, a large cedar tree. If 19
the trees at the ranch seem exceptionally tall, it's probably because their cousins next door are the biggest ones on earth. If you climb up to the top of the valley where it narrows and bear off to the left, in a mile or so you come to the rarely used back gate of Big Trees State Park, one of 75 groves, all on the gentle western face of the Sierra, where the Sequoia gigantea, the world's largest living things, are found. A hunter stumbled upon the Calaveras Grove in 1852 while chasing a wounded bear. News of the stupendous trees spread, and entrepreneurs soon arrived, eager to make money off the "vegetable monsters."

They decided to cut one of the largest sequoias down, strip off its bark, 20
and ship it to the east for exhibition. A 19th century writer described how five men attacked the tree for 22 days, "until at last, the noble monarch of the forest was forced to tremble, and then to fall, after braving 'the battle and the breeze,' for nearly three thousand years." He then cheerfully reported that the resulting stump "easily accommodates 32 dancers." An appalled John Muir remarked that removing the bark of the big trees to spread their fame was "as sensible a scheme as skinning our great men would be to prove their greatness."

We didn't skin any big trees, but we killed a lot of fledgling ones. We 21
spent our days clearing brush and small trees away from the oaks, snipping the little ones off with compound shears, cutting the big ones down with a chain saw and pulling the tiny ones right out of the ground.

One day we tried to burn, but the wind was too strong. The flames 22
jumped the perimeter and started making for the next brush pile. My uncle
and I had to attack the outlying flames with our McLeods, smashing the
burning grass down hard with the flat, heavy heads of our tools in the instant
we had before the superheated gusts of wind forced us to back off. We would
no sooner kill one hot spot than another would spring up. I got my eyebrows
singed. For a minute there was a whiff of panic in the air.

The day we left, the snow still lay in patches on the far side of the mead- 23
ow, but it would soon be gone. My cousin had cut through the fallen trees
blocking the trail with the chain saw. The stream was running, but we needed one more good rain. The velvety grass was getting longer. In a few weeks
the cold knife edge of spring, having only just come, would be gone.

The night before we left, we heard Canadian geese at dusk, barking and 24
snuffling like dogs, and saw them circling the lake before flying away.

On the last day, I walked through the little meadow where we'd seen the 25
deer. The smell was gone. I went over to look at the spot where it had been
lying and there was nothing. Something had taken it away.

Questions for Close Reading

1. What is the selection's thesis (or dominant impression)? Locate the sentence(s) in
   which Kamiya states his main idea. If he doesn't state his thesis explicitly, express
   it in your own words.
2. According to Kamiya, why is it difficult to experience spring in a city, particularly
   in San Francisco?
3. What role does the ranch play in Kamiya's family?
4. How have people helped shape the landscape of the ranch?
5. Refer to your dictionary as needed to define the following words used in the selection: *atavistic* (paragraph 2), *pyres* (2), *constitutions* (4), *harbinger* (5), *redolent* (7),
   grandiloquent (7), *infamous* (8), *ponderous* (14), *disconcerting* (14), *implacable*
   (16), *unfathomable* (18), *appalled* (20), and *singed* (22).

Questions About the Writer's Craft

1. **The pattern.** Through vivid language, descriptive writing evokes sensory experiences and emotions. In this essay, Kamiya overlays several sets of sensory details,
   from different times in the ranch's history. Which times seem most vivid? How do
   these glimpses of the ranch at different points in time relate to the essay's themes?
2. **Other patterns.** Narrative plays a big role in this essay. Identify passages in which
   Kamiya tells stories about events that happened on the ranch.
3. Kamiya's descriptive language and figures of speech powerfully evoke the ranch as
   a setting for the "Great Chain of Killing" (paragraph 16). Choose a passage about
   the ranch today or one of its animals, and analyze the sensory details and figures
   of speech, explaining how the language contributes to the main idea of the essay.
4. What does the title "Life, Death and Spring" suggest? Does the essay live up to its
   title? Do you think a more specific title would have been better? Why or why not?

Writing Assignments Using Description as a Pattern of Development

1. Several readers of this essay commented on *Salon.com* that Kamiya had evoked their memories of the Sierra by vividly describing the scent of pine trees and burning brush. Scents often trigger memories or associations. A perfume or the smell of cigarettes can evoke a particular person; the odor of crayons or paste can bring back childhood memories. Write an essay describing a place, thing, or person you associate with a particular scent. You need not limit your description to the sense of smell; use other sensory language as well. Enliven your writing with figures of speech, as Kamiya does.

2. Kamiya was fortunate that his family's ranch was not destroyed by wildfire. But many other special spots have been destroyed or are threatened by destruction, whether by natural disaster or the slow encroachment of human development. Write an essay describing a place (for example, a park, a school, an old-fashioned ice cream parlor) that doesn't exist any more. For your dominant theme, show which aspects of your subject made it worthy of being preserved for future generations. Before writing your essay, you might want to read Rachel Carson's "A Fable for Tomorrow" (page 359), an essay that laments the loss of a special place, and David Helvarg's "The Storm This Time" (page 103), which describes the devastation of the Gulf Coast by Hurricane Katrina.

Writing Assignments Combining Patterns of Development

3. Sometimes we, like Kamiya, are suddenly reminded of the nearness of death: a crushed animal lies in the road, a political leader is assassinated, a classmate is killed in a car crash. Write an essay about a time you were forced to think about mortality. *Narrate* what happened and *describe* your thoughts and feelings afterward.

4. Have your older relatives attempted to share with you some special experiences of their own? These experiences may center on a special family place, like Kamiya's family ranch, or they may have involved sharing photographs, stories, or heirlooms. Write an essay in which you *recount* how an older relative shared some experience with you. Explain the motivations of the older generation and the *effects* on the younger one. Judith Ortiz Cofer's "A Partial Remembrance of a Puerto Rican Childhood" (page 118) will spark some thoughts about special family times.

Writing Assignment Using a Journal Entry as a Starting Point

5. Review your pre-reading journal entry in which you described several places that are special for you. Select one of these places, and write an essay describing it. The place need not be a natural setting like Kamiya's ranch; it could be a city or building that has meant a great deal to you. Use sensory details and figurative language, as Kamiya does, to enliven your description and convey the place's significance for you. Before writing, read Maya Angelou's "Sister Flowers" (page 87) to see how another professional writer conveys the special qualities of a memorable childhood place.

Born in Puerto Rico, raised both on her native island and in the United States, and educated in sites that included Oxford University in England, Judith Ortiz Cofer (1952–) knows what it is to move between cultures, absorbing from each while keeping mindful of her own heritage. Cofer earned a master's degree in English from the University of Florida before spending a year in graduate study at Oxford. Following a stint as a bilingual teacher, Cofer taught English at several colleges and universities and currently teaches Creative Writing at the University of Georgia. She has published collections of poetry, including *Peregrine* (1986), *Terms of Survival* (1995), *Reaching for the Mainland and Selected New Poems* (1995), and *A Love Story Beginning in Spanish* (2005); novels, *The Line of the Sun* (1989), *The Meaning of Consuelo* (2003), and *Call Me Maria* (2004); and four books of essays, *Silent Dancing: A Partial Remembrance of a Puerto Rican Childhood* (1990), *The Latin Deli: Telling the Lives of Barrio Women* (1993), *An Island Like You: Stories of the Barrio* (1995), and *Woman in Front of the Sun* (2000). The following essay is taken from *Silent Dancing*.

Pre-Reading Journal Entry

Everyone loves a good story. But stories do more than merely entertain us. Use your journal to reflect on two or more stories that adults told you in your childhood as a way to teach an important lesson about life. In addition to sketching out the stories themselves, outline the circumstances of hearing the stories: who told them, where you were when you heard the stories, why the stories were recounted.

A Partial Remembrance of a Puerto Rican Childhood

At three or four o'clock in the afternoon, the hour of *café con leche*,[1] the women of my family gathered in Mamá's living room to speak of important things and retell familiar stories meant to be overheard by us young girls, their daughters. In Mamá's house (everyone called my grandmother Mamá) was a large parlor built by my grandfather to his wife's exact specifications so that it was always cool, facing away from the sun. The doorway was on the side of the house so no one could walk directly into her living room. First they had to take a little stroll through and around her beautiful garden where prize-winning orchids grew in the trunk of an ancient tree she had hollowed out for that purpose. This room was furnished with several mahogany rocking chairs, acquired at the births of her children, and one intricately carved rocker that had passed down to Mamá at the death of her own mother.

1

[1]Spanish for "coffee with milk" (editors' note).

It was on these rockers that my mother, her sisters, and my grand- 2
mother sat on these afternoons of my childhood to tell their stories, teaching each other, and my cousin and me, what it was like to be a woman, more
specifically, a Puerto Rican woman. They talked about life on the island, and
life in *Los Nueva Yores,* their way of referring to the United States from New
York City to California: the other place, not home, all the same. They told
real-life stories though, as I later learned, always embellishing them with a
little or a lot of dramatic detail. And they told *cuentos,* the morality and cautionary tales told by the women in our family for generations: stories that
became a part of my subconscious as I grew up in two worlds, the tropical
island and the cold city, and that would later surface in my dreams and in
my poetry.

One of these tales was about the woman who was left at the altar. Mamá 3
liked to tell that one with histrionic intensity. I remember the rise and fall
of her voice, the sighs, and her constantly gesturing hands, like two birds
swooping through her words. This particular story usually would come up
in a conversation as a result of someone mentioning a forthcoming engage-
ment or wedding. The first time I remember hearing it, I was sitting on the
floor at Mamá's feet, pretending to read a comic book. I may have been
eleven or twelve years old, at that difficult age when a girl was no longer a
child who could be ordered to leave the room if the women wanted freedom to take their talk into forbidden zones, nor really old enough to be
considered a part of their conclave. I could only sit quietly, pretending to
be in another world, while absorbing it all in a sort of unspoken agreement
of my status as silent auditor. On this day, Mamá had taken my long, tan-
gled mane of hair into her ever-busy hands. Without looking down at me
and with no interruption of her flow of words, she began braiding my hair,
working at it with the quickness and determination that characterized all
her actions. My mother was watching us impassively from her rocker across
the room. On her lips played a little ironic smile. I would never sit still for
her ministrations, but even then, I instinctively knew that she did not pos-
sess Mamá's matriarchal power to command and keep everyone's attention.
This was never more evident than in the spell she cast when telling a story.

"It is not like it used to be when I was a girl," Mamá announced. "Then, 4
a man could leave a girl standing at the church altar with a bouquet of fresh
flowers in her hands and disappear off the face of the earth. No way to track
him down if he was from another town. He could be a married man, with
maybe even two or three families all over the island. There was no way to
know. And there were men who did this. *Hombres*[2] with the devil in their
flesh who would come to a *pueblo,*[3] like this one, take a job at one of the

[2]Spanish for "men" (editors' note).
[3]Spanish for "community" (editors' note).

haciendas,[4] never meaning to stay, only to have a good time and to seduce the women."

The whole time she was speaking, Mamá would be weaving my hair   5
into a flat plait that required pulling apart the two sections of hair with little jerks that made my eyes water; but knowing how grandmother detested whining and *boba* (sissy) tears, as she called them, I just sat up as straight and stiff as I did at La Escuela San Jose, where the nuns enforced good posture with a flexible plastic ruler they bounced off of slumped shoulders and heads. As Mamá's story progressed, I noticed how my young Aunt Laura lowered her eyes, refusing to meet Mamá's meaningful gaze. Laura was seventeen, in her last year of high school, and already engaged to a boy from another town who had staked his claim with a tiny diamond ring, then left for Los Nueva Yores to make his fortune. They were planning to get married in a year. Mamá had expressed serious doubts that the wedding would ever take place. In Mamá's eyes, a man set free without a legal contract was a man lost. She believed that marriage was not something men desired, but simply the price they had to pay for the privilege of children and, of course, for what no decent (synonymous with "smart") woman would give away for free.

"María La Loca was only seventeen when *it* happened to her." I listened   6
closely at the mention of this name. María was a town character, a fat middle-aged woman who lived with her old mother on the outskirts of town. She was to be seen around the pueblo delivering the meat pies the two women made for a living. The most peculiar thing about María, in my eyes, was that she walked and moved like a little girl though she had the thick body and wrinkled face of an old woman. She would swing her hips in an exaggerated, clownish way, and sometimes even hop and skip up to someone's house. She spoke to no one. Even if you asked her a question, she would just look at you and smile, showing her yellow teeth. But I had heard that if you got close enough, you could hear her humming a tune without words. The kids yelled out nasty things at her, calling her *La Loca,*[5] and the men who hung out at the *bodega*[6] playing dominoes sometimes whistled mockingly as she passed by with her funny, outlandish walk. But María seemed impervious to it all, carrying her basket of *pasteles*[7] like a grotesque Little Red Riding Hood through the forest.

María La Loca interested me, as did all the eccentrics and crazies of our   7
pueblo. Their weirdness was a measuring stick I used in my serious quest for a definition of normal. As a Navy brat shuttling between New Jersey and the

[4]Spanish for "large estate" or "ranch" (editors' note).
[5]Spanish for "crazy one" (editors' note).
[6]Spanish for a neighborhood grocery store (editors' note).
[7]Spanish for "pastries" (editors' note).

pueblo, I was constantly made to feel like an oddball by my peers, who made fun of my two-way accent: a Spanish accent when I spoke English, and when I spoke Spanish I was told that I sounded like a *Gringa*.[8] Being the outsider had already turned my brother and me into cultural chameleons. We developed early on the ability to blend into a crowd, to sit and read quietly in a fifth story apartment building for days and days when it was too bitterly cold to play outside, or, set free, to run wild in Mamá's realm, where she took charge of our lives, releasing Mother for a while from the intense fear for our safety that our father's absences instilled in her. In order to keep us from harm when Father was away, Mother kept us under strict surveillance. She even walked us to and from Public School No. 11, which we attended during the months we lived in Paterson, New Jersey, our home base in the States. Mamá freed all three of us like pigeons from a cage. I saw her as my liberator and my model. Her stories were parables from which to glean the *Truth*.

"María La Loca was once a beautiful girl. Everyone thought she would 8 marry the Méndez boy." As everyone knew, Rogelio Méndez was the richest man in town. "But," Mamá continued, knitting my hair with the same intensity she was putting into her story, "this *macho* made a fool out of her and ruined her life." She paused for the effect of her use of the word "macho," which at that time had not yet become a popular epithet for an unliberated man. This word had for us the crude and comical connotation of "male of the species," stud; a *macho* was what you put in a pen to increase your stock.

I peeked over my comic book at my mother. She too was under Mamá's 9 spell, smiling conspiratorially at this little swipe at men. She was safe from Mamá's contempt in this area. Married at an early age, an unspotted lamb, she had been accepted by a good family of strict Spaniards whose name was old and respected, though their fortune had been lost long before my birth. In a rocker Papá had painted sky blue sat Mamá's oldest child, Aunt Nena. Mother of three children, stepmother of two more, she was a quiet woman who liked books but had married an ignorant and abusive widower whose main interest in life was accumulating wealth. He too was in the mainland working on his dream of returning home rich and triumphant to buy the *finca*[9] of his dreams. She was waiting for him to send for her. She would leave her children with Mamá for several years while the two of them slaved away in factories. He would one day be a rich man, and she a sadder woman. Even now her life-light was dimming. She spoke little, an aberration in Mamá's house, and she read avidly, as if storing up spiritual food for the long winters that awaited her in Los Nueva Yores without her family. But even Aunt Nena came alive to Mamá's words, rocking gently, her hands over a thick book in her lap.

---

[8]A negatively charged Latin American slang expression for a female foreigner (editors' note).
[9]Spanish for "farm" or "ranch" (editors' note).

Her daughter, my cousin Sara, played jacks by herself on the tile porch   10
outside the room where we sat. She was a year older than I. We shared a bed
and all our family's secrets. Collaborators in search of answers, Sara and I discussed everything we heard the women say, trying to fit it all together like a
puzzle that, once assembled, would reveal life's mysteries to us. Though she
and I still enjoyed taking part in boys' games—chase, volleyball, and even
vaqueros, the island version of cowboys and Indians involving cap-gun bat-
tles and violent shoot-outs under the mango tree in Mamá's backyard—we
loved best the quiet hours in the afternoon when the men were still at work,
and the boys had gone to play serious baseball at the park. Then Mamá's
house belonged only to us women. The aroma of coffee perking in the
kitchen, the mesmerizing creaks and groans of the rockers, and the women
telling their lives in *cuentos* are forever woven into the fabric of my imagination, braided like my hair that day I felt my grandmother's hands teaching
me about strength, her voice convincing me of the power of storytelling.

That day Mamá told how the beautiful María had fallen prey to a man   11
whose name was never the same in subsequent versions of the story; it was
Juan one time, José, Rafael, Diego, another. We understood that neither the
name or any of the *facts* were important, only that a woman had allowed love
to defeat her. Mamá put each of us in María's place by describing her wedding dress in loving detail: how she looked like a princess in her lace as she
waited at the altar. Then, as Mamá approached the tragic denouement of her
story, I was distracted by the sound of my Aunt Laura's violent rocking. She
seemed on the verge of tears. She knew the fable was intended for her. That
week she was going to have her wedding gown fitted, though no firm date
had been set for the marriage. Mamá ignored Laura's obvious discomfort,
digging out a ribbon from the sewing basket she kept by her rocker while
describing María's long illness, "a fever that would not break for days." She
spoke of a mother's despair: "that woman climbed the church steps on her
knees every morning, wore only black as a *promesa* to the Holy Virgin in
exchange for her daughter's health." By the time María returned from her
honeymoon with death, she was ravished, no longer young or sane. "As you
can see, she is almost as old as her mother already," Mamá lamented while
tying the ribbon to the ends of my hair, pulling it back with such force that
I just knew I would never be able to close my eyes completely again.

"That María's getting crazier every day." Mamá's voice would take a   12
lighter tone now, expressing satisfaction, either for the perfection of my
braid, or for a story well told—it was hard to tell. "You know that tune María
is always humming?" Carried away by her enthusiasm, I tried to nod, but
Mamá still had me pinned between her knees.

"Well, that's the wedding march." Surprising us all, Mamá sang out, "Da,   13
da, dara...da, da, dara." Then lifting me off the floor by my skinny shoulders,
she would lead me around the room in an impromptu waltz—another session

ending with the laughter of women, all of us caught up in the infectious joke of our lives.

Questions for Close Reading

1. What is the selection's thesis (or dominant impression)? Locate the sentence(s) in which Cofer states her main idea. If she doesn't state the thesis explicitly, express it in your own words.
2. Who are the women who participate in the storytelling sessions? Why is Cofer allowed to join them? Why aren't men or boys part of the group?
3. What lessons about men and women does Mamá intend the story of María La Loca to teach?
4. What information does Cofer provide about her aunts and her mother? What similarities and/or differences are there between each of their lives and the story of María La Loca?
5. Refer to your dictionary as needed to define the following words used in the selection: *intricately* (paragraph 1), *embellishing* (2), *cautionary* (2), *histrionic* (3), *conclave* (3), *auditor* (3), *impassively* (3), *ministrations* (3), *matriarchal* (3), *quest* (7), *chameleons* (7), *surveillance* (7), *conspiratorially* (9), *aberration* (9), *mesmerizing* (10), *denouement* (11), *ravished* (11), and *impromptu* (13).

Questions About the Writer's Craft

1. **The pattern.** Of all the women mentioned in the essay, only María La Loca is described in detail. What descriptive details does Cofer offer about her? Why do you suppose Cofer provides so much description about this particular woman?
2. In paragraph 7, Cofer provides some specifics about her childhood as a "Navy brat." What would have been lost if Cofer hadn't included this material?
3. **Other patterns.** Reread paragraphs 4, 6, 8, and 11–13, where Cofer *recounts* her grandmother's story. Why do you think Cofer doesn't tell the story straight through, without interruptions? What purpose do the interruptions serve? How does Cofer signal when she is moving away from the story or back to it?
4. Why might Cofer have mentioned in several spots the braiding of her hair, which goes on the whole time Mamá tells María's story? What similarities are there between the braiding and the storytelling session? What similarities are there between the braiding and Cofer's descriptive style (consider especially the last sentence of paragraph 10)?

Writing Assignments Using Description
as a Pattern of Development

1. Cofer paints a vivid picture of a childhood ritual: the telling of stories among the women in her family. Think of a specific scene, event, or ritual from your own childhood or youth that has special meaning for you. Then write a descriptive essay conveying the distinctive flavor of that occasion. Draw upon vivid sensory language to capture your dominant impression of that time. Consider using dialogue, as Cofer does, to texturize your description and to reveal character.

2. To Cofer, Mamá was a "liberator" and a "model." Think of a person in your life who served as a role model or opened doors for you, and write an essay describing that person. Like Cofer, place the person in a characteristic setting and supply vigorous details about the person's actions, speech, looks, and so forth. Make sure that all the descriptive details reinforce your dominant impression of the individual. You may want to read Maya Angelou's "Sister Flowers" (page 87) to see how one especially skilled writer describes a powerful, influential person.

Writing Assignments Combining Patterns of Development

3. Cofer's family is close-knit, but family life nowadays is more likely to be fragmented, with everyone going separate ways. Write an essay explaining what *steps* families could take to offset this tendency toward fragmentation. You might want to focus on a particular area of family life, such as mealtimes, after-supper hours, or vacations. Be sure to spend some time discussing the expected *outcomes* of the steps you propose. You might benefit from conducting research in the library and/or on the Internet into how to increase the quality and quantity of family time.

4. The stories Cofer heard taught her "what it was like to be a woman." What information and experiences shaped your understanding of your gender? Write an essay showing how your perception of your gender identity was *influenced* by what you heard, witnessed, and experienced as a child. Along the way, you might briefly *narrate* one or more of these gender-shaping interactions. Before writing your paper, you may wish to read some of the following essays, each of which provides insight into gender expectations: Marion Winik's "What Are Friends For?" (page 276), Ann Sutherland's "What Shamu Taught Me About a Happy Marriage" (page 310), and Dave Barry's "Beauty and the Beast" (page 370).

Writing Assignment Using a Journal Entry as a Starting Point

5. Write an essay narrating an experience that put to the test the moral of a story you were told when you were young. Select from your pre-reading journal entry the *one* story whose "truth" was most memorably validated *or* discredited by an experience later in your life. Your tone might be serious or humorous. In either case, be sure to make clear how you felt about the truth of the story after it was "tested" by experience.

Additional Writing Topics

DESCRIPTION

General Assignments

Write an essay using description to develop any of the following topics. Remember that an effective description focuses on a dominant impression and arranges details in a way that best supports that impression. Your details—vivid and appealing to the senses—should be carefully chosen so that the essay isn't overburdened with material of secondary importance. When writing, keep in mind that varied sentence structure and imaginative figures of speech are ways to make a descriptive piece compelling.

1. A favorite item of clothing
2. A school as a young child might see it
3. A hospital room you visited or stayed in
4. An individualist's appearance
5. A coffee shop, a bus shelter, a newsstand, or some other small place
6. A parade or victory celebration
7. A banana, a squash, or another fruit or vegetable
8. A particular drawer in a desk or bureau
9. A houseplant
10. A "media event"
11. A dorm room
12. An elderly person
13. An attractive man or woman
14. A prosthetic device or wheelchair
15. A TV, film, or music celebrity
16. A student lounge
17. A once-in-a-lifetime event
18. The inside of something, such as a cave, boat, car, shed, or machine
19. A friend, a roommate, or another person you know well
20. An essential gadget or a useless gadget

Assignments with a Specific Purpose, Audience, and Point of View

On Campus

1. For an audience of incoming first-year students, prepare a speech describing registration day at your college. Use specific details to help prepare students for the actual event. Choose an adjective that represents your dominant impression of the experience, and keep that word in mind as you write.
2. Your college has decided to replace an old campus structure (for example, a dorm or dining hall) with a new version. Write the administration a letter of

protest describing the place so vividly and appealingly that its value and need for preservation are unquestionable.

3. As a staff member of the campus newspaper, you have been asked to write a weekly column of social news and gossip. For your first column, you plan to describe a recent campus event—a dance, party, or concert, or other social activity. With a straightforward or tongue-in-cheek tone, describe where the event was held, the appearance of the people who attended, and so on.

At Home or in the Community

4. As a subscriber to a community-wide dating service, you've been asked to submit a description of the kind of person you'd like to meet. Describe your ideal date. Focus on specifics about physical appearance, personal habits, character traits, and interests.

5. As a resident of a particular town, you're angered by the appearance of a certain spot and by the activities that take place there. Write the town council a letter describing in detail the undesirable nature of this place (a video arcade, an adult bookstore, a bar, a bus station, a neglected park or beach). End with some suggestions about ways to improve the situation.

On the Job

6. You've noticed a recurring problem in your workplace, and you want to bring it to the attention of your boss, who is typically inattentive. Write a letter to your boss describing the problem. Your goal is not to provide solutions, but rather, to provide vivid description—complete with sensory details—so that your boss can no longer deny the problem.

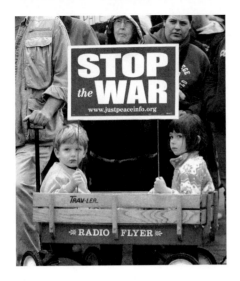

NARRATION

WHAT IS NARRATION?

Human beings are instinctively storytellers. In prehistoric times, our ancestors huddled around campfires to hear tales of hunting and magic. In ancient times, warriors gathered in halls to listen to bards praise in song the exploits of epic heroes. Things are no different today. Boisterous children invariably settle down to listen when their parents read to them; millions of people tune in day after day to the ongoing drama of their favorite soap operas; vacationers sit motionless on the beach, caught up in the latest best-sellers; and all of us enjoy saying, "Just listen to what happened to me today." Our hunger for story-telling is a basic part of us.

Narration means telling a single story or several related stories. The story can be a way to support a main idea or thesis. For instance, to demonstrate that television has become the constant companion of many children, you might narrate a typical child's day in front of the television—from frantic cartoons in the morning to dizzy situation comedies at night.

Narration is powerful. Every public speaker, from politician to classroom teacher, knows that stories capture the attention of listeners as nothing else can. Narration speaks to us strongly because it is about us; we want to know what happened to others, not simply because we're curious, but because their experiences shed light on the nature of our own lives. Narration lends force to opinions, triggers the flow of memory, and evokes places and times in ways that are compelling and affecting.

127

HOW NARRATION FITS YOUR PURPOSE AND AUDIENCE

Narration can appear in essays as a supplemental pattern of development. For example, if your purpose in a paper is to *persuade* apathetic readers that airport security regulations must be followed strictly, you might lead off with a brief account of a friend who inadvertently boarded a plane with a pocket knife in his backpack. In a paper *defining* good teaching, you might keep readers engaged by including satirical anecdotes about one hapless instructor, the antithesis of an effective teacher. An essay on the *effects* of an overburdened judicial system might provide a dramatic account of the way one clearly guilty murderer plea-bargained his way to freedom.

Narration can also serve as an essay's dominant pattern of development. You might choose to narrate the events of a day spent with your three-year-old nephew as a way of revealing how you rediscovered the importance of family life. Or you might relate the story of your roommate's mugging, evoking the powerlessness and terror of being a victim. Any story can form the basis for a narrative essay as long as you convey the essence of the experience and evoke its meaning.

At this point, you have a good sense of the way writers use narration to achieve their purpose and to connect with their readers. Now take a moment to look closely at the photograph at the beginning of this chapter. Imagine you're writing a "Recent Events" update, accompanied by the photo, for the website of an organization that supports (*or* opposes) the war in Iraq. Your purpose is to recount what happened at the protest in a way that supports the  website's position. Jot down some phrases you might use when *narrating* the events of the day.

SUGGESTIONS FOR USING NARRATION IN AN ESSAY

The suggestions here and in Figure 4.1 will be helpful whether you use narration as a dominant or a supportive pattern of development.

1. Identify the conflict in the event.   The power of many narratives is rooted in a special kind of tension that "hooks" readers and makes them want to follow

FIGURE 4.1
Development Diagram: Writing a Narration Essay

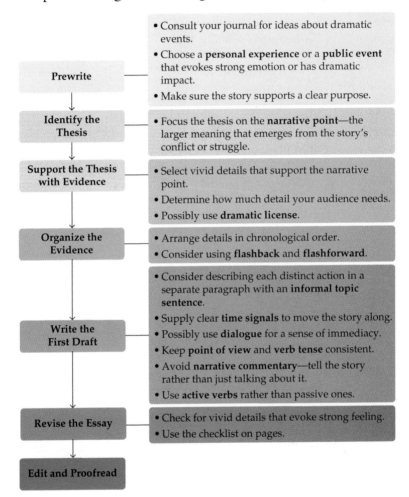

Prewrite
- Consult your journal for ideas about dramatic events.
- Choose a **personal experience** or a **public event** that evokes strong emotion or has dramatic impact.
- Make sure the story supports a clear purpose.

Identify the Thesis
- Focus the thesis on the **narrative point**—the larger meaning that emerges from the story's conflict or struggle.

Support the Thesis with Evidence
- Select vivid details that support the narrative point.
- Determine how much detail your audience needs.
- Possibly use **dramatic license**.

Organize the Evidence
- Arrange details in chronological order.
- Consider using **flashback** and **flashforward**.

Write the First Draft
- Consider describing each distinct action in a separate paragraph with an **informal topic sentence**.
- Supply clear **time signals** to move the story along.
- Possibly use **dialogue** for a sense of immediacy.
- Keep **point of view** and **verb tense** consistent.
- Avoid **narrative commentary**—tell the story rather than just talking about it.
- Use **active verbs** rather than passive ones.

Revise the Essay
- Check for vivid details that evoke strong feeling.
- Use the checklist on pages.

Edit and Proofread

the story to its end. This narrative tension is often a by-product of some form of *conflict* within the story. Many narratives revolve around an internal conflict experienced by a key person in the story. Or the conflict may be between people in the story or between a pivotal character and some social institution or natural phenomenon.

2. Identify the point of the narrative.   In *The Adventures of Huckleberry Finn*, Mark Twain warned: "Persons attempting to find a motive in this narrative will be prosecuted; persons attempting to find a moral in it will be banished; persons attempting to find a plot in it will be shot." Twain was, of course, being ironic; his novel's richness lies in its "motives" and "morals." Similarly, when you recount a narrative, it's your responsibility to convey the event's *significance* or *meaning*. In other words, be sure readers are clear about your *narrative point*, or thesis.

Suppose you decide to write about the time you got locked in a mall late at night. Your narrative might focus on the way the mall looked after hours and the way you struggled with mounting terror. But you would also use the narrative to make a point. Perhaps you want to emphasize that fear can be instructive. Or your point might be that malls have a disturbing, surreal underside. You could state this thesis explicitly. ("After hours, the mall shed its cheerful daytime demeanor and took on a more sinister quality.") Or you could rely on your details and language to convey the point of the narrative: "The mannequins stared at me with glazed eyes and frozen smiles" and "The steel grates pulled over each store's entrance glinted in the cold light, making each shop look like a prison cell."

3. Develop only those details that advance the narrative point. You know from experience that nothing is more boring than a storyteller who gets sidetracked and drags out a story with nonessential details. If a friend started to tell about the time his car broke down in the middle of an expressway—but interrupted his story to complain at length about the slipshod work done by his auto repair shop—you might become annoyed, wishing your friend would get back to the interesting part of the story.

Brainstorming ("What happened? When? Where? Who was involved? Why did it happen?") can be valuable for helping you amass narrative details. Then, after generating the specifics, you cull out the nonessential and devote your energies to the key specifics needed to advance your narrative point. When telling a story, you maintain an effective narrative pace by focusing on that point and eliminating details that don't support it. A good narrative depends not only on what is included, but also on what has been left out.

But how do you determine which specifics to omit, which to treat briefly, and which to emphasize? Having a clear sense of your narrative point and knowing your audience are crucial. Assume you're writing a narrative about a disastrous get-acquainted dance sponsored by your college the first week of the academic year. In addition to telling what happened, you want to make a point; perhaps you want to emphasize that, despite the college's good intentions, such official events actually make it difficult to meet people. So you might write about how stiff and unnatural students seemed, all dressed up in their best clothes; you might narrate snatches of strained conversation; you might describe the way males gathered on one side of the room, females on the other—reverting to behaviors supposedly abandoned in fifth grade. All these details would support your narrative point.

Because you don't want to get away from that point, you would leave out details about the topnotch band and the appetizing refreshments. The music and food may have been surprisingly good, but since these details don't advance the point you want to make, they should be omitted.

You also need to keep your audience in mind when selecting narrative details. If the audience consists of your instructor and other students—all of them familiar with the new student center where the dance was held—specific details about the center probably wouldn't have to be provided. But imagine that the essay is going to appear in the quarterly magazine published by the college's community relations office. Many of the magazine's readers are former graduates who haven't been on campus for several years. They may need some additional specifics about the student center: its location, how many people it holds, how it is furnished.

As you write, keep asking yourself, "Is this detail or character or snippet of conversation essential? Does my audience need this detail to understand the conflict in the situation? Does this detail advance or intensify the narrative action?" Summarize details that have some importance but do not deserve lengthy treatment ("Two hours went by..."). And try to limit *narrative commentary*—statements that tell rather than show what happened—since such remarks interrupt the narrative flow. Focus instead on the specifics that propel action forward in a vigorous way.

Sometimes, especially if the narrative re-creates an event from the past, you won't be able to remember what happened detail for detail. In such a case, you should take advantage of what is called *dramatic license*. Using as a guide your powers of recall as well as the perspective you now have of that particular time, feel free to reshape events to suit your narrative point.

4. Organize the narrative sequence.   Every narrative begins somewhere, presents a span of time, and ends at a certain point. Frequently, you'll want to use a straightforward time order, following the event *chronologically* from beginning to end: first this happened, next this happened, finally this happened.

But sometimes a strict chronological recounting may not be effective—especially if the high point of the narrative gets lost somewhere in the middle of the time sequence. To avoid that possibility, you may want to disrupt chronology, plunge the reader into the middle of the story, and then return in a *flashback* to the beginning of the tale. You're probably familiar with the way flashback is used on television and in film. You see someone appealing to the main character for financial help, then return to an earlier time when both were students in the same class, before learning how the rest of the story unfolds. Narratives can also use *flashforward*. You give readers a glimpse of the future (the main character being jailed) before the story continues in the present (the events leading to the arrest). These techniques shift the story onto several planes and keep it from becoming a step-by-step, predictable account. Reserve flashforwards and flashbacks, however, for crucial incidents only, since breaking out of chronological order acts as emphasis. Here are examples of how flashback and flashforward can be used:

Flashback

Standing behind the wooden counter, Greg wielded his knife expertly as he shucked clams—one every ten seconds—with practiced ease. The scene contrasted sharply with his first day on the job, when his hands broke out in blisters and when splitting each shell was like prying open a safe.

Flashforward

Rushing to move my car from the no-parking zone, I waved a quick goodbye to Karen as she climbed the steps to the bus. I didn't know then that by the time I picked her up at the bus station later that day, she had made a decision that would affect both our lives.

Whether or not you choose to include flashbacks or flashforwards in an essay, remember to limit the time span covered by the narrative. Otherwise, you will have trouble generating the details needed to give the story depth and meaning. Also, regardless of the time sequence you select, organize the tale so that it drives toward a strong finish. Be careful that your story doesn't trail off into minor, anticlimactic details.

5. Make the narrative easy to follow.   Describing each distinct action in a separate paragraph helps readers grasp the flow of events. Although narrative essays don't always have conventional topic sentences, each narrative paragraph should have a clear focus. Often this focus is indicated by a sentence early in the paragraph that directs attention to the action taking place. Such a sentence functions as a kind of *informal topic sentence;* the rest of the paragraph then develops that topic sentence. You should also be sure to use time signals when narrating a story. Words like *now, then, next, after,* and *later* ensure that your reader won't get lost as the story progresses.

6. Make the narrative vigorous and immediate.   A compelling narrative provides an abundance of specific details, making readers feel as if they're experiencing the story being told. Readers must be able to see, hear, touch, smell, and taste the event you're narrating. *Vivid sensory description* is, therefore, an essential part of an effective narrative. Not only do specific sensory details make writing a pleasure to read—we all enjoy learning the particulars about people, places, and things—but they also give the narrative the stamp of reality. The specifics convince the reader that the event actually did, or could, occur.

Compare the following excerpts from a narrative essay. The first version is lifeless and dull; the revised version, packed with sensory images, grabs readers with its sense of foreboding:

> That eventful day started out like every other summer day. My sister Tricia and I made several elaborate mud pies, which we decorated with care. A little later on, as we were spraying each other with the garden hose, we heard my father walk up the path.

> That sad summer day started out uneventfully enough. My sister Tricia and I spent a few hours mixing and decorating mud pies. Our hands caked with dry mud, we sprinkled each lopsided pie with alternating rows of dandelion and clover petals. Later when the sun got hotter, we tossed our white T-shirts over the red picket fence–forgetting my grandmother's frequent warnings to be more ladylike. Our sweaty backs bared to the sun, we doused each other with icy sprays from the garden hose. Caught up in the primitive pleasure of it all, we barely heard my father as he walked up the garden path, the gravel crunching under his heavy work boots.

A caution: Sensory language enlivens narration, but it also slows the pace. Be sure that the slower pace suits your purpose. For example, a lengthy description fits an account of a leisurely summer vacation but is inappropriate in a tale about a frantic search for a misplaced wallet.

Another way to create an aura of narrative immediacy is to use *dialogue.* Our sense of other people comes, in part, from what they say and how they sound. Dialogue allows the reader to experience characters directly. Compare the following fragments of a narrative, one with dialogue and one without, noting how much more energetic the second version is.

> When I finally found my way back to the campsite, the trail guide commented on my disheveled appearance.

> When I finally found my way back to the campsite, the trail guide took one look at me and drawled, "What on earth happened to you, Daniel Boone? You look as though you've been dragged through a haystack backwards."
> "I'd look a lot worse if I hadn't run back here. When a bullet whizzes by me, I don't stick around to see who's doing the shooting."

When using dialogue, begin a new paragraph to indicate a shift from one person's speech to another's (as in the second example above).

Using *varied sentence structure* is another strategy for making narratives lively and vigorous. Sentences that plod along predictably (subject-verb, subject-verb) put readers to sleep. Experiment with your sentences by juggling length and sentence type; mix long and short sentences, simple and complex. Compare the following original and revised versions to get an idea of how effective varied sentence rhythm can be in narrative writing.

Original

The store manager went to the walk-in refrigerator every day. The heavy metal door clanged shut behind her. I had visions of her freezing to death among the hanging carcasses. The shiny door finally swung open. She waddled out.

Revised

Each time the store manager went to the walk-in refrigerator, the heavy metal door clanged shut behind her. Visions of her freezing to death among the hanging carcasses crept into my mind until the shiny door finally swung open and she waddled out.

Original

The yellow-and-blue-striped fish struggled on the line. Its scales shimmered in the sunlight. Its tail waved frantically. I saw its desire to live. I decided to let it go.

Revised

Scales shimmering in the sunlight, tail waving frantically, the yellow-and-blue-striped fish struggled on the line. Seeing its desire to live, I let it go.

Finally, *vigorous verbs* lend energy to narratives. Use active verb forms ("The boss *yelled at* him") rather than passive ones ("He *was yelled at* by the boss"), and try to replace anemic *to be* verbs ("She *was* a good basketball player") with more dynamic constructions ("She *played* basketball well").

7. Keep your point of view and verb tense consistent.   All stories have a *narrator,* the person who tells the story. If you, as narrator, tell a story as you experienced it, the story is written in the *first-person point of view* ("*I* saw the dog pull loose"). But if you observed the event (or heard about it from others) and want to tell how someone else experienced the incident, you would use the *third-person point of view* ("*Anne* saw the dog pull loose"). Each point of view has advantages and limitations. First person allows you to express ordinarily private thoughts and to re-create an event as you actually experienced it. This point of view is limited, though, in its ability to depict the inner thoughts of other people involved in the event. By way of contrast, third person makes it easier to provide insight into the thoughts of all the participants. However, its objective, broad perspective may undercut some of the subjective immediacy of the "I was there" point of view. No matter which you select, stay with that vantage point throughout the narrative.

Knowing whether to use the *past* or *present tense* ("I *strolled* into the room" as opposed to "I *stroll* into the room") is important. In most narrations, the past tense predominates, enabling the writer to span a considerable period of time. Although more rarely used, the present tense can be powerful for events of short duration—a wrestling match or a medical emergency, for instance. A narrative in the present tense prolongs each moment, intensifying the reader's sense of participation. Be careful, though; unless the event is intense and fast-paced, the present tense can seem contrived. Whichever tense you choose, avoid shifting midstream—starting, let's say, in the past tense ("she skated") and switching to the present ("she runs").

REVISION STRATEGIES

Once you have a draft of the essay, you're ready to revise. The following checklist will help you and those giving you feedback apply to narration some of the revision techniques discussed on pages 60–62.

☑ NARRATION: A REVISION/PEER REVIEW CHECKLIST

Revise Overall Meaning and Structure

❏ What is the essay's main point? Is it stated explicitly or is it implied? Where? Could the point be conveyed more clearly? How?

❏ What is the narrative's conflict? Is it stated explicitly or is it implied? Where? Could the conflict be made more dramatic? How?

❏ From what point of view is the narrative told? Is it the most effective point of view for this essay? Why or why not?

Revise Paragraph Development

❏ Which paragraphs fail to advance the action, reveal character, or contribute to the story's mood? Should these sections be condensed or eliminated?

❏ Where should the narrative pace be slowed down or quickened?

❏ Where is it difficult to follow the chronology of events? Should the order of paragraphs be changed? How? Where would additional time signals help?

❏ How could flashback or flashforward paragraphs be used to highlight key events?

❏ Would dramatic dialogue or mood-setting description help make the essay's opening paragraph more compelling?

❏ What could be done to make the essay's closing paragraph more effective? Should the essay end earlier? Should it close by echoing an idea or image from the opening?

Revise Sentences and Words

❏ Where is sentence structure monotonous? Where would combining sentences, mixing sentence types, and alternating sentence length help?

❏ Where could dialogue replace commentary to convey character and propel the story forward?

❏ Which sentences and words are inconsistent with the essay's tone?

❏ Where do vigorous verbs convey action? Where could active verbs replace passive ones? Where could dull *to be* verbs be converted to more dynamic forms?

❏ Where are there inappropriate shifts in point of view or verb tense?

STUDENT ESSAY

The following student essay was written by Paul Monahan in response to this assignment:

> In "Shooting an Elephant," George Orwell tells about an incident that forced him to act in a manner that ran counter to his better instincts. Write a narrative about a time when you faced a disturbing conflict and ended up doing something you later regretted.

While reading Paul's paper, try to determine how well it applies the principles of narration. The annotations on Paul's paper and the commentary following it will help you look at the essay more closely.

If Only
by Paul Monahan

Introduction   Having worked at a 7-Eleven store for two years, I   1
thought I had become successful at what our manager calls
"customer relations." I firmly believed that a friendly smile and
an automatic "sir," "ma'am," and "thank you" would see me
through any situation that might arise, from soothing impa-

Narrative point
(thesis) ———— tient or unpleasant people to apologizing for giving out the
wrong change. But the other night an old woman shattered

my belief that a glib response could smooth over the rough spots of dealing with other human beings.

Informal topic sentence — The moment she entered, the woman presented a sharp   2
contrast to our shiny store with its bright lighting and neatly arranged shelves. Walking as if each step were painful, she slowly pushed open the glass door and hobbled down the nearest aisle. She coughed dryly, wheezing with each breath.

Sensory details — On a forty-degree night, she was wearing only a faded print dress, a thin, light beige sweater too small to button, and black vinyl slippers with the backs cut out to expose calloused heels. There were no stockings or socks on her splotchy, blue-veined legs.

After strolling around the store for several minutes, the old   3
woman stopped in front of the rows of canned vegetables. She picked up some corn niblets and stared with a strange intensity at the label. At that point, I decided to be a good, courteous

Informal topic sentence — employee and asked her if she needed help. As I stood close to her, my smile became harder to maintain; her red-rimmed eyes

Sensory details — were partially closed by yellowish crusts; her hands were covered with layer upon layer of grime; and the stale smell of sweat rose in a thick vaporous cloud from her clothes.

Start of dialogue — "I need some food," she muttered in reply to my bright   4
"Can I help you?"

"Are you looking for corn, ma'am?"   5

"I need some food," she repeated. "Any kind."   6

"Well, the corn is ninety-five cents," I said in my most   7
helpful voice. "Or, if you like, we have a special on bologna today."

"I can't pay," she said.   8

Conflict established — For a second, I was tempted to say, "Take the corn." But   9
the employee rules flooded into my mind: Remain polite, but do not let customers get the best of you. Let them know that you are in control. For a moment, I even entertained the idea that this was some sort of test, and that this woman was someone from the head office, testing my loyalty. I responded dutifully, "I'm sorry, ma'am, but I can't give away anything free."

Informal topic sentence — The old woman's face collapsed a bit more, if that were   10
possible, and her hands trembled as she put the can back on the shelf. She shuffled past me toward the door, her torn and dirty clothing barely covering her bent back.

Conclusion — Moments after she left, I rushed out the door with the   11
can of corn, but she was nowhere in sight. For the rest of my shift, the image of the woman haunted me. I had been

Echoing of narrative point in the introduction — young, healthy, and smug. She had been old, sick, and desperate. Wishing with all my heart that I had acted like a human being rather than a robot, I was saddened to realize how fragile a hold we have on our better instincts.

COMMENTARY

Point of view, tense, and conflict.   Paul chose to write "If Only" from the *first-person point of view*, a logical choice because he appears as a main character in his own story. Using the *past tense*, Paul recounts an incident filled with *conflicts*—between him and the woman and between his fear of breaking the rules and his human instinct to help someone in need.

Narrative point.   It isn't always necessary to state the *narrative point* of an essay; it can be implied. But Paul decided to express the controlling idea of his narrative in two places—in the introduction ("But the other night an old woman shattered my belief that a glib response could smooth over the rough spots of dealing with other human beings") and again in the conclusion, where he expands his idea about rote responses overriding impulses of independent judgment and compassion. All of the essay's *narrative details* contribute to the point of the piece; Paul does not include any extraneous information that would detract from the central idea he wants to convey.

Organization.   The narrative is *organized chronologically,* from the moment the woman enters the store to Paul's reaction after she leaves. Paul limits the narrative's time span. The entire incident probably occurs in under ten minutes, yet the introduction serves as a kind of *flashback* by providing some necessary background about Paul's past experiences. To help the reader follow the course of the narrative, Paul uses *time signals:* "*The moment* she entered, the woman presented a sharp contrast" (paragraph 2); "*At that point,* I decided to be a good, courteous employee" (3); "*For the rest of my shift,* the image of the woman haunted me" (11).

The paragraphs (except for those consisting solely of dialogue) also contain *informal topic sentences* that direct attention to the specific stage of action being narrated. Indeed, each paragraph focuses on a distinct event: the elderly woman's actions when she first enters the store, the encounter between Paul and the woman, Paul's resulting inner conflict, the woman's subsequent response, and Paul's delayed reaction.

Combining patterns of development.   This chronological chain of events, with one action leading to another, illustrates that the *cause-effect* pattern underlies the basic structure of Paul's essay. And by means of another pattern—*description*—Paul gives dramatic immediacy to the events being recounted. Throughout, he provides rich sensory details to engage the reader's interest. For instance, the sentence "her red-rimmed eyes were partially closed by yellowish crusts" (3) vividly re-creates the woman's appearance while also suggesting Paul's inner reaction to the woman.

Dialogue and sentence structure.   Paul dramatizes the conflict through *dialogue* that crackles with tension. And he achieves a vigorous narrative pace by *varying the length and structure of his sentences*. In the second paragraph, a short sentence ("There were no stockings or socks on her splotchy, blue-veined legs") alternates with a longer one ("On a forty-degree night, she was wearing only a faded print dress, a thin, light beige sweater too small to button, and black vinyl slippers with the backs cut out to expose calloused heels"). Some sentences open with a subject and verb ("She coughed dryly"), while others start with dependent clauses or participial phrases ("As I stood close to her, my smile became harder to maintain"; "Walking as if each step were painful, she slowly pushed open the glass door") or with a prepositional phrase ("For a second, I was tempted").

Revising the first draft.   Comparing the final version of the essay's third paragraph with the following preliminary version reveals some of the changes Paul made while revising the essay.

Original Version of the Third Paragraph

After sneezing and hacking her way around the store, the old woman stopped in front of the vegetable shelves. She picked up a can of corn and stared at the label. She stayed like this for several minutes. Then I walked over to her and asked if I could be of help.

After putting the original draft aside for a while, Paul reread his paper aloud and realized the third paragraph especially lacked power. So he decided to add compelling descriptive details about the woman ("the stale smell of sweat," for example). Also, by expanding and combining sentences, he gave the paragraph an easier, more graceful rhythm. Much of the time, revision involves paring down excess material. In this case, though, Paul made the right decision to elaborate his sentences. Furthermore, he added the following comment to the third paragraph: "I decided to be a good, courteous employee." These few words introduce an appropriate note of irony and serve to echo the essay's controlling idea.

Finally, Paul decided to omit the words "sneezing and hacking" because he realized they were too comic or light for his subject. Still, the first sentence in the revised paragraph is somewhat jarring. The word *strolling* isn't quite appropriate since it implies a leisurely grace inconsistent with the impression he wants to convey. Replacing *strolling* with, say, *shuffling* would bring the image more into line with the essay's overall mood.

Despite this slight problem, Paul's revisions are right on the mark. The changes he made strengthened his essay, turning it into a more evocative, more polished piece of narrative writing.

Activities: Narration

Prewriting Activities

1. Imagine you're writing two essays: One analyzes the *effect* of insensitive teachers on young children; the other *argues* the importance of family traditions. With the help of your journal or freewriting, identify different narratives you could use to open each essay.

2. For each of the situations below, identify two different conflicts that would make a story worth relating. Then prepare six to ten lines of natural-sounding dialogue for each potential conflict in *one* of the situations.
   a. Going to the supermarket with a friend
   b. Telling your parents which college you've decided to attend
   c. Participating in a demonstration
   d. Preparing for an exam in a difficult course

Revising Activities

3. Revise each of the following narrative sentence groups twice: once with words that carry negative connotations, and again with words that carry positive connotations. Use varied sentence structure, sensory details, and vigorous verbs to convey mood.
   a. The bell rang. It rang loudly. Students knew the last day of class was over.
   b. Last weekend, our neighbors burned leaves in their yard. We went over to speak with them.
   c. The sun shone in through my bedroom window. It made me sit up in bed. Daylight was finally here, I told myself.

4. The following paragraph is the introduction from the first draft of an essay proposing harsher penalties for drunk drivers. Revise this narrative paragraph to make it more effective. How can you make sentence structure less predictable? Which details should you delete? As you revise, provide

language that conveys the event's sights, smells, and sounds. Also, clarify the chronological sequence.

As I drove down the street in my bright blue sports car, I saw a car coming rapidly around the curve. The car didn't slow down as it headed toward the traffic light. The light turned yellow and then red. A young couple, dressed like models, started crossing the street. When the woman saw the car, she called out to her husband. He jumped onto the shoulder. The man wasn't hurt but, seconds later, it was clear the woman was. I ran to a nearby emergency phone and called the police. The ambulance arrived, but the woman was already dead. The driver, who looked terrible, failed the sobriety test, and the police found out that he had two previous offenses. It's apparent that better ways have to be found for getting drunk drivers off the road.

Audre Lorde

Named poet laureate of the state of New York in 1991, Audre Lorde (1934–92) was a New Yorker born of African-Caribbean parents. After earning degrees at Hunter College and Columbia University, Lorde held numerous teaching positions throughout the New York City area. She later toured the world as a lecturer, forming women's rights coalitions in the Caribbean, Africa, and Europe. Best known as a feminist theorist, Lorde combined social criticism and personal revelation in her writing on such topics as race, gender relations, and sexuality. Her numerous poems and nonfiction pieces were published in a variety of magazines and literary journals. Her books include *The Black Unicorn: Poems* (1978), *Sister Outsider: Essays and Speeches* (1984), and *A Burst of Light* (1988). The following selection is an excerpt from her autobiography, *Zami: A New Spelling of My Name* (1982).

For ideas about how this narration essay is organized, see Figure 4.2 on page 146.

Pre-Reading Journal Entry

When you were a child, what beliefs about the United States did you have? List these beliefs. For each, indicate whether subsequent experience maintained or shattered your childhood understanding of these beliefs. Take a little time to explore these issues in your journal.

The Fourth of July

The first time I went to Washington, D.C., was on the edge of the summer when I was supposed to stop being a child. At least that's what they said to us all at graduation from the eighth grade. My sister Phyllis graduated at the same time from high school. I don't know what she was supposed to stop being. But as graduation presents for us both, the whole family took a Fourth of July trip to Washington, D.C., the fabled and famous capital of our country.

It was the first time I'd ever been on a railroad train during the day. When I was little, and we used to go to the Connecticut shore, we always went at night on the milk train, because it was cheaper.

Preparations were in the air around our house before school was even over. We packed for a week. There were two very large suitcases that my father carried, and a box filled with food. In fact, my first trip to Washington was a mobile feast; I started eating as soon as we were comfortably ensconced in our seats, and did not stop until somewhere after Philadelphia. I remember it was Philadelphia because I was disappointed not to have passed by the Liberty Bell.

My mother had roasted two chickens and cut them up into dainty bite-size pieces. She packed slices of brown bread and butter and green pepper

1

2

3

4

and carrot sticks. There were little violently yellow iced cakes with scalloped edges called "marigolds," that came from Cushman's Bakery. There was a spice bun and rock-cakes from Newton's, the West Indian bakery across Lenox Avenue from St. Mark's School, and iced tea in a wrapped mayonnaise jar. There were sweet pickles for us and dill pickles for my father, and peaches with the fuzz still on them, individually wrapped to keep them from bruising. And, for neatness, there were piles of napkins and a little tin box with a washcloth dampened with rosewater and glycerine for wiping sticky mouths.

I wanted to eat in the dining car because I had read all about them, but   5
my mother reminded me for the umpteenth time that dining car food always costs too much money and besides, you never could tell whose hands had been playing all over that food, nor where those same hands had been just before. My mother never mentioned that Black people were not allowed into railroad dining cars headed south in 1947. As usual, whatever my mother did not like and could not change, she ignored. Perhaps it would go away, deprived of her attention.

I learned later that Phyllis's high school senior class trip had been   6
to Washington, but the nuns had given her back her deposit in private, explaining to her that the class, all of whom were white, except Phyllis, would be staying in a hotel where Phyllis "would not be happy," meaning, Daddy explained to her, also in private, that they did not rent rooms to Negroes. "We will take you to Washington, ourselves," my father had avowed, "and not just for an overnight in some measly fleabag hotel."

American racism was a new and crushing reality that my parents had   7
to deal with every day of their lives once they came to this country. They handled it as a private woe. My mother and father believed that they could best protect their children from the realities of race in america and the fact of american racism by never giving them name, much less discussing their nature. We were told we must never trust white people, but *why* was never explained, nor the nature of their ill will. Like so many other vital pieces of information in my childhood, I was supposed to know without being told. It always seemed like a very strange injunction coming from my mother, who looked so much like one of those people we were never supposed to trust. But something always warned me not to ask my mother why she wasn't white, and why Auntie Lillah and Auntie Etta weren't, even though they were all that same problematic color so different from my father and me, even from my sisters, who were somewhere in-between.

In Washington, D.C., we had one large room with two double beds and   8
an extra cot for me. It was a back-street hotel that belonged to a friend of my father's who was in real estate, and I spent the whole next day after Mass

squinting up at the Lincoln Memorial where Marian Anderson[1] had sung after the D.A.R.[2] refused to allow her to sing in their auditorium because she was Black. Or because she was "Colored," my father said as he told us the story. Except that what he probably said was "Negro," because for his time, my father was quite progressive.

I was squinting because I was in that silent agony that characterized all 9 of my childhood summers, from the time school let out in June to the end of July, brought about by my dilated and vulnerable eyes exposed to the summer brightness.

I viewed Julys through an agonizing corolla of dazzling whiteness and I 10 always hated the Fourth of July, even before I came to realize the travesty such a celebration was for Black people in this country.

My parents did not approve of sunglasses, nor of their expense. 11

I spent the afternoon squinting up at monuments to freedom and past 12 presidencies and democracy, and wondering why the light and heat were both so much stronger in Washington, D.C., than back home in New York City. Even the pavement on the streets was a shade lighter in color than back home.

Late that Washington afternoon my family and I walked back down 13 Pennsylvania Avenue. We were a proper caravan, mother bright and father brown, the three of us girls step-standards in-between. Moved by our historical surroundings and the heat of the early evening, my father decreed yet another treat. He had a great sense of history, a flair for the quietly dramatic and the sense of specialness of an occasion and a trip.

"Shall we stop and have a little something to cool off, Lin?" 14

Two blocks away from our hotel, the family stopped for a dish of vanil- 15 la ice cream at a Breyer's ice cream and soda fountain. Indoors, the soda fountain was dim and fan-cooled, deliciously relieving to my scorched eyes.

Corded and crisp and pinafored, the five of us seated ourselves one by 16 one at the counter. There was I between my mother and father, and my two sisters on the other side of my mother. We settled ourselves along the white mottled marble counter, and when the waitress spoke at first no one understood what she was saying, and so the five of us just sat there.

The waitress moved along the line of us closer to my father and spoke 17 again. "I said I kin give you to take out, but you can't eat here. Sorry." Then she dropped her eyes looking very embarrassed, and suddenly we heard what it was she was saying all at the same time, loud and clear.

[1]Acclaimed African-American opera singer (1902–93), famed for her renderings of Black spirituals (editors' note).
[2]Daughters of the American Revolution. A society, founded in 1890, for women who can prove direct lineage to soldiers or others who aided in winning American independence from Great Britain during the Revolutionary War (1775–83) (editors' note).

Straight-backed and indignant, one by one, my family and I got down 18
from the counter stools and turned around and marched out of the store,
quiet and outraged, as if we had never been Black before. No one would
answer my emphatic questions with anything other than a guilty silence.
"But we hadn't done anything!" This wasn't right or fair! Hadn't I written
poems about Bataan and freedom and democracy for all?

My parents wouldn't speak of this injustice, not because they had con- 19
tributed to it, but because they felt they should have anticipated it and avoided it. This made me even angrier. My fury was not going to be acknowledged
by a like fury. Even my two sisters copied my parents' pretense that nothing
unusual and anti-american had occurred. I was left to write my angry letter
to the president of the united states all by myself, although my father did
promise I could type it out on the office typewriter next week, after I showed
it to him in my copybook diary.

The waitress was white, and the counter was white, and the ice cream I 20
never ate in Washington, D.C., that summer I left childhood was white, and
the white heat and the white pavement and the white stone monuments of
my first Washington summer made me sick to my stomach for the whole
rest of that trip and it wasn't much of a graduation present after all.

Questions for Close Reading

1. What is the selection's thesis (or narrative point)? Locate the sentence(s) in which
   Lorde states her main idea. If she doesn't state the thesis explicitly, express it in
   your own words.
2. In paragraph 4, Lorde describes the elaborate picnic her mother prepared for the
   trip to Washington, D.C. Why did Lorde's mother make such elaborate preparations? What do these preparations tell us about Lorde's mother?
3. Why does Lorde have trouble understanding her parents' dictate that she "never
   trust white people" (paragraph 7)?
4. In general, how do Lorde's parents handle racism? How does the family as a whole
   deal with the racism they encounter in the ice-cream parlor? How does the family's
   reaction to the ice-cream parlor incident make Lorde feel?
5. Refer to your dictionary as needed to define the following words used in the selection: *fabled* (paragraph 1), *injunction* (7), *progressive* (8), *dilated* (9), *vulnerable*
   (9), *travesty* (10), *decreed* (13), and *pretense* (19).

Questions About the Writer's Craft

1. **The pattern.** What techniques does Lorde use to help readers follow the unfold-
   ing of the story as it occurs in both time and space?
2. When telling a story, skilled writers limit narrative commentary—statements that
   tell rather than show what happened—because it tends to interrupt the narrative
   flow. Lorde, however, provides narrative commentary in several spots. Find these
   instances. How is the information she provides essential to her narrative?

FIGURE 4.2

Essay Structure Diagram: "The Fourth of July" by Audre Lorde

Introductory paragraph: Narrative point (paragraph 1)	Going on a trip to Washington, D.C., as a graduation present. **Narrative point:** This experience marked the end of the narrator's childhood.
Narrative details (2–19) Also, descriptive and explanatory material (in parentheses at right)	Preparing for the train trip. (The food packed for the trip.) *Flashback:* Not allowed in the dining car. *Flashforward:* Learning later that her sister had been denied a trip to Washington because of racist hotel policies. (How the author's parents and relatives dealt with the "crushing reality" of racism.) (The hotel room and its location.) Spending the day "squinting up at monuments." Deciding to stop for ice cream at a soda fountain and waiting to be served. Waitress's refusing to serve the family. Leaving the soda fountain. (The parents' response and the author's anger.)
Concluding paragraph (20)	The incident at the soda fountain marked an end to the narrator's childhood.

3. In paragraphs 7 and 19, Lorde uses all lowercase letters for *America, American,* and *President of the United States.* Why do you suppose she doesn't follow the rules of capitalization? In what ways does her rejection of these rules reinforce what she is trying to convey through the essay's title?

4. What key word does Lorde repeat in paragraph 20? What effect do you think she hopes the repetition will have on readers?

Writing Assignments Using Narration as a Pattern of Development

1. Lorde recounts an incident during which she was treated unfairly. Write a narrative about a time when either you were treated unjustly or you treated someone else in an unfair manner. Like Lorde, use vivid details to make the incident come alive and to convey how it affected you. George Orwell's "Shooting an Elephant" (page 148) will prompt some ideas worth exploring.

2. Write a narrative about an experience that dramatically changed your view of the world. The experience might have been jarring and painful, or it may have been

positive and uplifting. In either case, recount the incident with compelling narrative details. To illustrate the shift in your perspective, begin with a brief statement of the way you viewed the world before the experience. The following essays provide insight into the way a single experience can alter one's understanding of the world: Maya Angelou's "Sister Flowers" (page 87) Langston Hughes's "Salvation" (page 160).

Writing Assignments Combining Patterns of Development

3. Lorde suggests that her parents use the coping mechanism of denial to deal with life's harsh realities, writing that whatever her mother "did not like and could not change, she ignored." Refer to a psychology textbook to learn more about denial. When is it productive? Counterproductive? Drawing upon your own experiences as well as those of friends, family, and classmates, write an essay *contrasting* effective and ineffective uses of denial. Near the end of the paper, present brief *guidelines* that will help readers identify when denial may be detrimental.

4. In her essay, Lorde decries and by implication takes a strong stance against racial discrimination. Brainstorm with friends, family members, and classmates to identify other injustices in American society. You might begin by considering attitudes toward the elderly, the overweight, the physically disabled; the funding of schools in poor and affluent neighborhoods; the portrayal of a specific ethnic group on television; and so on. Focusing on *one* such injustice, write an essay *arguing* that such an injustice indeed exists. To document the nature and extent of the injustice, use the library and/or Internet research. You should also consider *recounting* your own and other people's experiences. Acknowledge and, when you can, dismantle the views of those who think there isn't a problem.

Writing Assignment Using a Journal Entry as a Starting Point

5. Write an essay comparing and/or contrasting the beliefs you had about the United States as a child with those you have as an adult. Review your pre-reading journal entry, and select *one* American belief to focus on. Provide strong, dramatic examples that show why your childhood belief in this concept has been strengthened or weakened. Before writing, you should consider reading Yuh Ji-Yeon's "Let's Tell the Story of All America's Cultures" (page 520), a powerful account of personal disillusionment with American ideals, and Stanley Fish's "Free-Speech Follies" (page 508), a strongly argued examination of rights covered by the First Amendment of the Constitution. Jonathan Alter's "Time to Think About Torture" (page 551) and Henry Porter's "Now the Talk Is About Bringing Back Torture" (page 556) also address the painful clash of high national ideals with harsh realities.

Born Eric Blair in the former British colony of India, George Orwell (1903–50) is probably best known for his two novels, *Animal Farm* (1946) and *1984* (1949), both searing depictions of totalitarian societies. Orwell was also the author of numerous books and essays, many based on his diverse life experiences. He served with the Indian imperial police in Burma, worked at various jobs in London and Paris, and fought in the Spanish Civil War. His experiences in Burma provide the basis for the following essay, which is taken from his collection, *Shooting an Elephant and Other Essays* (1950).

Pre-Reading Journal Entry

Think of times when you were keenly aware of institutional injustice—an action, law, or regulation that was legally in the right but that you felt was wrong. In your journal, record several such examples. Why do you consider them wrong? Have you always felt that way? If not, what changed your opinion?

Shooting an Elephant

In Moulmein, in Lower Burma, I was hated by large numbers of people—the only time in my life that I have been important enough for this to happen to me. I was sub-divisional police officer of the town, and in an aimless, petty kind of way anti-European feeling was very bitter. No one had the guts to raise a riot, but if a European woman went through the bazaars alone somebody would probably spit betel juice over her dress. As a police officer I was an obvious target and was baited whenever it seemed safe to do so. When a nimble Burman tripped me up on the football field and the referee (another Burman) looked the other way, the crowd yelled with hideous laughter. This happened more than once. In the end the sneering yellow faces of young men that met me everywhere, the insults hooted after me when I was at a safe distance, got badly on my nerves. The young Buddhist priests were the worst of all. There were several thousand of them in the town and none of them seemed to have anything to do except stand on street corners and jeer at Europeans.

All this was perplexing and upsetting. For at that time I had already made up my mind that imperialism was an evil thing and the sooner I chucked up my job and got out of it the better. Theoretically—and secretly, of course—I was all for the Burmese and all against their oppressors, the British. As for the job I was doing, I hated it more bitterly than I can perhaps make clear. In a job like that you see the dirty work of Empire at close quarters. The wretched prisoners huddling in the stinking cages of the lockups, the grey, cowed faces of the long-term convicts, the scarred buttocks of the men who had been flogged with bamboos—all these oppressed me with an intolerable sense of guilt. But I could get nothing into perspective. I was young and ill-educated and I had had to think out my problems in the utter silence that is imposed on every Englishman in the East. I did not even know that the British Empire is dying, still less did I know that it is a great deal better than the younger empires that are going to supplant it. All I knew was that I was stuck between my hatred of the empire I served and my rage against the evil-spirited little beasts who tried to make my job impossible. With one part of my mind I thought of the British Raj as an unbreakable tyranny, as something clamped down, in *saecula saeculorum*,[1] upon the will of prostrate peoples; with another part I thought that the greatest joy in the world would be to drive a bayonet into a Buddhist priest's guts. Feelings like these are the normal by-products of imperialism; ask any Anglo-Indian official, if you can catch him off duty.

One day something happened which in a roundabout way was enlightening. It was a tiny incident in itself, but it gave me a better glimpse than I had had before of the real nature of imperialism—the real motives for which despotic governments act. Early one morning the sub-inspector at a police station at the other end of the town rang me up on the 'phone and said that an elephant was ravaging the bazaar. Would I please come and do something about it? I did not know what I could do, but I wanted to see what was happening and I got onto a pony and started out. I took my rifle, an old .44 Winchester and much too small to kill an elephant, but I thought the noise might be useful *in terrorem*.[2] Various Burmans stopped me on the way and told me about the elephant's doings. It was not, of course, a wild elephant, but a tame one which had gone "must." It had been chained up, as tame elephants always are when their attack of "must" is due, but on the previous night it had broken its chain and escaped. Its mahout, the only person who could manage it when it was in that state, had set out in pursuit, but had taken the wrong direction and was now twelve hours' journey away, and in the morning the elephant had suddenly reappeared in the town. The Burmese population had no weapons and were quite helpless against it. It had already destroyed somebody's bamboo hut, killed a cow and raided some fruit-stalls and devoured the stock; also it had met the municipal rubbish van and, when the driver jumped out and took to his heels, had turned the van over and inflicted violence upon it.   3

The Burmese sub-inspector and some Indian constables were waiting for me in the quarter where the elephant had been seen. It was a very poor quarter, a labyrinth of squalid bamboo huts, thatched with palm-leaf, winding all over a steep hillside. I remember that it was a cloudy, stuffy morning at the beginning of the rains. We began questioning the people as to where   4

[1]For ever and ever (editors' note).
[2]As a warning (editors' note).

the elephant had gone and, as usual, failed to get any definite information. That is invariably the case in the East; a story always sounds clear enough at a distance, but the nearer you get to the scene of events the vaguer it becomes. Some of the people said that the elephant had gone in one direction, some said that he had gone in another, some professed not even to have heard of any elephant. I had almost made up my mind that the whole story was a pack of lies, when we heard yells a little distance away. There was a loud, scandalized cry of "Go away, child! Go away this instant!" and an old woman with a switch in her hand came round the corner of a hut, violently shooing away a crowd of naked children. Some more women followed, clicking their tongues and exclaiming; evidently there was something that the children ought not to have seen. I rounded the hut and saw a man's dead body sprawling in the mud. He was an Indian, a black Dravidian coolie, almost naked, and he could not have been dead many minutes. The people said that the elephant had come suddenly upon him round the corner of the hut, caught him with its trunk, put its foot on his back and ground him into the earth. This was the rainy season and the ground was soft, and his face had scored a trench a foot deep and a couple of yards long. He was lying on his belly with arms crucified and head sharply twisted to one side. His face was coated with mud, the eyes wide open, the teeth bared and grinning with an expression of unendurable agony. (Never tell me, by the way, that the dead look peaceful. Most of the corpses I have seen looked devilish.) The friction of the great beast's foot had stripped the skin from his back as neatly as one skins a rabbit. As soon as I saw the dead man I sent an orderly to a friend's house nearby to borrow an elephant rifle. I had already sent back the pony, not wanting it to go mad with fright and throw me if it smelt the elephant.

The orderly came back in a few minutes with a rifle and five cartridges, and meanwhile some Burmans had arrived and told us that the elephant was in the paddy fields below, only a few hundred yards away. As I started forward practically the whole population of the quarter flocked out of the houses and followed me. They had seen the rifle and were all shouting excitedly that I was going to shoot the elephant. They had not shown much interest in the elephant when he was merely ravaging their homes, but it was different now that he was going to be shot. It was a bit of fun to them, as it would be to an English crowd; besides they wanted the meat. It made me vaguely uneasy. I had no intention of shooting the elephant—I had merely sent for the rifle to defend myself if necessary—and it is always unnerving to have a crowd following you. I marched down the hill, looking and feeling a fool, with the rifle over my shoulder and an ever-growing army of people jostling at my heels. At the bottom, when you got away from the huts, there was a metalled road and beyond that a miry waste of paddy fields a thousand yards across, not yet ploughed but soggy from the first rains and dotted with

5

coarse grass. The elephant was standing eight yards from the road, his left side towards us. He took not the slightest notice of the crowd's approach. He was tearing up bunches of grass, beating them against his knees to clean them and stuffing them into his mouth.

I had halted on the road. As soon as I saw the elephant I knew with perfect certainty that I ought not to shoot him. It is a serious matter to shoot a working elephant—it is comparable to destroying a huge and costly piece of machinery—and obviously one ought not to do it if it can possibly be avoided. And at that distance, peacefully eating, the elephant looked no more dangerous than a cow. I thought then and I think now that his attack of "must" was already passing off; in which case he would merely wander harmlessly about until the mahout came back and caught him. Moreover, I did not in the least want to shoot him. I decided that I would watch him for a little while to make sure that he did not turn savage again, and then go home. 6

But at that moment I glanced round at the crowd that had followed me. It was an immense crowd, two thousand at the least and growing every minute. It blocked the road for a long distance on either side. I looked at the sea of yellow faces above the garish clothes—faces all happy and excited over this bit of fun, all certain that the elephant was going to be shot. They were watching me as they would watch a conjurer about to perform a trick. They did not like me, but with the magical rifle in my hands I was momentarily worth watching. And suddenly I realized that I should have to shoot the elephant after all. The people expected it of me and I had got to do it; I could feel their two thousand wills pressing me forward, irresistibly. And it was at this moment, as I stood there with the rifle in my hands, that I first grasped the hollowness, the futility of the white man's dominion in the East. Here was I, the white man with his gun, standing in front of the unarmed native crowd—seemingly the leading actor of the piece; but in reality I was only an absurd puppet pushed to and fro by the will of those yellow faces behind. I perceived in this moment that when the white man turns tyrant it is his own freedom that he destroys. He becomes a sort of hollow, posing dummy, the conventionalized figure of a sahib. For it is the condition of his rule that he shall spend his life in trying to impress the "natives," and so in every crisis he has got to do what the "natives" expect of him. He wears a mask, and his face grows to fit it. I had got to shoot the elephant. I had committed myself to doing it when I sent for the rifle. A sahib has got to act like a sahib; he has got to appear resolute, to know his own mind and do definite things. To come all that way, rifle in hand, with two thousand people marching at my heels, and then to trail feebly away, having done nothing—no, that was impossible. The crowd would laugh at me. And my whole life, every white man's life in the East, was one long struggle not to be laughed at. 7

But I did not want to shoot the elephant. I watched him beating his bunch of grass against his knees, with that preoccupied grandmotherly air 8 that elephants have. It seemed to me that it would be murder to shoot him. At that age I was not squeamish about killing animals, but I had never shot an elephant and never wanted to. (Somehow it always seems worse to kill a *large* animal.) Besides, there was the beast's owner to be considered. Alive, the elephant was worth at least a hundred pounds; dead, he would only be worth the value of his tusks, five pounds, possibly. But I had got to act quickly. I turned to some experienced-looking Burmans who had been there when we arrived, and asked them how the elephant had been behaving. They all said the same thing: he took no notice of you if you left him alone, but he might charge if you went too close to him.

It was perfectly clear to me what I ought to do. I ought to walk up to   9
within, say, twenty-five yards of the elephant and test his behavior. If he charged, I could shoot; if he took no notice of me, it would be safe to leave him until the mahout came back. But also I knew that I was going to do no such thing. I was a poor shot with a rifle and the ground was soft mud into which one would sink at every step. If the elephant charged and I missed him, I should have about as much chance as a toad under a steam-roller. But even then I was not thinking particularly of my own skin, only of the watchful yellow faces behind. For at that moment, with the crowd watching me, I was not afraid in the ordinary sense, as I would have been if I had been alone. A white man mustn't be frightened in front of "natives"; and so, in general, he isn't frightened. The sole thought in my mind was that if anything went wrong those two thousand Burmans would see me pursued, caught, trampled on and reduced to a grinning corpse like that Indian up the hill. And if that happened it was quite probable that some of them would laugh. That would never do. There was only one alternative. I shoved the cartridges into the magazine and lay down on the road to get a better aim.

The crowd grew very still, and a deep, low, happy sigh, as of people who   10
see the theatre curtain go up at last, breathed from innumerable throats. They were going to have their bit of fun after all. The rifle was a beautiful German thing with cross-hair sights. I did not then know that in shooting an elephant one would shoot to cut an imaginary bar running from ear-hole to ear-hole. I ought, therefore, as the elephant was sideway on, to have aimed straight at his ear-hole; actually I aimed several inches in front of this, thinking the brain would be further forward.

When I pulled the trigger I did not hear the bang or feel the kick—one   11
never does when a shot goes home—but I heard the devilish roar of glee that went up from the crowd. In that instant, in too short a time, one would have thought, even for the bullet to get there, a mysterious, terrible change had come over the elephant. He neither stirred nor fell, but every line of his body had altered. He looked suddenly stricken, shrunken, immensely old, as though the frightful impact of the bullet had paralyzed him without knocking him down. At last, after what seemed a long time—it might have been

five seconds, I dare say—he sagged flabbily to his knees. His mouth slobbered. An enormous senility seemed to have settled upon him. One could have imagined him thousands of years old. I fired again into the same spot. At the second shot he did not collapse but climbed with desperate slowness to his feet and stood weakly upright, with legs sagging and head drooping. I fired a third time. That was the shot that did for him. You could see the agony of it jolt his whole body and knock the last remnant of strength from his legs. But in falling he seemed for a moment to rise, for as his hind legs collapsed beneath him he seemed to tower upward like a huge rock toppling, his trunk reaching skywards like a tree. He trumpeted, for the first and only time. And then down he came, his belly towards me, with a crash that seemed to shake the ground even where I lay.

I got up. The Burmans were already racing past me across the mud. It 12 was obvious that the elephant would never rise again, but he was not dead. He was breathing very rhythmically with long rattling gasps, his great mound of a side painfully rising and falling. His mouth was wide open—I could see far down into caverns of pale pink throat. I waited a long time for him to die, but his breathing did not weaken. Finally I fired my two remaining shots into the spot where I thought his heart must be. The thick blood welled out of him like red velvet, but still he did not die. His body did not even jerk when the shots hit him, the tortured breathing continued without a pause. He was dying, very slowly and in great agony, but in some world remote from me where not even a bullet could damage him further. I felt that I had got to put an end to that dreadful noise. It seemed dreadful to see the great beast lying there, powerless to move and yet powerless to die, and not even to be able to finish him. I sent back for my small rifle and poured shot after shot into his heart and down his throat. They seemed to make no impression. The tortured gasps continued as steadily as the ticking of a clock.

In the end I could not stand it any longer and went away. I heard later 13 that it took him half an hour to die. Burmans were bringing dahs and baskets even before I left, and I was told they had stripped the body almost to the bones by the afternoon.

Afterwards, of course, there were endless discussions about the shooting 14 of the elephant. The owner was furious, but he was only an Indian and could do nothing. Besides, legally I had done the right thing, for a mad elephant has to be killed, like a mad dog, if its owner fails to control it. Among the Europeans opinion was divided. The older men said I was right, the younger men said it was a damn shame to shoot an elephant for killing a coolie, because an elephant was worth more than any damn Coringhee coolie. And afterwards I was very glad that the coolie had been killed; it put me legally in the right and it gave me a sufficient pretext for shooting the elephant. I often wondered whether any of the others grasped that I had done it solely to avoid looking a fool.

Questions for Close Reading

1. What is the selection's thesis (or narrative point)? Locate the sentence(s) in which Orwell states his main idea. If he doesn't state the thesis explicitly, express it in your own words.
2. How does Orwell feel about the Burmans? What words does he use to describe them?
3. What reasons does Orwell give for shooting the elephant?
4. In paragraph 3, Orwell says that the elephant incident gave him a better understanding of "the real motives for which despotic governments act." What do you think he means? Before you answer, reread paragraph 7 carefully.
4. Refer to your dictionary as needed to define the following words used in the selection: *imperialism* (paragraph 2), *prostrate* (2), *despotic* (3), *mahout* (3), *miry* (5), *conjurer* (7), *futility* (7), and *sahib* (7).

Questions About the Writer's Craft

1. **The pattern.** Most effective narratives encompass a restricted time span. How much time elapses from the moment Orwell gets his gun to the death of the elephant? What time signals does Orwell provide to help the reader follow the sequence of events in this limited time span?
2. Orwell doesn't actually begin his narrative until the third paragraph. What purposes do the first two paragraphs serve?
3. **Other patterns.** In paragraph 6, Orwell says that shooting a working elephant "is comparable to destroying a huge and costly piece of machinery." This kind of *comparison* is called an *analogy*—describing something unfamiliar, often abstract, in terms of something more familiar and concrete. Find at least three additional analogies in Orwell's essay. What effect do they have?
4. **Other patterns.** Much of the power of Orwell's narrative comes from his ability to convey sensory impressions—what he saw, heard, smelled. Orwell's *description* becomes most vivid when he writes about the death of the elephant in paragraphs 11 and 12. Find some evocative words and phrases that give the description its power.

Writing Assignments Using Narration as a Pattern of Development

1. Orwell recounts a time he acted under great pressure. Write a narrative about an action you once took simply because you felt pressured. Perhaps you were attempting to avoid ridicule or to fulfill someone else's expectations. Like Orwell, use vivid details to bring the incident to life and to convey its effect on you. Langston Hughes's "Salvation" (page 160) may lead you to some insights about the way stress influences behavior.

2. Write a narrative essay about an experience that gave you, like Orwell, a deeper insight into your own nature. You may have discovered, for instance, that you can be surprisingly naive, compassionate, petty, brave, rebellious, or good at something. Consider first reading Joan Murray's "Someone's Mother" (page 156), David Helvarg's "The Storm This Time" (page 103), and Adam Mayblum's "The Price

We Pay" (page 164), essays showing how the authors' responses to a challenge revealed much about their character.

Writing Assignments Combining Patterns of Development

3. Was Orwell justified in shooting the elephant? Write an essay *arguing* that Orwell was either justified *or* not justified. To develop your thesis, cite several specific reasons, each supported by *examples* drawn from the essay. Here are some points you might consider: the legality of Orwell's act, the elephant's temperament, the crowd's presence, the aftermath of the elephant's death, the death itself.

4. Orwell's essay concerns, in part, the tendency to conceal indecision and confusion behind a facade of authority. Focusing on one or two groups of people (parents, teachers, doctors, politicians, and so on), write an essay *arguing* that people in authority sometimes *pretend* to know what they're doing so that subordinates won't suspect their insecurity or incompetence. Part of your essay should focus on the *consequences* of such behaviors.

Writing Assignment Using a Journal Entry as a Starting Point

5. Review your pre-reading journal entry, and select *one* action, law, or regulation that you consider indefensible. Interview friends, family, and classmates in an effort to gather views on all sides of the issue. Also consider supplementing this informal research with information gathered in the library and/or on the Internet. After weighing all your material, formulate a thesis; then write an essay convincing readers of the validity of your position.

Joan Murray

Joan Murray—a poet, writer, editor, and playwright—was born in New York City in 1945. She attended Hunter College and New York University, and published her first volume of poetry, which she also illustrated, in 1975. Three of her poetry books—*Queen of the Mist, Looking for the Parade,* and *The Same Water*—have won prizes. Her most recent volume of poetry is *Dancing on the Edge,* published in 2002. This essay appeared in the "Lives" section of the weekly *New York Times Magazine* on May 13, 2007.

Pre-Reading Journal Entry

We are used to having our mothers care for us, but sometimes we have to care for our mothers. Reflect on an occasion when you had to do something important for your mother or other caregiver. What was the situation? How did you help? How did you feel about helping someone who normally helped you? Use your journal to respond to these questions.

Someone's Mother

Hitchhiking is generally illegal where I live in upstate New York, but it's 1 not unusual to see someone along Route 20 with an outstretched thumb or a handmade sign saying "Boston." This hitchhiker, though, was waving both arms in the air and grinning like a president boarding Air Force One.

I was doing 60—eager to get home after a dental appointment in 2 Albany—and I was a mile past the hitchhiker before something made me turn back. I couldn't say if the hitchhiker was a man or a woman. All I knew was that the hitchhiker was old.

As I drove back up the hill, I eyed the hitchhiker in the distance: dark 3 blue raincoat, jaunty black beret. Thin arms waving, spine a little bent. Wisps of white hair lilting as the trucks whizzed by. I made a U-turn and pulled up on the gravel, face to face with an eager old woman who kept waving till I stopped. I saw no broken-down vehicle. There was no vehicle at all. She wore the same broad grin I noticed when I passed her.

I rolled my window down. "Can I call someone for you?" 4

"No, I'm fine—I just need a ride." 5

"Where are you going?" 6

"Nassau." 7

That was three miles away. "Are you going there to shop?" 8

"No. I live there." 9

"What are you doing here?" I asked with a tone I hadn't used since my 10 son was a teenager.

"I was out for a walk." 11

I glanced down the road: Jet's Autobody. Copeland Coating. Thoma 12 Tire Company. And the half-mile hill outside Nassau—so steep that there's a second lane for trucks. She must have climbed the shoulder of that hill. And the next one. And the next. Until something made her stop and throw her hands in the air.

"Did you get lost?" I asked, trying to conceal my alarm. 13

"It was a nice day," she said with a little cry. "Can't an old lady go for a 14 walk on a nice day and get lost?"

It wasn't a question meant to be answered. She came around to the pas- 15 senger side, opened the door and sat down. On our way to Nassau, she admitted to being 92. Though she ducked my questions about her name, her address and her family. "Just leave me at the drugstore," she said.

"I'll take you home," I said. "Then you can call someone." 16

"Please," she said, "just leave me at the drugstore." 17

"I can't leave you there," I replied just as firmly. "I'm going to take you 18 to your house. Or else to the police station."

"No, no," she begged. She was agitated now. "If my son finds out, he'll 19 put me in a home."

Already I was seeing my own mother, who's 90. A few years ago, she was 20 living in her house on Long Island, surrounded by her neighbors, her bird feeders, her azaleas. Then one morning she phoned my brother to say she didn't remember how to get dressed anymore. A few weeks later, with sorrow and worry, we arranged her move to a nursing home.

I noticed that the hitchhiker had a white dove pinned to her collar. "Do 21 you belong to a church?" I tried. "Yes," she said. She was grinning. "I'd like to take you there," I said. "No, please," she said again. "My son will find out."

Things were getting clearer. "You've gotten lost before?" 22

"A few times," she shrugged. "But I always find my way home. Just take 23 me to the drugstore."

As we drove, I kept thinking about my mother, watched over and cared 24 for in a bright, clean place. I also thought about her empty bird feeders, her azaleas blooming for no one, the way she whispers on the phone, "I don't know anyone here."

When I pulled into the parking strip beside the drugstore, the hitchhik- 25 er let herself out. "I just need to sit on the step for a while," she said before closing the door. I stepped out after her. "Can't I take you home?" I asked as gently as I could.

She looked into my eyes for a moment. "I don't know where I live," she 26 said in the tiniest voice. "But someone will come along who knows me. They always do."

I watched as she sat herself down on the step. Already she had dismissed 27 me from her service. She was staring ahead with her grin intact, waiting for the next person who would aid her.

I should call the police, I thought. But then surely her son would be told. 28 I should speak with the pharmacists. Surely they might know her—though they might know her son as well. Yet who was I to keep this incident from him? And yet how could I help him put the hitchhiker in a home?

"Promise me you'll tell the druggist if no one comes soon," I said to her with great seriousness.   29

"I promise," she said with a cheerful little wave.   30

Questions for Close Reading

1. What is the selection's thesis? Locate the sentence(s) in which Murray states her main idea. If she doesn't state her thesis explicitly, express it in your own words.
2. What is the external conflict Murray experiences in this essay? What is the internal conflict?
3. In paragraph 22, the author says "Things were getting clearer." What does she mean by this?
4. Why does Murray finally go along with the hitchhiker's wishes?
5. Refer to your dictionary as needed to define the following words used in the selection: *jaunty* (paragraph 3), *beret* (3), *lilting* (3), *shoulder* (12), *agitated* (19), and *azaleas* (20).

Questions About the Writer's Craft

1. **The pattern.** How does Murray organize the events in this essay? How does she keep the reader oriented as her story progresses?
2. **Other patterns.** In some passages, Murray *describes* the hitchhiker's appearance. What do these descriptions contribute to the narrative?
3. In paragraphs 12, 20, 24 and 28, Murray tells us her thoughts. What effect do these sections have on the pace of the narrative? How do they affect our understanding of what is happening?
4. Murray uses a lot of dialogue in this essay. Explain why the use of dialogue is (or is not) effective. What function does the dialogue have?

Writing Assignments Using Narration as a Pattern of Development

1. Murray's encounter with the hitchhiker happens as she is driving home. Recall a time when you were traveling in a car, bus, or other vehicle and something surprising occurred. Were you frightened, puzzled, amused? Did you learn something about people or about yourself? Tell the story using first-person narration, being sure to include your thoughts as well as your actions and the actions of others.
2. Write a narrative about an incident in your life in which a stranger helped you, and explain how this made you feel. The experience might have made you grateful, resentful, or anxious like the hitchhiker. Use either flashback or flashforward to emphasize an event in your narrative. To read an essay that uses flashback, see Gary Kamiya's "Life, Death and Spring" (page 111), Audre

Lordes' "The Fourth of July" (page 142) and Beth Johnson's "Bombs Bursting in Air" (page 215).

Writing Assignments Combining Patterns of Development

3. Did Murray do the right thing when she left the elderly woman sitting in front of the drugstore? Write an essay in which you *argue* that Murray did or did not act properly. You can support your argument using *examples* from the essay showing the hitchhiker's state of mental and physical health. You can also support your argument by presenting the possible positive or negative effects of Murray's action, depending on your point of view.

4. Murray is concerned that the hitchhiker, like Murray's own mother, may not able to take care of herself sufficiently. Do some research on the Internet or in the library about options available for elderly people who can no longer live alone. Write an essay in which you give *examples* of these options and *compare* them in terms of price, services, and quality of life.

Writing Assignment Using a Journal Entry as a Starting Point

5. Review your pre-reading journal entry in which you described a time when you had to help your mother or other caregiver. Compare your experience to those of Joan Murray, who helped her own mother as well as the hitchhiker, who was "someone's mother." How did your experience differ from hers? How was it similar? If you were to do it again, would you do so the same way, or would you do it differently? Why?

Langston Hughes

One of the foremost members of the 1920s literary movement known as the Harlem Renaissance, Langston Hughes (1902–67) committed himself to portraying the richness of Black life in the United States. A poet and a writer of short stories, Hughes was greatly influenced by the rhythms of blues and jazz. In his later years, he published two autobiographical works, *The Big Sea* (1940) and *I Wonder as I Wander* (1956), and he wrote a history of the National Association for the Advancement of Colored People (NAACP). The following selection is from *The Big Sea*.

Pre-Reading Journal Entry

Young people often feel pressured by family and community to adopt certain values, beliefs, or traditions. In your journal, reflect on some of the pressures that you've experienced. What was your response to these pressures? What have been the consequences of your response? Do you think your experience with these family or community pressures was unique or fairly common?

Salvation

I was saved from sin when I was going on thirteen. But not really saved. 1
It happened like this. There was a big revival at my Auntie Reed's church. Every night for weeks there had been much preaching, singing, praying, and shouting, and some very hardened sinners had been brought to Christ, and the membership of the church had grown by leaps and bounds. Then just before the revival ended, they held a special meeting for children, "to bring the young lambs to the fold." My aunt spoke of it for days ahead. That night I was escorted to the front row and placed on the mourners' bench with all the other young sinners, who had not yet been brought to Jesus.

My aunt told me that when you were saved you saw a light, and some- 2
thing happened to you inside! And Jesus came into your life! And God was with you from then on! She said you could see and hear and feel Jesus in your soul. I believed her. I had heard a great many old people say the same thing and it seemed to me they ought to know. So I sat there calmly in the hot, crowded church, waiting for Jesus to come to me.

The preacher preached a wonderful rhythmical sermon, all moans and 3
shouts and lonely cries and dire pictures of hell, and then he sang a song about the ninety and nine safe in the fold, but one little lamb was left out in the cold. Then he said: "Won't you come? Won't you come to Jesus? Young lambs, won't you come?" And he held out his arms to all us young sinners there on the mourners' bench. And the little girls cried. And some of them jumped up and went to Jesus right away. But most of us just sat there.

A great many older people came and knelt around us and prayed, old 4
women with jet-black faces and braided hair, old men with work-gnarled

hands. And the church sang a song about the lower lights are burning, some poor sinners to be saved. And the whole building rocked with prayer and song.

Still I kept waiting to *see* Jesus. 5

Finally all the young people had gone to the altar and were saved, but 6
one boy and me. He was a rounder's son named Westley. Westley and I were surrounded by sisters and deacons praying. It was very hot in the church, and getting late now. Finally Westley said to me in a whisper: "God damn! I'm tired o' sitting here. Let's get up and be saved." So he got up and was saved.

Then I was left all alone on the mourners' bench. My aunt came and 7
knelt at my knees and cried, while prayers and songs swirled all around me in the little church. The whole congregation prayed for me alone, in a mighty wail of moans and voices. And I kept waiting serenely for Jesus, waiting, waiting—but he didn't come. I wanted to see him, but nothing happened to me. Nothing! I wanted something to happen to me, but nothing happened.

I heard the songs and the minister saying: "Why don't you come? My 8
dear child, why don't you come to Jesus? Jesus is waiting for you. He wants you. Why don't you come? Sister Reed, what is this child's name?"

"Langston," my aunt sobbed. 9

"Langston, why don't you come? Why don't you come and be saved? 10
Oh, Lamb of God! Why don't you come?"

Now it was really getting late. I began to be ashamed of myself, holding 11
everything up so long. I began to wonder what God thought about Westley, who certainly hadn't seen Jesus either, but who was now sitting proudly on the platform, swinging his knickerbockered legs and grinning down at me, surrounded by deacons and old women on their knees praying. God had not struck Westley dead for taking his name in vain or for lying in the temple. So I decided that maybe to save further trouble, I'd better lie, too, and say that Jesus had come, and get up and be saved.

So I got up. 12

Suddenly the whole room broke into a sea of shouting, as they saw me rise. 13
Waves of rejoicing swept the place. Women leaped in the air. My aunt threw her arms around me. The minister took me by the hand and led me to the platform.

When things quieted down, in a hushed silence, punctuated by a few 14
ecstatic "Amens," all the new young lambs were blessed in the name of God. Then joyous singing filled the room.

That night, for the last time in my life but one—for I was a big boy 15
twelve years old—I cried. I cried, in bed alone, and couldn't stop. I buried my head under the quilts, but my aunt heard me. She woke up and told my uncle I was crying because the Holy Ghost had come into my life, and because I had seen Jesus. But I was really crying because I couldn't bear to tell her that I had lied, that I had deceived everybody in the church, and I

hadn't seen Jesus, and that now I didn't believe there was a Jesus any more, since he didn't come to help me.

Questions for Close Reading

1. What is the selection's thesis (or narrative point)? Locate the sentence(s) in which Hughes states his main idea. If Hughes doesn't state the thesis explicitly, express it in your own words.
2. During the revival meeting, what pressures are put on the young Langston to get up and be saved?
3. How does Westley's attitude differ from Hughes's?
4. Does the narrator's Auntie Reed really understand him? Why can't he tell her the truth about his experience in the church?
5. Refer to your dictionary as needed to define the following words used in the selection: *revival* (paragraph 1), *knickerbockered* (11), *punctuated* (14), and *ecstatic* (14).

Questions About the Writer's Craft

1. The pattern. A narrative's power can often be traced to a conflict within the event being recounted. What conflict does the narrator of "Salvation" experience? How does Hughes create tension about this conflict?
2. What key role does Westley serve in the resolution of the narrator's dilemma? How does Hughes's inclusion of Westley in the story help us to understand the narrator better?
3. Other patterns. The thirteenth paragraph presents a *metaphor* of the church as an ocean. What images develop this metaphor? What does the metaphor tell us about Hughes's feelings and those of the church people?
4. The singing of hymns is a major part of this religious service. Why do you think Hughes has the narrator reveal the subjects and even the lyrics of some of the hymns?

Writing Assignments Using Narration as a Pattern of Development

1. Like Hughes, we sometimes believe that deception is our best alternative. Write a narrative about a time you felt deception was the best way either to protect those you care about or to maintain the respect of those important to you.
2. Write a narrative essay about a chain of events that caused you to become disillusioned about a person or institution you had previously regarded highly. Begin as Hughes does by presenting your initial beliefs. Relate the sequence of events that changed your evaluation of the person or organization. In the conclusion, explain the short- and long-term effects of the incident. For more accounts of childhood disillusionment, read Audre Lorde's "The Fourth of July" (page 142) and Beth Johnson's "Bombs Bursting in Air" (page 215).

Writing Assignments Combining
Patterns of Development

3. Hughes writes, "My aunt told me that when you were saved, you saw a light, and something happened to you inside! And Jesus came into your life!" What *causes* people to change their beliefs? Do such changes come from waiting calmly, as Hughes tried to do in church, or must they come from a more active process? Write an essay explaining your viewpoint. You may use *process analysis, causal analysis,* or some other organizational pattern to develop your thesis. Be sure to include specific examples to support your understanding of the way beliefs change.

4. Write a *persuasive* essay *arguing* either that lying is sometimes right or that lying is always wrong. Apply your thesis to particular situations and show how lying is or is not the right course of action. Be sure to keep your *narration* of these situations brief and focused on your point. Remember to acknowledge the opposing viewpoint. Charles Sykes's "The 'Values' Wasteland" (page 197) and Stephanie Ericsson's "The Ways We Lie" (page 253) may help you define your position. You might even mention these authors' perspectives in your essay.

Writing Assignment Using a Journal
Entry as a Starting Point

5. Review your pre-reading journal entry, and select *one* family or community pressure with which you've had to contend. Then write an essay examining the effect that this pressure has had on you. Refer to your journal as you prepare to explain the values, beliefs, or traditions that you were expected to adopt. Discuss your response to this pressure and how your reaction has affected you.

Adam Mayblum

On September 11, 2001, as thirty-five-year-old Adam Mayblum worked in his investment firm's office on the eighty-seventh floor of the World Trade Center's North
Tower, a terrorist-hijacked plane crashed into the building. His presence of mind—
and a great deal of good fortune—allowed him to escape from the tower before it
collapsed. The day after the attacks, he sent an e-mail to friends and family describing his experiences. The e-mail, later titled "The Price We Pay," was soon being for-
warded around the world and reprinted in newspapers and magazines and on websites. (Mayblum's account appears below in much the same form as when he sent it;
it has not been corrected for grammar or mechanics.) Today, Mayblum works at a
new firm located just a few blocks from the site of the former World Trade Center.
He lives with his wife and three children in New Rochelle, New York.

Pre-Reading Journal Entry

The terrorist attacks against the United States on September 11, 2001, had a profound impact the world over. Where were you that morning? What was your reaction
when you learned of the attacks? What was the reaction of those around you? How
did your feelings change over time? How, if at all, did the event alter your perspectives about larger issues? Explore these questions in your pre-reading journal.

The Price We Pay

My name is Adam Mayblum. I am alive today. I am committing this to   1
"paper" so I never forget. SO WE NEVER FORGET. I am sure that this
is one of thousands of stories that will emerge over the next several days
and weeks.

I arrived as usual a little before 8am. My office was on the 87th floor of   2
1World Trade Center, AKA: Tower 1, AKA: the North Tower. Most of my
associates were in by 8:30am. We were standing around, joking around, eating breakfast, checking emails, and getting set for the day when the first
plane hit just a few stories above us. I must stress that we did not know that
it was a plane. The building lurched violently and shook as if it were an earthquake. People screamed. I watched out my window as the building seemed
to move 10 to 20 feet in each direction. It rumbled and shook long enough
for me to get my wits about myself and grab a co-worker and seek shelter
under a doorway. Light fixtures and parts of the ceiling collapsed. The
kitchen was destroyed. We were certain that it was a bomb. We looked out
the windows. Reams of paper were flying everywhere, like a ticker tape
parade. I looked down at the street. I could see people in Battery Park City
looking up. Smoke started billowing in through the holes in the ceiling. I
believe that there were 13 of us.

We did not panic. I can only assume that we thought that the worst was   3
over. The building was standing and we were shaken but alive. We checked the

halls. The smoke was thick and white and did not smell like I imagined smoke should smell. Not like your BBQ or your fireplace or even a bonfire. The phones were working. My wife had taken our 9 month old for his check up. I called my nanny at home and told her to page my wife, tell her that a bomb went off, I was ok, and on my way out. I grabbed my laptop. Took off my tee shirt and ripped it into 3 pieces. Soaked it in water. Gave 2 pieces to my friends. Tied my piece around my face to act as an air filter. And we all started moving to the staircase. One of my dearest friends said that he was staying until the police or firemen came to get him. In the halls there were tiny fires and sparks. The ceiling had collapsed in the men's bathroom. It was gone along with anyone who may have been in there. We did not go in to look. We missed the staircase on the first run and had to double back. Once in the staircase we picked up fire extinguishers just in case. On the 85th floor a brave associate of mine and I headed back up to our office to drag out my partner who stayed behind. There was no air, just white smoke. We made the rounds through the office calling his name. No response. He must have succumbed to the smoke. We left defeated in our efforts and made our way back to the stairwell. We proceeded to the 78th floor where we had to change over to a different stairwell. 78 is the main junction to switch to the upper floors. I expected to see more people. There were some 50 to 60 more. Not enough. Wires and fires all over the place. Smoke too. A brave man was fighting a fire with the emergency hose. I stopped with two friends to make sure that everyone from our office was accounted for. We ushered them and confused people into the stairwell. In retrospect, I recall seeing Harry, my head trader, doing the same several yards behind me. I am only 35. I have known him for over 14 years. I headed into the stairwell with 2 friends.

We were moving down very orderly in Stair Case A. very slowly. No panic. At least not overt panic. My legs could not stop shaking. My heart was pounding. Some nervous jokes and laughter. I made a crack about ruining a brand new pair of Merrells.[1] Even still, they were right, my feet felt great. We all laughed. We checked our cell phones. Surprisingly, there was a very good signal, but the Sprint network was jammed. I heard that the Blackberry 2-way email devices worked perfectly. On the phones, 1 out of 20 dial attempts got through. I knew I could not reach my wife so I called my parents. I told them what happened and that we were all okay and on the way down. Soon, my sister in law reached me. I told her we were fine and moving down. I believe that was about the 65th floor. We were bored and nervous. I called my friend Angel in San Francisco. I knew he would be watching. He was amazed I was on the phone. He told me to get out that there was another plane on its way. I did not know what he was talking about. By now the second plane had struck Tower 2. We were so deep into the middle of our building that we did

4

---

[1]A brand of men's shoes (editors' note).

not hear or feel anything. We had no idea what was really going on. We kept making way for wounded to go down ahead of us. Not many of them, just a few. No one seemed seriously wounded. Just some cuts and scrapes. Everyone cooperated.

Everyone was a hero yesterday. No questions asked. I had co-workers in another office on the 77th floor. I tried dozens of times to get them on their cell phones or office lines. It was futile. Later I found that they were alive. One of the many miracles on a day of tragedy.   5

On the 53rd floor we came across a very heavyset man sitting on the stairs. I asked if he needed help or was he just resting. He needed help. I knew I would have trouble carrying him because I have a very bad back. But my friend and I offered anyway. We told him he could lean on us. He hesitated, I don't know why. I said do you want to come or do you want us to send help for you. He chose for help. I told him he was on the 53rd floor in Stairwell A and that's what I would tell the rescue workers. He said okay and we left.   6

On the 44th floor my phone rang again. It was my parents. They were hysterical. I said relax, I'm fine. My father said get out, there is third plane coming. I still did not understand. I was kind of angry. What did my parents think? Like I needed some other reason to get going? I couldn't move the thousand people in front of me any faster. I know they love me, but no one inside understood what the situation really was. My parents did. Starting around this floor the firemen, policemen, WTC K-9 units without the dogs, anyone with a badge, started coming up as we were heading down. I stopped a lot of them and told them about the man on 53 and my friend on 87. I later felt terrible about this. They headed up to find those people and met death instead.   7

On the 33rd floor I spoke with a man who somehow knew most of the details. He said 2 small planes hit the building. Now we all started talking about which terrorist group it was. Was it an internal organization or an external one? The overwhelming but uninformed opinion was Islamic Fanatics. Regardless, we now knew that it was not a bomb and there were potentially more planes coming. We understood.   8

On the 3rd floor the lights went out and we heard & felt this rumbling coming towards us from above. I thought the staircase was collapsing upon itself. It was 10am now and that was Tower 2 collapsing next door. We did not know that. Someone had a flashlight. We passed it forward and left the stairwell and headed down a dark and cramped corridor to an exit. We could not see at all. I recommended that everyone place a hand on the shoulder of the person in front of them and call out if they hit an obstacle so others would know to avoid it. They did. It worked perfectly. We reached another stairwell and saw a female officer emerge soaking wet and covered in soot. She said we could not go that   9 way it was blocked. Go up to 4 and use the other exit. Just as we started up she said it was ok to go down instead. There was water everywhere. I called out for hands on shoulders again and she said that was a great idea. She stayed behind instructing people to do that. I do not know what happened to her.

We emerged into an enormous room. It was light but filled with 10
smoke. I commented to a friend that it must be under construction. Then we realized where we were. It was the second floor. The one that overlooks the lobby. We were ushered out into the courtyard, the one where the fountain used to be. My first thought was of a TV movie I saw once about nuclear winter and fallout. I could not understand where all of the debris came from. There was at least five inches of this gray pasty dusty drywall soot on the ground as well as a thickness of it in the air. Twisted steel and wires. I heard there were bodies and body parts as well, but I did not look. It was bad enough. We hid under the remaining overhangs and moved out to the street. We were told to keep walking towards Houston Street. The odd thing is that there were very few rescue workers around. Less than five. They all must have been trapped under the debris when Tower 2 fell. We did not know that and could not understand where all of that debris came from. It was just my friend Kern and I now. We were hugging but sad. We felt certain that most of our friends ahead of us died and we knew no one behind us.

We came upon a post office several blocks away. We stopped and looked 11
up. Our building, exactly where our office is (was), was engulfed in flame and smoke. A postal worker said that Tower 2 had fallen down. I looked again and sure enough it was gone. My heart was racing. We kept trying to call our families. I could not get in touch with my wife. Finally I got through to my parents. Relieved is not the word to explain their feelings. They got through to my wife, thank God and let her know I was alive. We sat down. A girl on a bike offered us some water. Just as she took the cap off her bottle we heard a rumble. We looked up and our building, Tower 1 collapsed. I did not note the time but I am told it was 10:30am. We had been out less than 15 minutes.

We were mourning our lost friends, particularly the one who stayed in 12
the office as we were now sure that he had perished. We started walking towards Union Square. I was going to Beth Israel Medical Center to be looked at. We stopped to hear the President speaking on the radio. My phone rang. It was my wife. I think I fell to my knees crying when I heard her voice. Then she told me the most incredible thing. My partner who had stayed behind called her. He was alive and well. I guess we just lost him in the commotion. We started jumping and hugging and shouting. I told my wife that my brother had arranged for a hotel in midtown. He can be very resourceful in that way. I told her I would call her from there. My brother

and I managed to get a gypsy cab to take us home to Westchester instead. I cried on my son and held my wife until I fell asleep.

As it turns out my partner, the one who I thought had stayed behind   13 was behind us with Harry Ramos, our head trader. This is now second-hand information. They came upon Victor, the heavyset man on the 53rd floor. They helped him. He could barely move. My partner bravely/stupidly tested the elevator on the 52nd floor. He rode it down to the sky lobby on 44. The doors opened, it was fine. He rode it back up and got Harry and Victor. I don't yet know if anyone else joined them. Once on 44 they made their way back into the stairwell. Someplace around the 39th to 36th floors they felt the same rumble I felt on the 3rd floor. It was 10am and Tower 2 was coming down. They had about 30 minutes to get out. Victor said he could no longer move. They offered to have him lean on them. He said he couldn't do it. My partner hollered at him to sit on his butt and scooch down the steps. He said he was not capable of doing it. Harry told my partner to go ahead of them. Harry had once had a heart attack and was worried about this mans heart. It was his nature to be this way. He was/is one of the kindest people I know. He would not leave a man behind. My partner went ahead and made it out. He said he was out maybe 10 minutes before the building came down. This means that Harry had maybe 25 minutes to move Victor 36 floors. I guess they moved 1 floor every 1.5 minutes. Just a guess. This means Harry was around the 20th floor when the building collapsed. As of now 12 of 13 people are account-ed for. As of 6pm yesterday his wife had not heard from him. I fear that Harry is lost. However, a short while ago I heard that he may be alive. Apparently there is a website with survivor names on it and his name appears there. Unfortunately, Ramos is not an uncommon name in New York. Pray for him and all those like him.[2]

With regards to the firemen heading upstairs, I realize that they were   14 going up anyway. But, it hurts to know that I may have made them move quicker to find my friend. Rationally, I know this is not true and that I am not the responsible one. The responsible ones are in hiding somewhere on this planet and damn them for making me feel like this. But they should know that they failed in terrorizing us. We were calm. Those men and women that went up were heroes in the face of it all. They must have known what was going on and they did their jobs. Ordinary people were heroes too. Today the images that people around the world equate with power and democracy are gone but "America" is not an image it is a concept. That concept is only strengthened by our pulling together as a team. If you want to kill us, leave us alone because we will do it by ourselves. If you want to

[2]Sadly, it later was confirmed that Harry Ramos did not survive the collapse of the towers that day (editors' note).

make us stronger, attack and we unite. This is the ultimate failure of terrorism against The United States and the ultimate price we pay to be free, to decide where we want to work, what we want to eat, and when & where we want to go on vacation. The very moment the first plane was hijacked, democracy won.

Questions for Close Reading

1. What is the selection's thesis (or narrative point)? Locate the sentence(s) in which Mayblum states his main idea. If he doesn't state the thesis explicitly, express it in your own words.
2. Strong narrative involves conflict (see page 128). What is the main conflict in "The Price We Pay"?
3. What reason does Mayblum give for writing his account? What additional reasons might he have?
4. In Mayblum's view, the World Trade Center attacks were part of "the price we pay." What is it that he believes Americans paid for on September 11, 2001? Do you agree? Why or why not?
5. Refer to your dictionary as needed to define the following terms used in the selection: *aka* (paragraph 2), *lurched* (2), *reams* (2), *ticker tape* (2), *succumbed* (3), *junction* (3), *ushered* (3), *retrospect* (3), *nuclear winter* (10), *fallout* (10), *debris* (10), *engulfed* (11), *commotion* (12), and *gypsy cab* (12).

Questions About the Writer's Craft

1. **The pattern.** Mayblum tells his story primarily in past tense. However, he occasionally uses present tense. Identify some of these instances. What effect does his use of present tense have on the narrative?
2. Mayblum's essay is marked by two clear stylistic characteristics: First, he uses many sentence fragments and short sentences, and second, he omits quotation marks around people's exact words. How do these choices affect the narrative?
3. Many of Mayblum's sentences begin with *We*—for example, "We did not panic" (3), "We all laughed" (4), and "We understood" (7). How does the prevalent use of *we* and *our* fit with Mayblum's theme?
4. Mayblum says American freedom is the freedom to "decide where we want to work, what we want to eat, and when & where we want to go on vacation" (14). Do you find these examples effective and appropriate? Why or why not?

Writing Assignments Using Narration as a Pattern of Development

1. Mayblum tells a story of courage, compassion, and quick thinking in the face of horror. Think back and take a few moments to freewrite about a situation in which you experienced terror or alarm. Maybe you got lost in the woods or witnessed a crime. Write an essay in which you recount your frightening situation. What exactly took

place? How did you react? How did others react? What did you learn from the experience? Be sure to provide vivid details to recreate the sights, sounds, and feelings surrounding the event. For additional accounts of weathering a harrowing situation, read George Orwell's "Shooting an Elephant" (page 148) or Beth Johnson's "Bombs Bursting in Air" (page 215).

2. Americans cherish their personal liberties. Recall a time when, in your view, you were wrongly deprived of some freedom. Perhaps you were punished for expressing your opinion or ordered not to associate with particular people. Write an essay that narrates the unjust incident, focusing on the main conflict. What were the circumstances? Who was involved? Discuss your treatment and why you felt it was unjust. In addition, provide some thoughts on whether now, in retrospect, you have a different perspective on the event than you did at the time.

Writing Assignments Combining Patterns of Development

3. In an emergency, some people stay calm; others panic. Think of the person you would most want to be with in a crisis. Next, think of the person you would *least* want to be with. Freewrite thoughts about each of these people in your journal. Then, in a serious or humorous piece, *contrast* these two people's personalities, revealing why one would probably be a reliable partner in a crisis whereas the other would probably be a disastrous one. Be sure to provide *examples* of these people's behavior to *illustrate* why you regard each of them as you do.

 4. As new structures are erected on the site of the destroyed World Trade Center towers, several groups continue to have an interest in how the site is developed. The commercial developer wants to ensure that there are profitable office buildings. The city and state governments, as well as local residents and businesses, want any development to revitalize the surrounding area. And families of September 11th victims want to make sure that those who died are properly memorialized. Write an essay in which you *describe* the current development plans for the site and *argue* whether they are meeting the needs of these various interest groups. Research the development progress and plans in the library and/or on the Internet, making sure to consult reputable sources.

Writing Assignment Using a Journal Entry as a Starting Point

5. It is clear from Mayblum's account that the events of September 11, 2001, had a profound impact on his life. But a person need not have been actively involved in the events to have felt their repercussions. Review the thoughts you recorded in your pre-reading journal. Then write an essay about how the events of that day have *affected* you. You might organize the essay by first considering your immediate response to the events, perhaps as part of a *narrative* of when and how you found out. What kinds of emotions and thoughts did you experience at the time? Then you might proceed by discussing longer-term effects on your thoughts or feelings. For instance, has the attack made you feel any closer to your family and friends? Has it left you feeling unsafe or depressed? Has it changed your view of America or the rest of the world?

Additional Writing Topics

NARRATION

General Assignments

Prepare an essay on any of the following topics, using narration as the paper's dominant method of development. Be sure to select details that advance the essay's narrative purpose; you may even want to experiment with flashback or flashforward. In any case, keep the sequence of events clear by using transitional cues. Within the limited time span covered, use vigorous details and varied sentence structure to enliven the narrative. Tell the story from a consistent point of view.

1. An emergency that brought out the best or worst in you
2. The hazards of taking children out to eat
3. An incident that made you believe in fate
4. Your best or worst day at school or work
5. A major decision
6. An encounter with a machine
7. An important learning experience
8. A narrow escape
9. Your first date, first day on the job, or first anything
10. A memorable childhood experience
11. A fairy tale the way you would like to hear it told
12. A painful moment
13. An incredible but true story
14. A significant family event
15. An experience in which a certain emotion (pride, anger, regret, or some other) was dominant
16. A surprising coincidence
17. An act of heroism
18. An unpleasant confrontation
19. A cherished family story
20. An imagined meeting with an admired celebrity or historical figure

Assignments with a Specific Purpose, Audience, and Point of View

On Campus

1. Write an article for your old high school newspaper. The article will be read primarily by seniors who are planning to go away to college next year. In the article, narrate a story that points to some truth about the "breaking away" stage of life.
2. A friend of yours has seen someone cheat on a test, plagiarize an entire paper, or seriously violate some other academic policy. In a letter, convince this friend to

inform the instructor or a campus administrator by narrating an incident in which a witness did (or did not) speak up in such a situation. Tell what happened as a result.

At Home or in the Community

3. You have had a disturbing encounter with one of the people who seems to have "fallen through the cracks" of society—a homeless person, an unwanted child, or anyone else who is alone and abandoned. Write a letter to the local newspaper describing this encounter. Your purpose is to arouse people's indignation and compassion and to get help for such unfortunates.
4. Your younger brother, sister, relative, or neighborhood friend can't wait to be your age. Write a letter in which you narrate a dramatic story that shows the young person that your age isn't as wonderful as he or she thinks. Be sure to select a story that the person can understand and appreciate.

On the Job

5. As fund-raiser for a particular organization (for example, the Red Cross, the SPCA, Big Brothers/Big Sisters), you're sending a newsletter to contributors. Support your cause by telling the story of a time when your organization made all the difference—the blood donation that saved a life, the animal that was rescued from abuse, and so on.
6. A customer has written a letter to you (or your boss) telling about a bad experience that he or she had with someone in your workplace. On the basis of that single experience, the customer now regards your company and its employees with great suspicion. It's your responsibility to respond to this complaint. Write a letter to the customer balancing his or her negative picture by narrating a story that shows the "flip side" of your company and its employees.

A GUIDE TO USING SOURCES

Many assignments in *The Longman Reader* suggest that you might want to do some research in the library and/or on the Internet. Such research enlarges your perspective and enables you to move beyond off-the-top-of-your-head opinions to those that are firmly supported. This appendix will be useful if you do decide to draw upon outside sources when preparing a paper. The appendix explains how to (1) evaluate articles, books, and Web sources; (2) analyze and synthesize sources you find; (3) use quotation, summary, and paraphrase correctly to avoid plagiarism; (4) integrate source material into your writing; and (5) document print, Internet, and other sources.

EVALUATING SOURCE MATERIALS

The success of your essay will depend in large part on the evidence you provide (see pages 34–38 on the characteristics of evidence). Evidence from sources, whether print or electronic, needs to be evaluated for its *relevance, timeliness, seriousness of approach*, and *objectivity*.

Relevance

Titles can be misleading. To determine if a source is relevant for your paper, review it carefully. For a book, read the preface or introduction, skim the table of contents, and check the index to see whether the book is likely to contain information that's important to your topic. If the source is an influential text in the field, you may want to read the entire book for background and specific ideas. Or if a text devotes just a few pages to your topic, you might read those pages, taking notes on important information. For an article, read the abstract of the article, if there is one. If not, read the first few paragraphs and skim the rest to determine if it might be useful. As you read a source, make use of the reading checklists on pages 2–3 to get the most from the material. If a source turns out to be irrelevant, just make a note to yourself that you consulted the source and found it didn't relate to your topic.

Timeliness

To some extent, the topic and the kind of research you're doing will determine whether a work is outdated. If you're researching a historical topic such as the internment of Japanese Americans during World War II, you would most likely consult sources published in the 1940s and 1950s, as well as more up-to-date sources. In contrast, if you're investigating a recent scientific development—cloning, for example—it would make sense to restrict your search to current material. For most college research, a source older than ten years is considered outdated unless it was the first to present key concepts in a field.

Seriousness of Approach

As you review a source, ask yourself if it is suitable for your purpose and your instructor's requirements. Articles from *general* periodicals (newspapers and widely read magazines like *Time* and *Newsweek*) and *serious* publications (such as *National Geographic* and *Scientific American*) may be sufficient to provide support in a personal essay. But an in-depth research paper in your major field of study will require material from *scholarly* journals and texts (for example, *American Journal of Public Health* and *Film Quarterly*).

Objectivity

As you examine your sources for possible bias, keep in mind that a strong conclusion or opinion is *not in itself* a sign of bias. As long as a writer doesn't ignore opposing positions or distort evidence, a source can't be considered biased. A biased source presents only those facts that fit the writer's predetermined conclusions. Such a source is often marked by emotionally charged language (see page 19). Publications sponsored by special interest groups—a particular industry, religious association, advocacy group, or political party—are usually biased. Reading such materials *does* familiarize you with a specific point of view, but remember that contrary evidence has probably been ignored or skewed.

The following checklist provides some questions to ask yourself as you evaluate print sources.

☑ EVALUATING ARTICLES AND BOOKS: A CHECKLIST

❏ If the work is scholarly, is the author well-known in his or her field? Is the author affiliated with an accredited college or university? A nonscholarly author, such as a journalist, should have a reputation for objectivity and thoroughness.

❏ Is the publication reputable? If a scholarly publication is *peer-reviewed*, experts in the field have a chance to comment on the author's work before it is published. Nonscholarly publications such as newspapers and magazines should be well-established and widely respected.

❏ Is the source recently published and up to date? Alternatively, is it a classic in its field? In the sciences and social sciences, recent publication is particularly critical.

❏ Is the material at an appropriate level—neither too scholarly nor too general—for your purpose and audience? Make sure you can understand and digest the material for your readers.

❏ Does the information appear to be accurate, objectively presented, and complete? Statistics and other evidence should be not be distorted or manipulated to make a point.

Special care must be taken to evaluate the worth of material found on the Web. Electronic documents often seem to appear out of nowhere and can disappear without a trace. And anyone—from scholar to con artist—can create a Web page. How, then, do you know if an Internet source is credible? The following checklist provides some questions to ask when you work with online material.

☑ EVALUATING INTERNET MATERIALS: A CHECKLIST

❏ Who is the author of the material? Does the author offer his or her credentials in a résumé or biographical note? Do these credentials qualify the author to provide reliable information on the topic? Does the author provide an e-mail address so you can request more information? The less you know about an author, the more suspicious you should be about using the data.

❏ Can you verify the accuracy of the information presented? Does the author refer to studies or to other authors you can investigate? If the author doesn't cite other works or other points of view, that may suggest the document is opinionated and one-sided. In such a case, it's important to track down material addressing alternative points of view.

❑ Who's sponsoring the Web site? Check for an "About Us" link on the home page, which may tell you the site's sponsorship and goals. Many sites are established by organizations—businesses, agencies, lobby groups—as well as by individuals. If a sponsor pushes a single point of view, you should use the material with great caution. Once again, make an extra effort to locate material addressing other sides of the issue.

❑ Is the cited information up-to-date? Being on the Internet doesn't guarantee that information is current. To assess the timeliness of Internet materials, check at the top or bottom of the document for copyright date, publication date, and/or revision date. Those dates will help you determine whether the material is recent enough for your purposes.

❑ Is the information original or taken from another source? Is quoted material accurate? Some Web pages may reproduce material from other sources without identifying them. Watch out for possible plagiarism. Nonoriginal material should be accurately quoted and acknowledged on the site.

ANALYZING AND SYNTHESIZING SOURCE MATERIAL

As you read your sources and begin taking notes, you may not be able to judge immediately how helpful a source will be. At that time, you probably should take fairly detailed notes. After a while, you'll become more selective. You'll find that you are thinking more critically about the material you read, isolating information and ideas that are important to your thesis, and formulating questions about your topic.

Analyzing Source Material

To begin with, you should spend some time analyzing each source for its *central ideas, main supporting points,* and *key details.* (See Chapter 1 for tips on effective reading techniques.) As you read, keep asking yourself how the source's content meshes with your working thesis and with what you know about your subject. Does the source repeat what you already know, or does it supply new information? If a source provides detailed support for important ideas or suggests a new angle on your subject, read carefully and take full notes. If the source refers to other sources, you might decide to consult those.

Make sure you have all necessary citation information for every source you consult. (See pages 606–637 for information you will need for documenting citations.) Then, as you read relevant sources, make sure to take plenty of notes. Articles you have printed out can be highlighted and annotated with your comments. (See the checklist on pages 608–609 for annotation techniques.) In addition, you may wish to photocopy selected book pages to annotate. However, you will also have to take handwritten or typewritten notes on some material. When you do so, make sure to put quotation marks around direct quotes. Annotating and note-taking will help you think through and respond to the source's ideas. (For help with analyzing images in your sources—for example, graphs and illustrations—see page 609.)

Your notes might include any of the following: facts, statistics, anecdotal accounts, expert opinion, case studies, surveys, reports, results of experiments. When you are recording data, check that you have copied the figures accurately. Also note how and by whom the statistics were gathered, as well as where and when they were first reported.

Take down your source's interpretation of the statistics, but be sure to scrutinize the interpretation for any "spin" that distorts them. For example, if 80 percent of Americans think violent crime is our number one national problem, that doesn't mean that violent crime *is* our main problem; it simply means that 80 percent of the people polled *think* it is. And if a "majority" of people think that homelessness should be among our top national priorities, it may be that a mere 51 percent—a bare majority—feel that way. In short, make sure the statistics mean what your sources say they mean. If you have any reason to suspect distortion, it's a good idea to corroborate such figures elsewhere; tracking down the original source of a statistic is the best way to ensure that numbers are being reported fairly.

Synthesizing Source Materials

As you go along, you may come across material that challenges your working thesis and forces you to think differently about your subject. Indeed, the more you learn, the more difficult it may be to state anything conclusively. This is a sign that you're synthesizing and weighing all the evidence. In time, the confusion will lessen, and you'll emerge with a clearer understanding of your subject.

Suppose you find sources that take positions contrary to the one that you had previously considered credible. When you come across such conflicting material, you can be sure you've identified a pivotal issue within your topic. To decide which position is more valid, you need to take good notes or carefully annotate your photocopies or printed documents. Then evaluate the sources for bias. On this basis alone, you might discover serious flaws in one or several sources. Also compare the key points and supporting evidence in the sources. Where do they agree? Where do they disagree? Does one source argue against another's position, perhaps even discrediting some of the opposing view's evidence? The answers to these questions may very well cause you to question the quality, completeness, or fairness of one or more sources.

To resolve such a conflict, you can also research your subject more fully. For example, if your conflicting sources are at the general or serious level, you should probably turn to more scholarly sources. By referring to more authoritative material, you may be able to determine which of the conflicting sources is more valid.

When you attempt to resolve discrepancies among sources, be sure not to let your own bias come into play. Try not to favor one position over the other simply because it supports your working thesis. Remember, your goal is to arrive at the most well-founded position you can. In fact, researching a topic may lead you to change your original viewpoint. In this case, you shouldn't hesitate to revise your working thesis to accord with the evidence you gather.

☑ ANALYZING AND SYNTHESIZING SOURCE MATERIAL: A CHECKLIST

❏ As you read sources, note central ideas, main supporting points, and key details.

❏ Make sure to record all bibliographic information carefully, identify any quotations, and copy statistical data accurately.

❏ Annotate or take full notes on sources that deal with ideas that are important to your topic or suggest a new angle on your subject.

❏ Examine statistics and other facts for any distortions.

❏ Read carefully material that causes you to take a different view of your subject. Keep an open mind and do additional research to confirm or change your thesis.

USING QUOTATION, SUMMARY, AND PARAPHRASE WITHOUT PLAGIARIZING

Your paper should contain your own ideas stated in your own words. To support your ideas, you can introduce evidence from sources in three ways—with direct quotations, summaries, and paraphrases. Knowing how and when to use each type is an important part of the research process.

Quotation

A *quotation* reproduces, word for word, that which is stated in a source. Although quoting can demonstrate the thoroughness with which you reviewed relevant sources, don't simply use one quotation after another without any intervening commentary or analysis. To do so would mean you hadn't evaluated and synthesized your sources sufficiently. Aim for one to three quotations from each major source; more than that can create a problem in your paper. Consider using quotations in the following situations:

- If a source's ideas are unusual or controversial, include a representative quotation in your paper to show you have accurately conveyed the source's viewpoint.
- Record a quotation if a source's wording is so eloquent or convincing that it would lose its power if you restated the material in your own words.
- Use a quotation if a source's ideas reinforce your own conclusions. If the source is a respected authority, such a quotation will lend authority to your own ideas.
- In an analysis of a literary work, use quotation from the work to support your interpretations.

Remember to clearly identify quotes in your notes so that you don't confuse the quotation with your own comments when you begin drafting your paper. Record the author's statement *exactly* as it appears in the original work, right down to the punctuation. In addition, make sure to properly document the quotation. See "How to Document: MLA In-Text References" and "How to Document: MLA List of Works Cited" on pages 629–630.

Original Passage 1

In this excerpt from *The Canon: A Whirligig Tour of the Beautiful Basics of Science*, by Natalie Angier, page 22, the author is discussing the subject of scientific reasoning.

> Much of the reason for its success is founded on another fundamental of the scientific bent. Scientists accept, quite staunchly, that there is a reality capable of being understood, and understood in a way that can be shared with and agreed upon by others. We can call this "objective" reality if we like, as opposed to subjective reality, or opinion, or "whimsical set of predilections." The concept is deceptive, however, because it implies that the two are discrete entities with remarkably little in common.

Original Passage 2

The following is the entire text of Amendment I of the Constitution of the United States.

> Congress shall make no law respecting an establishment of religion, or prohibiting the free exercise thereof; or abridging the freedom of speech, or of the press; or the right of the people peaceably to assemble, and to petition the Government for a redress of grievances.

Acceptable Uses of Quotation   For a paper on society's perception of important freedoms, a student writer used this quotation in its entirety:

The First Amendment of the Constitution of the United States delineates what were thought to be society's most cherished freedoms: "Congress shall make no law respecting an establishment of religion, or prohibiting the free exercise thereof; or abridging the freedom of speech, or of the press; or the right of the people peaceably to assemble, and to petition the Government for a redress of grievances."

In a paper on science education in schools, one student writer used this quotation:

In explaining scientific reasoning, Angier says, "Scientists accept, quite staunchly, that there is a reality capable of being understood, and understood in a way that can be shared with and agreed upon by others" (22).

Notice that both quotations are reproduced exactly as they appear in the source and are enclosed in quotation marks. The parenthetical reference to the page number in the second example is a necessary part of documenting the quotation. (See page 625–627 for more on in-text references.) The first example requires no page number because quotations from well-known sources such as the Constitution and the Bible are sufficiently identified by their own numbering systems, in this case, the text's use of "First Amendment of the Constitution."

Incorrect Use of Quotation   Another student writer, attempting to provide some background on the scientific method, used the source material incorrectly.

To understand the scientific method, it is important to understand that scientists believe there is a reality capable of being understood (Angier 22).

The phrase "a reality capable of being understood," which are the source's exact words, should have quotations around it. Even though the source is identified correctly in the parenthetical reference, the lack of quotation marks actually constitutes plagiarism, the use of someone's words or ideas without proper acknowledgement (see page 611–612).

Summary

A *summary* is a condensation of a larger work. You extract the essence of someone's ideas and restate it in your own words. The length of a summary depends on your topic and purpose, but generally a summary is *much* shorter than the item you are summarizing. For example, you may summarize the plot of a novel in a few short paragraphs, or you might summarize a reading from this book in a few sentences. You might choose to use a summary for the following reasons:

- To give a capsule presentation of the main ideas of a book or an article, use a summary.
- If the relevant information is too long to be quoted in full, use a summary.
- Use a summary to give abbreviated information about such elements as such as plot, background, or history.
- To present an idea from a source without including all the supporting details, use a summary.

To summarize a source, read the material; jot down or underline the main idea, main supporting points, and key details; and then restate the information in shortened form in your own words. Your summary should follow the order of information in the original. Also, be sure to treat any original wording as quotations in your summary. *A caution:* When summarizing, don't use the ellipsis to signal that you have omitted some ideas. The ellipsis is used only when quoting.

Original Passage 3

This excerpt is from *The Homeless and History* by Julian Stamp, page 8.

The key to any successful homeless policy requires a clear understanding of just who are the homeless. Since fifty percent of shelter residents have drug and alcohol addictions, programs need to provide not only a place to sleep but also comprehensive treatment for addicts and their families. Since roughly one-third of the homeless population is mentally ill, programs need to offer psychiatric care, perhaps even institutionalization, and not just housing subsidies. Since the typical head of a homeless family (a young woman with fewer than six months' working experience) usually lacks the know-how needed to maintain a job and a home, programs need to supply employment and life skills training; low-cost housing alone will not ensure the family's stability.

However, if we switch our focus from the single person to the larger economic issues, we begin to see that homelessness cannot be resolved solely at the level of individual treatment. Beginning in the 1980s and through the 1990s, the gap between the rich and the poor has widened, buying power has stagnated, industrial jobs have fled overseas, and federal funding for low-cost housing has been almost eliminated. Given these developments, homelessness begins to look like a product of history, our recent history, and only by addressing shifts in the American economy can we begin to find effective solutions for people lacking homes. Moreover, these solutions—ranging from renewed federal spending to tax laws favoring job-creating companies—will require a sustained national commitment that transcends partisan politics.

Acceptable Use of Summary   The following summary was written by a student working on a paper related to the causes of homelessness.

In his *The Homeless and History*, Stamp asserts that society must not only provide programs to help the homeless with their personal problems, it must also develop government programs to deal with the economic causes of homelessness (8).

The writer gives the gist of Stamp's argument in his own words. The parenthetical reference at the end tells the reader that the material being summarized is on page 8 of the source (see pages 618–625 for more on in-text references).

Incorrect Use of Summary   The student who wrote the following has incorrectly summarized ideas from the Stamp passage.

Who are the homeless? According to Stamp, the homeless are people with big problems like addiction, mental illness, and poor job skills. Because they haven't been provided with proper treatment and training, the homeless haven't been able to adapt to a changing economy. So their numbers soared in the 1990s (8).

The writer was so determined to put things her way that she added her own ideas and ended up distorting Stamp's meaning. For instance, note the way she emphasizes personal problems over economic issues, making the former the cause of the latter. Stamp does just the opposite and highlights economic solutions rather than individual treatment.

Paraphrase

Unlike a summary, which condenses the original, a *paraphrase* recasts material by using roughly the same number of words and retaining the same level of detail as the original. The challenge with paraphrasing is to capture the information without using the original language of the material. Paraphrasing is useful in these situations:

- If you want to include specific details from a source but you want to avoid using a long quotation or string of quotations, paraphrase the material.
- To interpret or explain material as you include it, try using a paraphrase.
- Paraphrase to avoid injecting another person's style into your own writing.

One way to compose a paraphrase is to read the original passage and then set it aside while you draft your restatement. As you write, make sure to use appropriate synonyms and to vary the sentence structure from that of the original. Then compare the passages to make sure you have not used any of the original language, unless you have enclosed it in quotation marks.

Acceptable Use of Paraphrase   In the following example, the student writer paraphrases the second paragraph of Stamp's original, fitting the restatement into her argument.

Can we work together as a society to eliminate homelessness? One historian urges us to look at larger economic issues, claiming that the problem cannot be solved simply by the treatment of personal problems such as substance abuse. Economic conditions for the poor have worsened in the last few decades, with fewer jobs and substantially diminished federal support for low-cost housing. To find a solution to homelessness, society must deal with these economic causes. A "sustained national commitment," regardless of political ideology, to stepped-up federal spending and tax laws that promote the creation of jobs, as well as to other initiatives, is needed (Stamp 8).

Note that the paraphrase is nearly as long as the original. Apart from the single instance of original language, enclosed in quotation marks, the writer has not used phrases or even sentence structures from the original. Notice also that it is easy to see where the paraphrase starts and ends: The phrase "One historian" begins the paraphrase, and the parenthetical reference ends it. Because the text does not identify the source by name, the source's name is included in the parenthetical reference.

Incorrect Use of Paraphrase   When preparing the following paraphrase, the student stayed too close to the source and borrowed much of Stamp's language word for word (underlined). Because the student did not enclose the original phrases in quotation marks, this paraphrase constitutes plagiarism, *even though* this student acknowledged Stamp in the paper. The lack of quotation marks implies that the language is the student's when, in fact, it is Stamp's.

Only by addressing changes in the American economy—from the gap between the wealthy and the poor to the loss of industrial jobs to overseas markets—can we begin to find solutions for the homeless. And these solutions, ranging from renewed federal spending to tax laws favoring job-creating companies, will not be easy to find or implement (Stamp 8).

As the following example shows, another student believed, erroneously, that if he changed a word here and omitted a word there, he'd be preparing an effective paraphrase. Note that the language is all Stamp's *except* for the underlined words, which are the student's.

Only by addressing shifts in the economy can we find solutions for the homeless. These solutions will require a sustained federal commitment that avoids partisan politics (Stamp 8).

The student in the immediately preceding example occasionally deleted a word from Stamp's original, thinking that such changes would result in a legitimate paraphrase. For example, in "Only by addressing shifts in the [American] economy can we [begin to] find [effective] solutions" the brackets show where the student has omitted Stamp's words. The student couldn't place quotation marks around these near-quotes because his wording isn't identical to that of the source. Yet the near-quotes are deceptive; the lack of quotation marks suggests that the language is the student's when actually it's substantially (but not exactly) Stamp's. Such near-quotes are also considered plagiarism, even if, when writing the paper, the student supplies a parenthetical reference citing the source.

☑ USING QUOTATION, SUMMARY, AND PARAPHRASE: A CHECKLIST

❑ For a *quotation*, give the statement *exactly* as it was originally written.

❑ Always accompany quotations with your own commentary or analysis.

❑ Don't string quotations together one after the other without intervening text.

❑ Avoid using too many quotations. One to three quotations from any major source is sufficient.

❑ For a *summary*, restate ideas from the source in your own words.

❑ Keep summaries much shorter than the original material.

❑ Make sure your summary does not distort the meaning or tone of the original.

❑ For a *paraphrase*, recast ideas with the same level of detail as the original.

❑ Make sure to use your own language in a paraphrase—finding appropriate synonyms and varying sentence structure from that of the original.

❑ Check that any original source language used in a summary or paraphrase is enclosed in quotation marks.

Avoiding Plagiarism

Plagiarism occurs when a writer borrows someone else's ideas, facts, or language but doesn't properly credit that source. Summarizing and paraphrasing, in particular, can lead to plagiarism, but improper use of quotation can also constitute plagiarism.

Copyright law and the ethics of research require that you give credit to those whose words and ideas you borrow; that is, you must represent the source's words and ideas accurately and provide full documentation (see pages 625–637). Missing or faulty documentation can constitute plagiarism and undermine your credibility. For one thing, readers may suspect that you're hiding something if you fail to identify your sources clearly. Further, readers planning follow-up research of their own will be perturbed if they have trouble locating your sources. Finally, weak documentation makes it difficult for readers to distinguish your ideas from those of your sources.

To avoid plagiarizing, you must provide proper documentation in the following situations:

- When you include a word-for-word quotation from a source.
- When you paraphrase or summarize ideas or information from a source, unless that material is commonly known and accepted (whether or not you yourself were previously aware of it) or is a matter of historical or scientific record.
- When you combine a summary or paraphrase with a quotation.

One exception to formal documentation occurs in writing for the general public. For example, you may have noticed that while the authors of this book's essays, as well as newspaper and magazine writers, identify sources they have used, these writers don't use full documentation. Academic writers, though, must provide full documentation for all borrowed information.

INTEGRATING SOURCES INTO YOUR WRITING

On the whole, your paper should be written in your own words. As you draft your paper, indicate places where you might want to add evidence from sources to support your ideas. Depending on the source and the support you need, you may choose to use quotations, paraphrases, or summaries to present this evidence, as discussed in the preceding section.

Take care to blend the evidence seamlessly into your own writing through the use of introductions (see pages 48, 53–55, 68), transitions (see pages 51–52, 68), and conclusions (see pages 48, 55–56, 70). At a minimum, each paragraph should have a topic sentence, and it may also be useful to introduce evidence with an *attribution*, a phrase that identifies the source and forms part of the documentation you will need to use (see pages 619–620).

A quotation, by itself, won't always make your case for you. In addition, you will need to interpret quotations, showing why they are significant and explaining how they support your central points. Indeed, such commentary is often precisely what's needed to blend source material gracefully into your discussion. Also, use quotations sparingly; draw upon them only when they dramatically illustrate key points you want to make or when they lend authority to your own conclusions. A string of quotations signals that you haven't sufficiently evaluated and distilled your sources.

Awkward Use of a Quotation   In the following example, note how the quotation is dropped awkwardly into the text, without any transition or commentary. (For an explanation of the parenthetical reference at the end of the quotation, see page 626–627.)

Recent studies of parenting styles are designed to control researcher bias. "Recent studies screen out researchers whose strongly held attitudes make objectivity difficult" (Layden 10).

Effective Use of Quotation   Adding brief interpretive remarks in this example provides a transition that smoothly merges the quotation with the surrounding material:

Recent studies of parenting styles are designed to control researcher bias. The psychologist Marsha Layden, a harsh critic of earlier studies, acknowledges that nowadays most investigations "screen out researchers whose strongly held beliefs make objectivity difficult" (10).

Introducing a Source

Try to avoid such awkward constructions as these: *According to Julian Stamp, he says that...* and *In the book by Julian Stamp, he argues that...* Instead, follow these hints for writing smooth, graceful attributions.

Identifying the Source   An introduction to a source may specify the author's name, it may inform readers of an author's expertise, or it may refer to a source more generally. To call attention to an author who is prominent in the field, important to your argument, or referred to many times in your paper, you may give the author's full name and identifier at the first mention in the text. Then in subsequent mentions, you may give only the last name. Don't use personal titles such as *Mr.* or *Ms.*

Natalie Angier, a Pulitzer Prize–winning journalist who writes about science, says that....Angier goes on to explain....

The historian Julian Stamp argues that....As Stamp explains....

For other sources, use a more general attribution and include the source's name, along with any page numbers, in the parenthetical citation.

One writer points out...(Angier 22).

According to statistics, fifty percent...(Stamp 8).

As part of an introduction, you may mention the title of the book, article, or other source.

In *The Homeless and History*, Stamp maintains that....

According to the National Aeronautics and Space Administration (NASA),...

A recent article in *National Geographic* demonstrates that....

When the author's name is provided in the text, don't repeat the name in the parenthetical reference. (See pages 625–627 for more details on parenthetical references.)

One psychologist who is a harsh critic of earlier studies acknowledges that nowadays most investigations "screen out researchers whose strongly held beliefs make objectivity difficult" (Layden 10).

The psychologist Marsha Layden acknowledges that...(10).

Using Variety in Attributions   Don't always place attributions at the beginning of the sentence; experiment by placing them in the middle or at the end:

The key to any successful homeless policy, Stamp explains, "requires a clear understanding of just who are the homeless" (8).

Half of homeless individuals living in shelters are substance abusers, according to statistics (Stamp 8).

Try not to use a predictable subject-verb sequence (*Stamp argues that, Stamp explains that*) in all your attributions. Aim for variations like the following:

The information compiled by Stamp shows....

In Stamp's opinion,...

Stamp's study reveals that....

Rather than repeatedly using the verbs *says* or *writes* in your introductions, seek out more vigorous verbs, making sure the verbs you select are appropriate to the tone and content of the piece you're quoting. The list on page 621 offers a number of options.

Shortening or Clarifying Quotations

To make the best use of quotations, you will often need to shorten or excerpt them. It's acceptable to omit parts of quotations as long as you do not change the wording or distort the meaning of the original.

acknowledges	demonstrates	reports
adds	endorses	responds
admits	grants	reveals
argues	implies	says
asserts	insists	shows
believes	maintains	speculates
compares	notes	states
confirms	points out	suggests
contends	questions	wonders
declares	reasons	writes

Quoting a Single Word, a Phrase, or Part of a Sentence   Put double quotation marks around a quoted element you are integrating into your own sentence.

Angier says that to speak of "objective" and "subjective" realities is to imply that these are "discrete entities" (22).

Making these changes will necessitate "a sustained national commitment that transcends partisan politics," according Stamp (8).

Omitting Material in the Middle of the Original Sentence   Insert three spaced periods, called an *ellipsis* (...), in place of the deleted words. Leave a space before the first period of the ellipsis and leave a space after the third period of the ellipsis before continuing with the quoted matter.

"However, if we switch our focus ... to the larger economic issues, we begin to see that homelessness cannot be resolved solely at the level of individual treatment" (Stamp 8).

Omitting Material at the End of the Original Sentence   If no parenthetical reference is needed, insert a period before the first ellipsis period and provide the closing quotation mark, as in the first example below. If a parenthetical reference is needed, use only the ellipsis and add the period after the parentheses.

The First Amendment of the Constitution of the United States lays the foundation for the doctrine of free speech: "Congress shall make no law respecting an establishment of religion, or prohibiting the free exercise thereof; or abridging the freedom of speech, or of the press.... "

In discussing scientific reasoning, Angier states, "We can call this 'objective' reality if we like, as opposed to subjective reality ... " (22).

Speaking of the scientific method, Angier says, "Much of the reason for its success is founded on another fundamental. . . . Scientists accept . . . that there is a reality capable of being understood . . . in a way that can be shared with and agreed upon by others" (22).

Omitting Material at the Start of a Quotation   No ellipses are required. Simply place the quotation marks where you begin quoting directly. Capitalize the first word if the resulting quotation forms a complete sentence.

Simply providing housing for homeless will not suffice: "Programs need to supply employment and life skills training" (Stamp 8).

Adding Material to a Quotation   If, for the sake of clarity or grammar, you need to add a word or short phrase to a quotation (for example, by changing a verb tense or replacing a vague pronoun with a noun), enclose your insertion in brackets:

Moreover, Angier discredits the concept that "the two [objective reality and subjective reality] are discrete entities with remarkably little in common" (22).

Capitalizing and Punctuating Short Quotations

The way a short quotation is used in a sentence determines whether it begins or doesn't begin with a capital letter and whether it is or isn't preceded by a comma. For the formatting and punctuation of a long (block) quotation, see page 628–629.

Introducing a Quotation That Can Stand Alone as a Sentence   If a quotation can stand alone as a grammatical sentence, capitalize the quotation's first word. Also, precede the quotation with a comma:

Stamp observes, "Beginning in the 1980s and through the 1990s, the gap between the rich and the poor has widened . . ." (8).

According to Stamp, "Federal funding for low-cost housing has been almost eliminated" (8).

Using That, Which, _or_ Who _(Stated or Implied)_   If you use _that, which,_ or _who_ to blend a quotation into the structure of your own sentence, don't capitalize the quotation's first word and don't precede it with a comma.

Stamp observes that "beginning in the 1980s and through the 1990s, the gap between the rich and the poor has widened, buying power has stagnated, industrial jobs have fled overseas, and federal funding for low-cost housing has been almost eliminated" (8).

Angier describes scientists as firmly believing there is "a reality capable of being understood" (22).

Even if, as in the first example above, the material being quoted originally started with a capital letter, you still use lowercase when incorporating the quotation into your own sentence. Note that in the second example, the word *that* is implied (before the word *there*).

Interrupting a Full-Sentence Quotation with an Attribution   Place commas on both sides of the attribution, and resume the quotation with a lowercase letter.

"The key to any successful homeless policy," Stamp comments, "requires a clear understanding of just who are the homeless" (8).

Using a Quotation with a Quoted Word or Phrase   When a source you're quoting contains a quoted word or phrase, place single quotation marks around the quoted words. (See page 628 for how to treat a source that is quoting another source.)

"We can call this 'objective' reality if we like, as opposed to subjective reality, or opinion, or 'whimsical set of predilections,'" Angier posits (22).

Punctuating with a Question Mark or Exclamation Point   If the question mark or exclamation point is part of the quotation, place it inside the quotation marks. If the mark is part of the structure of the framing sentence, as in the second example below, place it outside the quotation marks and after any parenthetical reference.

Discussing a child's epileptic attack, the psychoanalyst Erik Erikson asks, in *Childhood and Society*, "What was the psychic stimulus?" (26).

But what does Stamp see as the "key to any successful homeless policy" (8)?

Presenting Statistics

Citing statistics can be an successful strategy for supporting your ideas. Be careful, though, not to misinterpret the data or twist their significance, and remember to provide an attribution indicating the source. Also, be sure not to overwhelm readers with too many statistics; include only those that support your central points in compelling ways. Keep in mind, too, that statistics won't speak for themselves. You need to interpret them for readers, showing how the figures cited reinforce your key ideas.

Ineffective Use of Statistics   For a paper showing that Medicare reform is needed to control increasing costs, one student writer presented the following statistics.

The Centers for Medicaid and Medicare Services reports that 1992 revenues ($185 billion) exceeded spending ($120 billion). But in 1997, revenues ($204 billion) and spending ($208 billion) were almost the same. It is projected that by the year 2010, revenues will be $310 billion and spending $410 billion (Mohr 14).

The student gave one statistic after the other, without explanatory commentary or attribution. This presentation makes it hard for the reader to understand the meaning of the statistics.

Effective Use of Statistics   Instead of including so many statistics, the writer could have presented only the most telling statistics, being sure to explain their significance.

The Centers for Medicaid and Medicare Services reports that in 1992, Medicare revenues actually exceeded spending by about $65 billion. But five years later, costs had increased so much that they exceeded revenues by about $4 billion. This trend toward escalated costs is expected to continue. It's projected that by the year 2010, revenues will be only $310 billion, while spending—if not controlled—will climb to at least $410 billion (Mohr 14).

☑ INTEGRATING SOURCES INTO YOUR WRITING: A CHECKLIST

❑ Introduce an important or oft-used source by giving the author's full name and credentials at the first mention. Thereafter, refer to author by last name only. Don't use personal titles such as *Mr.* or *Ms.*

❑ Use general introductions (*One historian says...*) for less important sources.

❑ Vary the style of attributions by sometimes positioning them at the middle or end, using different verbs, or blending quotations into your own sentences.

❑ Words may be deleted from a quotation as long as the author's original meaning isn't changed. Insert an ellipsis (...) in place of the deleted words. An ellipsis is not needed when material is omitted from the start of a quotation. Use a period plus an ellipsis when the end of a sentence is deleted.

❑ Use brackets to add clarifying information to quotations.

❑ If a quotation can stand alone as a grammatical sentence, capitalize its first word and precede it with a comma. If a quotation is blended

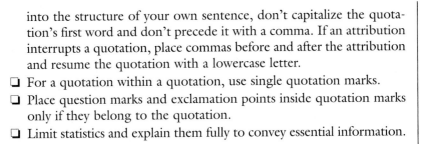

into the structure of your own sentence, don't capitalize the quotation's first word and don't precede it with a comma. If an attribution interrupts a quotation, place commas before and after the attribution and resume the quotation with a lowercase letter.
❑ For a quotation within a quotation, use single quotation marks.
❑ Place question marks and exclamation points inside quotation marks only if they belong to the quotation.
❑ Limit statistics and explain them fully to convey essential information.

DOCUMENTING SOURCES: MLA STYLE

In Chapter 11, you learned the importance of documentation—giving credit to the print and electronic sources whose words and ideas you borrow in an essay (see page 481). That earlier discussion showed you how to document sources in informal papers. The following pages will show you how to use the documentation system of the Modern Language Association (MLA)[1] when citing sources in more formal papers.

To avoid plagiarism, you must provide documentation when you include quotations from a source or you summarize or paraphrase in your own words ideas or information from a source. However, if the information you are including is commonly known or is a matter of historical or scientific record (the date of the Gettyburg Address or the temperature at which water boils, for example), you need not document it.

The discussion here covers key features of the MLA system. For more detailed coverage, you may want to consult a recent composition handbook or the latest edition of the *MLA Handbook for Writers of Research Papers*. For a sample paper that uses MLA documentation, turn to the student essay on pages 497–502.

HOW TO DOCUMENT: MLA IN-TEXT REFERENCES

The MLA documentation system uses the *parenthetical reference*, a brief note in parentheses inserted into the text after borrowed material. The parenthetical reference doesn't provide full bibliographic information, but it presents

---

[1]MLA documentation is appropriate in papers written for humanities courses, such as your composition class. If you're writing a paper for a course in the social sciences (for example, psychology, economics, or sociology), your professor will probably expect you to use the citation format developed by the American Psychological Association (APA). For information about APA documentation, consult *The Longman Writer* or the most recent edition of the *Publication Manual of the American Psychological Association*.

enough so that readers can turn to the Works Cited list (see pages 501–502) at the end of the paper for complete information.

Whenever you quote or summarize material from an outside source, you must do two things: (1) identify the source (usually an author) and (2) specify the page(s) in your source on which the material appears. The author's name may be given either in an introduction (often called the *attribution*) or in the parentheses following the borrowed material. The page number always appears in parentheses, usually at the end of the sentence just before the period. The examples below illustrate the MLA documentation style. You may also consult pages 619–623 for additional examples of attributions and parenthetical references.

Single Source: Parentheses Only

In the following two examples, a complete parenthetical reference follows a summary.

Counseling and support services are not enough to solve the problem of homelessness; proposed solutions must also address the complex economic issues at the heart of homelessness (Stamp 8).

If a source is alphabetized by title in your Works Cited list, use a shortened version of the title in place of the author's name in the parenthetical reference. In the following example, the full title of the source is "Supreme Court of the United States."

The U.S. Supreme Court is fundamentally an appeals court, responsible for "cases arising under the Constitution, laws, or treaties of the United States" among others ("Supreme Court").

Complete parenthetical references follow these uses of quotation. Note the punctuation in the second example, where the comma in the quotation is part of the original sentence.

If we look beyond the problems of homelessness, to "larger economic issues," it is clear that "homelessness cannot be resolved solely at the level of the individual" (Stamp 8).

Given the fact that a significant percentage of the homeless suffer from mental illness, "programs need to offer psychiatric care..., not just housing subsidies" (Stamp 8).

Single Source: Parentheses and Attributions

The attribution should make it clear where the quotation, summary, or paraphrase begins.

Julian Stamp argues that homelessness must be addressed in terms of economics, not simply in terms of individual counseling, addiction therapy, or job training (8).

As Stamp explains, "The key to any successful homeless policy requires a clear understanding of just who are the homeless" (8).

Because half of those taking refuge in shelters have problems with drugs and alcohol, Stamp reasons that "programs need to provide not only a place to sleep but also comprehensive substance-abuse treatment" (8).

According to statistics, half of the homeless individuals living in shelters are substance abusers (Stamp 8).

In *The Homeless and History*, Stamp maintains that economic issues, rather than difficulties in people's personal lives, are at the core of the homeless problem (8).

Stamp points out that "homelessness cannot be resolved solely at the level of the individual" (8), although other experts disagree.

Note that in the immediately preceding example, the parenthetical reference follows the quotation in the middle of the sentence; placing the reference at the end of sentence would erroneously imply that idea expressed by "although other experts disagree" is Stamp's.

More Than One Source by the Same Author

When your paper includes references to more than one work by the same author, you must specify—either in the parenthetical reference or in the attribution—the particular work being cited. You do this by providing the title, as well as the author's name and the page(s). Here are examples from a paper in which two works by the psychologist Jean Piaget were used.

In *The Language and Thought of the Child*, Jean Piaget states that "discussion forms the basis for a logical point of view" (240).

Piaget considers dialogue essential to the development of logical thinking (*Language and Thought* 240).

The Child's Conception of the World shows that young children think that the name of something can never change (Piaget 81).

Young children assume that everything has only one name and that no others are possible (Piaget, *Child's Conception* 81).

Notice that when a work is named in the attribution, the full title appears; when a title is given in the parenthetic citation, though, only the first few significant words appear. (However, don't use the ellipsis to indicate that some words have been omitted from the title; the ellipsis is used only in actual quotations.) Note also that when name, title, and page number all appear in the parenthetical reference, a comma follows the author's name.

Source Within a Source

If you quote or summarize a *secondary source* (a source whose ideas come to you only through another source), you need to make this clear. The parenthetical documentation should indicate "as quoted in" with the abbreviation *qtd. in*:

According to Sherman, "Recycling has, in several communities, created unanticipated expenses" (qtd. in Pratt 3).

Sherman explains that recycling can be surprisingly costly (qtd. in Pratt 3).

If the material you're quoting includes a quotation, place single quotation marks around the secondary quotation:

Pratt believes that "recycling efforts will be successful if, as Sherman argues, 'communities launch effective public-education campaigns' " (3).

Note: Your Works Cited list should include the source you actually read (Pratt), rather than the source you refer to secondhand (Sherman).

Long (Block) Quotations

A quotation longer than four lines starts on a new line and is indented, throughout, one inch from the left margin. Since this block format indicates a quotation, quotation marks are unnecessary. Double-space the block quotation, as you do the rest of your paper. Don't leave extra space above or below the quotation. Long quotations, always used sparingly, require a lead-in. A lead-in that isn't a full sentence is followed by a comma; a lead-in that is a full sentence (see below) is followed by a colon:

Stamp cites changing economic conditions as the key to a national homeless policy:

Beginning in the 1980s and through the 1990s, the gap between the rich and the poor has widened, buying power has stagnated, industrial jobs have fled overseas, and federal funding for low-cost housing has been almost eliminated. Given these developments, homelessness begins to look like a product of history, our recent history, and only by addressing shifts in the American economy can we begin to find effective solutions for people lacking homes. (8)

Douglas, Susan, and Meredith Michaels. *The Mommy Myth: The Idealization of Motherhood and How It Has Undermined Women.* New York: Free Press, 2004. Print.

Gunningham, Neil A., Robert Kagan, and Dorothy Thornton. *Shades of Green: Business, Regulation, and Environment.* Palo Alto: Stanford UP, 2003. Print.

Book by Four or More Authors

For a work by four or more authors, give only the first author's name followed by a comma and *et al.* (Latin for "and others"). Do not italicize "et al."

Brown, Michael K., et al. *Whitewashing Race: The Myth of a Color-Blind Society.* Berkeley: U of California P, 2003. Print.

Two or More Works by the Same Author

If you use more than one work by the same author, list each book separately. Give the author's name in the first entry only; begin the entries for other books by that author with three hyphens followed by a period. Arrange the works alphabetically by title.

McChesney, Robert W. *The Problem of the Media: U.S. Communication Politics in the 21st Century.* New York: Monthly Review, 2004. Print.

---. *Rich Media, Poor Democracy: Communication Politics in Dubious Times.* Champaign: U of Illinios P, 1999. Print.

Revised Edition

Indicate a revised edition (*Rev. ed., 2nd ed., 3rd ed., 4th ed.,* and so on) after the title.

Weiss, Thomas G., David P. Forsythe, and Roger A. Coate. *The United Nations and Changing World Politics.* 3rd ed. Boulder: Westview, 2001. Print.

Zinn, Howard. *A People's History of the United States: 1492-Present.* Rev. ed. New York: Perennial, 2003. Print.

Book with an Editor or Translator

Following the title, type *Ed.* or *Trans.* (for "Edited by" or "Translated by"), followed by the name of the editor or translator.

Douglass, Frederick. *My Bondage and My Freedom.* Ed. John David Smith. New York: Penguin, 2003. Print.

Anthology or Compilation of Works by Different Authors

List anthologies according to editors' names, followed by *ed.* or *eds.* (for "editor" or "editors").

Kasser, Tim, and Allen D. Kanner, eds. *Psychology and Consumer Culture: The Struggle for a Good Life in a Materialistic World.* Washington, DC: American Psychological Association, 2004. Print.

Section of an Anthology or Compilation

Begin this entry with the author and title of the selection (in quotation marks), followed by the title of the anthology. The editors' names are listed after the anthology title and are preceded by *Ed.* (for "Edited by"). Note that the entry gives the page numbers on which the selection appears.

Levin, Diane E., and Susan Linn. "The Commercialization of Childhood: Understanding the Problem and Finding Solutions." *Psychology and Consumer Culture: The Struggle for a Good Life in a Materialistic World.* Ed. Tim Kasser and Allen D. Kanner. Washington, DC: American Psychological Association, 2004. 212-28. Print.

Section or Chapter in a Book by One Author

Wolfson, Evan. "Is Marriage Equality a Question of Civil Rights?" *Why Marriage Matters: America, Equality, and Gay People's Right to Marry.* New York: Simon, 2004. 242-69. Print.

Reference Work

"Temperance Movements." *Columbia Encyclopedia.* 6th ed. New York: Columbia UP, 2000. Print.

Book by an Institution or Corporation

Give the name of the institution or corporation in the author position, even if the same institution is the publisher.

United Nations. Department of Economic and Social Affairs. *Human Development, Health, and Education: Dialogues at the Economic and Social Council.* New York: United Nations, 2004.

CITING PRINT SOURCES—PERIODICALS

Titles of periodicals should be italicized (or underlined if your instructor prefers). Abbreviate names of months, except for *May, June,* and *July.* If the article is printed on multiple, nonconsecutive pages, simply list the first page (including any section letters) followed by a plus sign (+). Include the medium of publication (*Print*) at the end of the citation.

Article in a Weekly or Biweekly Magazine

Provide the author's name (if the article is signed) and article title (in quotation marks). Then give the periodical name (italicized and with *no* period) and date of publication (day, month, year), followed by a colon and the page number(s) of the article. End with the medium of publication (*Print*).

Leo, John. "Campus Censors in Retreat." *U.S. News & World Report* 16 Feb. 2004: 64–65. Print.

Article in a Monthly or Bimonthly Magazine

Wheeler, Jacob. "Outsourcing the Public Good." *Utne* Sept.-Oct. 2004: 13–14. Print.

Article in a Daily Newspaper

Omit the initial *The* from newspaper names.

Doolin, Joseph. "Immigrants Deserve a Fair Deal." *Boston Globe* 19 Aug. 2003: A19+ Print.

Editorial, Letter to the Editor, or Reply to a Letter

List as you would any signed or unsigned article, but indicate the type of piece after the article's title.

Johnson, Paul. "Want to Prosper? Then Be Tolerant." Editorial. *Forbes* 21 June 2004: 41. Print.

"Playing Fair with Nuclear Cleanup." Editorial. *Seattle Times* 5 Oct. 2003: D2. Print.

Article in a Scholarly Journal

Most journals, like the one cited in the second example below, are paginated continuously; the first issue of each year starts with page 1, and each subsequent issue picks up where the previous one left off. Some journals do not paginate continuously; they start each new issue in a year with page 1.

Regardless of how a journal is paginated, include *both* the issue number (if available) and the volume number. After the title, give the volume number followed by a period, then the issue number, and then the year in parentheses. Use arabic, not roman, numerals, without either *volume* or *vol.* The article's page(s) appear at the end, separated from the year by a colon. Give the medium of publication (*Print*) at the end.

Chew, Cassie. "Achieving Unity through Diversity." *Black Issues in Higher Education* 21.5 (2004): 8-11. Print.

Manning, Wendy D. "Children and the Stability of Cohabiting Couples." *Journal of Marriage & Family* 66.3 (2004): 674-89. Print.

CITING SOURCES FOUND ON A WEBSITE

Citations for sources found on the Internet require much of the same information used in citations for print sources. Internet addresses (URLs) change so frequently that unless you judge that a source would be very difficult to find without one, do not give the URL in the citation. (See "Personal and Professional Website" for an example using a URL.) To cite an item from a website, supply the following information:

- Author's name
- Selection's title (in quotation marks)
- Source—generally the title of the website (italicized or underlined)
- Version or edition of the website, if relevant
- Publisher or sponsor of the website—often found at the bottom of the Web page (or *N.p.* for "no publisher")
- Publication date (or *n.d.* for "no date")
- Publication medium (*Web*)
- The date you retrieved the information (day, month, year)

Newspaper or Magazine Article

Orecklin, Michele. "Stress and the Superdad." *Time.* Time.com, 16 Aug. 2004. Web. 2 Dec. 2008.

Nachtigal, Jeff. "We Own What You Think." *Salon.com.* Salon Media Group, 18 Aug. 2004. Web. 17 Mar. 2005.

"Restoring the Wetlands." Editorial. *Los Angeles Times.* Los Angeles Times, 26 July 2008. Web. 6 Jan. 2009.

Online Reference Work

"Salem Witch Trials." *Encyclopaedia Britannica Online.* Encyclopaedia Britannica, 2008. Web. 3 Jan. 2009.

Scholarly Journal Found on the Internet

For articles accessed from a website, follow the citation format for print articles, but specify *Web* as the medium and give the date of access. If no page numbers are available, insert *n. pg.* See also the entry for "Scholarly Journal Found in an Online Database."

Njeng, Eric Sipyinyu, "Achebe, Conrad, and the Postcolonial Strain." *CLCWeb: Comparative Literature and Culture* 10.1 (2008): 1-8. Web. 12 Dec. 2008.

Qin, Desiree Baolian. "The Role of Gender in Immigrant Children's Educational Adaptation." *Current Issues in Comparative Education* 9.1 (2006): 8-19. Web. 5 Jan. 2009.

Personal and Professional Website

Because the site would otherwise be difficult to access, the first entry below contains a URL, enclosed in angle brackets and followed by a period. Note that long Web addresses should be broken up only after slashes. In the second entry below, *Uncle Tom's Cabin* is *not* italicized. It's a title that would ordinarily be italicized, but since the rest of the website title is italicized, the book title is set off in regular type.

Finney, Dee. *Native American Culture.* 23 May 2008. Web. 6 June 2008. <http://www.greatdreams.com/native.htm>.

Railton, Stephen, ed. Uncle Tom's Cabin & *American Culture: A Multi-Media Archive.* Dept. of English, U of Virginia, 2007. Web. 9 Apr. 2006.

Blog

If the blog has no title, insert "Online posting" in place of the title, without quotation marks or italics.

Waldman, Deane. "'Care' Has Deserted Managed Care." *Huffington Post.* HuffingtonPost.com, 26 June 2008. Web. 18 Nov. 2008.

Podcast

Elisabeth Arnold. "Tale of Two Alaska Villages." *NPR.org.* Natl. Public Radio. 29 July 2008. Web. 13 Dec. 2008.

CITING SOURCES FOUND THROUGH AN ONLINE DATABASE OR SCHOLARLY PROJECT

Specify the database or project, but do not include the URL or information about the library system used.

Scholarly Journal Found in an Online Database

For articles accessed through an online database, begin with the same information as for online periodicals. After the publication information (volume, issue, date, and page numbers), give the title of the database (italicized or underlined) and the medium of publication (*Web*). Complete the entry with the date you accessed the information. See also the entry "Scholarly Journal Found on the Internet."

Weiler, Angela M. "Using Technology to Take Down Plagiarism." *Community College Week* 16.16 (2004): 4-6. *EBSCOhost*. Web. 17 Oct. 2008.

Book Found in an Online Scholarly Project

When it's available, include the book's original publication information. Also include (when available) the name of the site's editor, its electronic publication date, its sponsoring organization, your date of access, and the Web address.

Franklin, Benjamin. *The Autobiography of Benjamin Franklin*. London, 1793. *Electronic Text Center*. Ed. Judy Boss. Web. 16 Jan. 2009.

CITING OTHER COMMON SOURCES

Include the medium through which you accessed the source, for example, *CD* for "compact disc" or *E-mail* for an e-mail message you received.

Television or Radio Program

"A Matter of Choice? Gay Life in America." Part 4 of 5. *Nightline*. Narr. Ted Koppel. ABC. WPVI-TV, Philadelphia. 23 May 2002. Television.

Movie, Recording, Videotape, DVD, Filmstrip, or Slide Program

Provide the author or composer of the piece (if appropriate); title (italicized or underlined); director, conductor, or performer; manufacturer or distributor; and year of release. Give the medium at the end of the citation.

Fahrenheit 911. Dir. Michael Moore. Sony, 2004. DVD.

CD-ROM or DVD-ROM

Cite the following information (when available): author, title (italicized or underlined), version, place of publication, publisher, year of publication, and medium (CD-ROM or DVD-ROM).

World Book Encyclopedia. 2006 Edition. Renton, WA: Topics Entertainment, 2006. CD-ROM.

Personal or Telephone Interview

Specify "Personal interview" for an interview you conducted in person and "Telephone interview" for an interview you conducted over the telephone.

Langdon, Paul. Personal interview. 26 Jan. 2008.

Lecture, Speech, Address, or Reading

Blacksmith, James. "Urban Design in the New Millennium." Cityscapes Lecture Series. Urban Studies Institute. Metropolitan College, Washington, DC. 18 Apr. 2005. Lecture.

Papa, Andrea. "Reforming the Nation's Tax Structure." Accounting 302. Cypress College, Astoria, NY. 3 Dec. 2004. Lecture.

E-mail Message

Start with the sender's name. Then give the title (from the subject line) in quotation marks, a description, the date of the message, and the medium (*E-mail*).

Mack, Lynn. "New Developments in Early Childhood Education." Message to the author. 30 Aug. 2006. E-mail.